SACRIFICE IN THE BIBLE

SACRIFICE
IN THE
BIBLE

Editors:

ROGER T. BECKWITH
and
MARTIN J. SELMAN

CARLISLE, UNITED KINGDOM

BAKER BOOK HOUSE
Grand Rapids, Michigan

First published 1995 jointly
in the U.K. by Paternoster Press, P.O. Box 300, Carlisle CA3 0QS
and in the U.S.A. by Baker Book House, Box 6287, Grand Rapids, MI 49516

01 00 99 98 97 96 95   7   6   5   4   3   2   1

British Library Cataloguing in Publication Data

Sacrifice in the Bible
I. Beckwith, R. T. II. Selman, Martin J.
220.6

ISBN 0–85364–611–2

Baker ISBN 0–8010–2044–1

Typeset by Photoprint, Torquay, Devon
and printed by The Guernsey Press Co. Ltd., Guernsey, Channel Islands

In grateful memory of
John Patrick Baker,
scholar and pastor,
secretary of the Biblical Theology study group
of the Tyndale Fellowship
from its inception
until his death in 1988

Contents

Abbreviations

BIBLICAL BOOKS

Old Testament

Gen.	Genesis	Ezr.	Ezra	Dan.	Daniel
Exod.	Exodus	Neh.	Nehemiah	Hos.	Hosea
Lev.	Leviticus	Est.	Esther	Joel	
Num.	Numbers	Job		Amos	
Deut.	Deuteronomy	Ps. (Pss.)	Psalms	Obad.	Obadiah
Jos.	Joshua	Prov.	Proverbs	Jon.	Jonah
Jdg.	Judges	Eccl.	Ecclesiastes	Mic.	Micah
Ruth		Cant.	Song of Solomon	Nah.	Nahum
1 Sam.	1 Samuel		(Canticles)	Hab.	Habakkuk
2 Sam.	2 Samuel	Isa.	Isaiah	Zeph.	Zephaniah
1 Ki.	1 Kings	Jer.	Jeremiah	Hag.	Haggai
2 Ki.	2 Kings	Lam.	Lamentations of	Zech.	Zechariah
1 Chr.	1 Chronicles		Jeremiah	Mal.	Malachi
2 Chr.	2 Chronicles	Ezek.	Ezekiel		

New Testament

Matt.	Matthew	Phil.	Philippians	Jas.	James
Mk.	Mark	Col.	Colossians	1 Pet.	1 Peter
Lk.	Luke	1 Thess.	1 Thessalonians	2 Pet.	2 Peter
Jn.	John	2 Thess.	2 Thessalonians	1 Jn.	1 John
Acts	Acts of the	1 Tim	1 Timothy	2 Jn.	2 John
	Apostles	2 Tim.	2 Timothy	3 Jn.	3 John
Rom.	Romans	Tit.	Titus	Jude	
1 Cor.	1 Corinthians	Phlm.	Philemon	Rev.	The Revelation of
2 Cor.	2 Corinthians	Heb.	Hebrews		John (Apocalypse)
Gal.	Galatians				
Eph.	Ephesians				

Note: Transliteration of Hebrew and Greek words follows the system used in the *Illustrated Bible Dictionary* (Leicester: IVP, 1980).

ANCIENT SOURCES

Did.	Didache
Dio Chrys.	Dio Cocceianus, later called Chrysostomos
Diod. Sic.	Diodorus Siculus
Eth.Enoch	Ethiopic Book of Enoch, or 1 Enoch
Exod.Rab.	*Exodus Rabba*
Ignatius, *Eph.*	Ignatius, *Letter to the Ephesians*
Josephus, *Ant.*	Josephus, *Jewish Antiquities*
Josephus, *War*	Josephus, *The Jewish War*
Justin, *Apol.*	Justin, *Apology*

Justin, *Dial.*	Justin, *Dialogue with Trypho*
Mart. Isa.	Martyrdom of Isaiah
Mek.	*Mekhilta*
Midr.Rab.	*Midrash Rabba*
Pes.	Pesahim
Philo, *Congr.*	Philo, *De Congressu Eruditionis Gratia*
Philo, *Plant.*	Philo, *De Plantatione*
Philo, *Rer.Div.Her.*	Philo, *Quis Rerum Divinarum Heres Sit*
Philo, *Som.*	Philo, *De Somniis*
Philo, Vit.Mos.	Philo, *De Vita Mosis*
Plut.	Plutarch
Pss.Sol.	Psalms of Solomon
1QpHab	*Pesher on Habakkuk* from Qumran Cave 1
1QS	*Serek hayyahad (Rule of the Community, Manual of Discipline)*
11QMelch	*Melchizedek* text from Qumran Cave 11
Sir.	The Book of Sirach, or Ecclesiasticus
Sl.Enoch	Slavonic Book of Enoch, or Book of the Secrets of Enoch, or 2 Enoch
Sukk.	Sukkah
Test.Lev.	Testament of Levi
Tr. Isa.	*Targum of Isaiah*
Tg. Ezk.	*Targum of Ezekiel*

REFERENCE WORKS AND JOURNALS

AB	Anchor Bible
Afo	*Archiv für Orientforschung*
AHW	W. von Soden, *Akkadisches Handwörterbuch*
AnBib	Analecta Biblica
ANET	J.B. Pritchard (ed.), *Ancient Near Eastern Texts*
ASOR	*American School of Oriental Research*
ASORDS	*American Schools of Oriental Research, Dissertation Series*
BAG	W. Bauer, W.F. Arndt, and F.W. Gingrich, *Greek–English Lexicon of the NT*
BBB	Bonner Biblische Beiträge
BDB	F. Brown, S.R. Driver, and C.A. Briggs, *Hebrew and English Lexicon of the Old Testament*
BETL	Bibliotheca ephemeridum theologicarum lovaniensium
Bib	*Biblica*
BJRL	*Bulletin of the John Rylands University Library of Manchester*
BKAT	Biblischer Kommentar: Altes Testament
BTB	*Biblical Theology Bulletin*
BZAW	Beihefte zur *ZAW*
CAD	*The Assyrian Dictionary of the Oriental Institute of the University of Chicago*
CBC	Cambridge Bible Commentary
CT	*Cuneiform Texts from Babylonian Tablets in the British Museum*
CTA	A. Herdner, *Corpus des tablettes en cunéiformes alphabétiques découvertes à Ras Shamra-Ugarit*
ET	English translation
Ev Q	*Evangelical Quarterly*
Exp Tim	*Expository Times*
FS	Festschrift
GKC	*Gesenius' Hebrew Grammar*, ed. E. Kautzsch, tr. A.E. Cowley
GNB	*Good News Bible*
HSM	Harvard Semitic Monographs
ICC	International Critical Commentary
Int	*Interpretation*
ITC	International Theological Commentary
JAOS	*Journal of the American Oriental Society*
JB	*Jerusalem Bible*

JBL	*Journal of Biblical Literature*
JCS	*Journal of Cuneiform Studies*
JES	*Journal of Ecumenical Studies*
JPS	Jewish Publication Society
JRAS	*Journal of the Royal Asiatic Society*
JSNT	*Journal for the Study of the New Testament*
JSNTS	Journal for the Study of the New Testament, Supplement Series
JSOT	*Journal for the Study of the Old Testament*
JSOTS	Journal for the Study of the Old Testament, Supplement Series
JTS	*Journal of Theological Studies*
KTU	M. Dietrich, O. Loretz, J. Sanmartin, *Die keilalphabetischen Texte aus Ugarit*
MANE	Monographs on the Ancient Near East
MM	J.H. Moulton and G. Milligan, *The Vocabulary of the Greek New Testament*
NCB	*New Century Bible*
NEB	*New English Bible*
NICOT	New International Commentary on the Old Testament new series
NIDNTT	L. Coenen, F. Bayreuther, H. Bietenhard and C. Brown (eds.), *New International Dictionary of New Testament Theology*
NIV	*New International Version*
NovT	*Novum Testamentum*
NovTSup	Novum Testamentum, Supplements
NRSV	*New Revised Standard Version*
ns	new series
NTS	*New Testament Studies*
OTL	Old Testament Library
par.	parallel
RA	*Révue d'assyriologie et d'archéologie orientale*
RB	*Révue Biblique*
REB	*Revised English Bible*
RSV	*Revised Standard Version*
SANE	Sources from the Ancient Near East
SAP	Sheffield Academic Press
SBL	Society for Biblical Literature
SBLDS	SBL Dissertation Series
SBT	Studies in Biblical Theology
SJT	*Scottish Journal of Theology*
SJLS	Studies in Judaism and Late Antiquity
SNTSMS	Society for New Testament Studies Monograph Series
StudNeot	Studia neotestamentica, Studia
TDNT	G. Kittel and G. Friedrich (eds.), *Theological Dictionary of the New Testament*
TDOT	H. Botterweck and H. Ringgren (eds.), *Theological Dictionary of the Old Testament*
TNTC	Tyndale New Testament Commentaries
TOTC	Tyndale Old Testament Commentaries
Tyn.B.	*Tyndale Bulletin*
TS	*Theological Studies*
UF	*Ugaritische Forschungen*
VE	*Vox Evangelica*
VKGNT	K. Aland (ed.), *Vollständige Konkordanz zum griechischen Neuen Testament*
VT	*Vetus Testamentum*
VTSup	Vetus Testamentum, Supplements
WBC	Word Biblical Commentary
WEC	Wycliffe Exegetical Commentary
WMANT	Wissenschaftriche Monographien zum Alten und Neuen Testament
WUNT	Wissenschaftriche unter Suchungen zum Neuen Testament
ZAW	*Zeitschrift für die alttestamentliche Wissenschaft*
ZDPV	*Zeitschrift des deutschen Palästina-Vereins*

Preface and Dedication

To write a book on *Sacrifice in the Bible* is to recognize the central place of the idea and practice of sacrifice in biblical religion. What began in the Old Testament as the ceremonial way of worship and atonement became, later in the Old Testament and especially in the New, the pattern for the way of human life and also for the way of divine salvation, through the work of the divine-human Saviour Jesus Christ. How far these developed ideas were implicit in the ceremonial practice from which they arose is one of the questions which has to be discussed in such a book.

Beginning from the ceremonial practice, especially as exemplified in the Passover sacrifice and the sacrificial regulations of Leviticus, the book passes on to the interpretation of sacrifice in the Psalms and the Prophets, before summing up the Old Testament material in a chapter on the theology of sacrifice and a chapter on sacrifice among the nations who were Israel's neighbours. The New Testament section begins with a chapter on the Jewish and Gentile backgrounds, and then surveys the main bodies of New Testament teaching in two chapters, before concluding with another theological chapter and a chapter which attempts to draw out the relevance for today of the whole book.

Sacrifice in the Bible originated in a conference of the Biblical Theology study group of the Tyndale Fellowship for Biblical and Theological Research, which was held at Tyndale House, Cambridge, in July 1987. The conference had been organized, and the speakers invited, by the Rev John P Baker, rector of Newick, Sussex, who had been the able and enthusiastic secretary of the group for many years. It was the last of these conferences that he was able to attend, as he was already suffering from leukaemia, which was the cause of his premature death the following year. From the outset it had been hoped that the papers read at the conference might form the basis of a book on the same theme, and now that the book is at last appearing, the editors would like to dedicate it, with respect and gratitude, to John Baker's memory.

After John Baker's death, two of the speakers at the conference undertook to edit the papers, with help in the initial stages from David Deboys, then librarian of Tyndale House. The general division of responsibility was for Roger Beckwith to edit the New Testament material and Martin Selman the Old Testament, though overall responsibility for the shape of the book and the greater part of the labour has been borne by the latter.

RTB
MJS

1

The Passover Sacrifice

T.D. ALEXANDER

I. CONTEMPORARY APPROACHES TO THE PASSOVER

The Passover is undoubtedly the best known of all the Jewish festivals. This is due in part to its prominence in the remarkable events surrounding the Israelite exodus from Egypt, and in part to the association of the death of Jesus Christ with the killing of the Passover sacrifice, as reflected in the famous words of Paul, 'For Christ, our Passover, has been sacrificed' (1 Cor. 5:7). Yet behind this casual familiarity there is much uncertainty about the Passover in the Old Testament period.

While we are primarily interested in the sacrificial element of the Passover, we must take as our starting point current theories regarding the origin and development of the Passover as a whole. This is necessary because scholarly research over the past century has led to a radically new understanding of the Passover's early history, challenging the authenticity of two central components of the biblical tradition. Firstly, it is now widely accepted that the Passover and the Feast of Unleavened Bread, in spite of their close association in Exodus 12 and elsewhere, were originally unrelated religious feasts. Secondly, it is often suggested that the real origin of the Passover is an ancient nomadic practice concerning the well-being of the flocks, and not the Israelite exodus from Egypt. The present biblical portrayal of the Passover arose out of a concern to provide later religious rites with an historical etiology. This reappraisal of the Passover's history, not surprisingly, has serious implications for our understanding of its sacrificial nature.

The modern rejection of the biblical Passover tradition is rooted in the theory that almost all of the Pentateuch comes from four sources, designated Yahwistic (J), Elohistic (E), Deuteronomistic (D) and Priestly (P), and dated respectively to the tenth/ninth, ninth/eighth, seventh and sixth/fifth centuries BC. This theory of four sources, known as the Documentary Hypothesis, received its most influential formulation over a century ago in the writings of Julius Wellhausen.[1] Significantly, to support his dating of the Pentateuchal sources, Wellhausen posited, in part, a totally new picture of the origin and development of the Passover. By comparing Ex. 23:15–16 and Ex. 34:18–22 (both J) with Dt. 16:1–17 (D) he concluded that in ancient Israel there were three main feasts: Unleavened Bread, Weeks and Tabernacles/Booths. On the basis of their earliest titles (Unleavened Bread, Harvest and Ingathering, as reflected in Ex. 23 and 34) they were clearly agricultural in origin, probably taken over by the Israelites from the Canaanites. Furthermore, because the J sections of the Pentateuch never mention it, the Passover could not have existed when J was composed.[2] Wellhausen then suggested, on the basis of Dt. 16:1–8 (D), that the Passover and the Feast of Unleavened Bread were amalgamated about the time of Josiah's reforms in 621 BC.[3] Prior to this they were totally unconnected. Subsequent developments, as revealed in the Priestly Writer's portrayal of the Passover (as found in Ex. 12:1–20, 28, 43–49; 13:1–2; Lv. 23:5–8; Nu. 9:1–14; Nu. 28:16–25), confirmed this major innovation.[4] By concluding that the Passover and the Feast of Unleavened Bread were unrelated prior to about 620 BC, Wellhausen overturned the longstanding tradition, highlighted especially in Exodus 12–13, that both originated as commemorations of the Israelite exodus from Egypt. So cogent were his arguments for the original independence of the Passover and Unleavened Bread that Wellhausen's work heralded a new era in the study of the early history of these sacred feasts.

If the Passover was unconnected to the Feast of Unleavened Bread prior to the time of Josiah, how did it originate and what form did it take? For his part, Wellhausen suggested that the Passover developed in a pastoral, rather than an agricultural setting, as the offering of the firstfruits of sheep and cattle.[5] Expressing gratitude to God for fruitful flocks and herds, it was the oldest of the feasts and was not tied to any particular time in the year. Although the offering of firstfruits originated in Israel's nomadic past, it was only rarely observed during the early monarchy; hence it is not mentioned in the Book of the Covenant (Ex. 22:29–30). It was revived in Judah after the fall of the northern kingdom in 721 BC, to be amalgamated almost a century later with the Feast of Unleavened Bread. Only at this stage was the name *pesaḥ* 'Passover' introduced.

While accepting the validity of Wellhausen's general approach, other writers substantially revised his picture of the Passover's origin. G.B. Gray sought to isolate various ancient features of the Passover by focusing on its later customs.[6] He concluded that the Passover was originally observed by nomadic Israelites on the night of the full moon nearest the Spring equinox. In its earliest form it consisted of a sacrificial meal in which the entire victim was eaten raw, with the blood still in it.[7] This custom was later modified; the victim was now cooked and its blood smeared on the door posts. The blood ritual had an apotropaic purpose; it was intended to protect those within from some power outside by providing a 're-inforced closed door'. With the centralization of sacrificial worship in Jerusalem in 621 BC, the practice of smearing the blood on the door was abandoned; the sacrificial meal alone continued to be observed.

According to R. de Vaux, the Passover began as the spring-time sacrifice of a young animal, not necessarily the firstborn, by nomadic or semi-nomadic shepherds in order to guarantee the prosperity of the flock.[8] It occurred prior to the tribal migration, and required neither a priest nor an altar. An important feature of the feast, which took place at the full moon, was the smearing of blood on the tent-poles in order to drive away evil powers. Various features of the later Passover celebration reflect its nomadic origin:

> The victim was roasted over a fire without any kitchen utensils; it was eaten with unleavened bread (which is still the normal bread of Bedouin to-day), and with bitter herbs (which does not mean vegetables grown in the garden, but the desert plants which Bedouin pick to season their food). The ritual prescribed that those eating it should have their belts already fastened, sandals on their feet (as if they were going to make a long journey on foot), and a shepherd's stick in one hand.[9]

Before the Israelite settlement of Canaan, the Passover was a common feast celebrated at the central sanctuary of the tribal federation. With the decentralization of cultic worship, after Israel's occupation of Canaan, it became a family feast. Much later, as a result of Josiah's decision to have all cultic worship centralized in Jerusalem, it reverted to a common feast.

Recently, the speculative nature of such histories has been highlighted by J. Van Seters. On methodological grounds he rejects these traditio-historical attempts to reconstruct the Passover's origin through either the backward projection of later features or the use of comparative customs.

> For all its ingenious reconstructions the disadvantages of the traditio-historical method are considerable. Since it speculates about the shape of the pre-literate tradition its theories cannot be falsified by an appeal to the present texts. There is also no way to make any judgment between radically different proposals and thus theories about the cult have greatly proliferated. Furthermore, those who follow this method have never demonstrated by comparative literature that tradition- history is anything but a completely artificial construction of biblical scholars.[10]

Because they cannot be substantiated, traditio-historical theories about the Passover's origin must be treated with the utmost caution. They clearly do not provide a very secure foundation upon which to base our investigation of the sacrificial nature of the Passover.

Although Van Seters affirms emphatically the priority of source analysis for uncovering the true history of the Passover, he rejects Wellhausen's approach on a number of specific points. Firstly, he is convinced that the J material should be dated to the period of the exile, making D the earliest source, with J coming midway between D and P. Secondly, whereas Wellhausen maintained that the Passover and the Feast of Unleavened Bread were first amalgamated in Deuteronomy 16, Van Seters views all the references to Unleavened Bread in Deuteronomy 16 as later additions. Thirdly, he supports the view of J. Halbe that the Feast of Unleavened Bread did not originate as an ancient Canaanite agricultural festival.[11] Rather he dates it to the exilic period when the eating of the Passover sacrifice could no longer be observed due to the destruction of the temple; the eating of unleavened bread became the basis of a substitute festival. Fourthly, he reassigns some of the material in Exodus 12–13 to different sources from those proposed by Wellhausen: 12:29–39 and 13:3–16 come from J; the remaining verses (12:1–28 and 13:1–2) are the product of P.[12]

In the light of these considerations, Van Seters proposes the following reconstruction of the Passover's history. The Passover, as reflected in the earliest source D, was a one day festival in the spring at a local sanctuary. After the slaughter of an animal from the flock or herd, there was a meal, eaten at night without unleavened bread. D restricted the celebration of the festival to a central sanctuary, and introduced the idea that it was a commemoration of the exodus. About a century and a half later, with the destruction of the temple, it was no longer possible to celebrate the Passover. As a result the Feast of Unleavened Bread was instituted by J as a substitute. This new feast, however, lasted for a week, and prominence was given to the eating of unleavened bread, the one significant element retained from the Passover celebration. With the restoration of the temple after the exile further modifications occurred, as witnessed in P. The revived Passover celebration was combined with the Feast of Unleavened Bread. This, however, presented a problem for Jews living in the Diaspora. How could they, far removed from the sanctuary, participate in the new combined feast? To resolve the problem each household was sanctified by means of a blood rite: 'A small animal could be slaughtered as a sacrifice, its blood used to purify the house, and the animal cooked in such a way as to resemble an offering by fire.'[13] To legitimize this activity the Priestly Writer created the etiology of the blood rite of the exodus story.[14]

The proposals of Wellhausen and Van Seters highlight the variety of reconstructions which are possible for the history of the Passover. Their differing conclusions depend heavily upon the source analysis of the relevant Pentateuchal passages and their dating in relation to one another. Since it is not possible in this present study to explore in detail the vast and complex issue of Pentateuchal criticism, several observations must suffice.

Firstly, at the present time the whole question of the source analysis of the Pentateuch is in a state of flux. The once assured results of the Documentary Hypothesis no longer enjoy widespread acceptance. Recent studies have challenged both the validity of the criteria used to distinguish sources[15] and the order in which they should be dated.[16] In the light of these developments, caution should be exercised about any attempt to reconstruct the history of the Passover on the basis of one particular theory of source analysis.

Secondly, in the past it has generally been assumed that if a Pentateuchal source shows no knowledge of a particular custom or practice, that feature did not exist when the source was composed. Yet conclusions drawn from the silence of the text may prove unwarranted. Two factors make this likely. On the one hand, some passages about the Passover are exceptionally brief (e.g. Ex. 34:25; Lv. 23:5; Nu. 28:16). The absence of particular details may be due entirely to the succinct nature of the material. On the other hand, if two sources have been combined, specific details in one source may be omitted for editorial reasons.[17] This is especially relevant regarding the narrative in Exodus 12–13, which is generally understood to be comprised of two, if not more, sources. Little allowance is made for the fact that the editor(s) who combined these sources may have deliberately omitted details already present in one source in favour of parallel details found in another of the sources. For example, while J alone mentions the use of a basin for catching the blood and of hyssop for smearing it on the door-posts (Ex. 12:21–27), we should not suppose that P's silence about these matters means that he had no knowledge of them. We must allow for the possibility that some material became redundant when the sources were combined.[18] Unfortunately, we have no way of knowing how little or how much material has been lost in the editorial process.

In the light of these observations it is apparent that the task of reconstructing the history of the Passover will continue to present a major challenge, even if scholars arrive at a new consensus regarding the source analysis of the Pentateuch. Two factors, however, suggest that greater authenticity should be attributed to the biblical account of the Passover's early history.

First, almost every passage which refers to the Passover associates it with either the Feast of Unleavened Bread or with the eating of unleavened bread.[19] Although Wellhausen and Van Seters maintain that the two feasts were originally unconnected in J and D respectively, their arguments are not convincing. M. Haran has demonstrated, *contra* Wellhausen, that J knew of both feasts; there is no reason to delete the term *pesaḥ* Passover in Ex. 34:25.[20] Nor is it necessary to remove, as Van Seters suggests, all references to Unleavened Bread in Deuteronomy 16.[21] Given the unanimity of the biblical tradition, there are surely good grounds for believing that both feasts were united from their inception. The evidence to the contrary is not compelling.

Second, all the Pentateuchal sources link the Passover with the Israelite exodus.[22] The assumption that later writers created an historical etiology is not supported by the evidence. No alternative explanation for the designation *pesaḥ* 'Passover' has gained widespread support, and although scholars have expressed reservations concerning with the explanation given in Exodus 12–13, it is by far the most suitable.[23]

For these reasons we shall treat seriously the biblical tradition which links the origin of both the Passover and the Feast of Unleavened Bread with the Israelite exodus from Egypt. Even if the reliability of this tradition is rejected, it still merits detailed consideration as it stands, if only because later generations unreservedly accepted it as trustworthy. To appreciate how the Passover was perceived in the post-biblical period and beyond, we must begin with the biblical tradition as we now have it.

II. ANALYSIS OF INDIVIDUAL PASSAGES

We shall consider initially the account of the very first Passover in Exodus 12–13. The uniqueness of this occasion sets it apart from all others. Unfortunately, modern historical reconstructions tend to blur this distinction. After considering this passage we shall survey the remaining texts. Throughout we shall give special consideration to the sacrificial nature of the Passover.

Exodus 12:1–13:16

By far the most detailed description of the Passover comes in Ex. 12:1–13:16. Set in the context of Israel's deliverance from Egypt we have here a description of the first Passover, together with instructions for future annual commemorations.

As it stands, the text of Exodus 12–13 draws an important distinction between this Passover and later commemorations. Comments regarding the first Passover focus primarily on the activities associated with the sacrifice made on the fourteenth day of the first month (Ex. 12:2–13, 21–23). This Passover is so significant that the Israelites are instructed to commemorate it for an entire week annually.[24] However, their imminent departure from Egypt prohibits any prolonged celebration at that time. Only in subsequent years will this be possible. These future commemorations will centre on a seven day festival marked by the eating of unleavened bread (Ex. 12:14–20; 13:3–10). While the Feast of Unleavened Bread will form the basis of future celebrations, the Passover night itself will also be remembered. It will be commemorated on the evening of the fourteenth of Abib, with the Feast of Unleavened Bread beginning on the fifteenth day of the month and lasting until the evening of the twenty-first day of the month.[25]

At the heart of the first Passover ritual is the slaying of a lamb or kid, the smearing of its blood on the door posts, and the eating of its meat. The detailed instructions for this ritual parallel closely those relating to sacrifices. Thus, the specifications concerning the victims are similar to those given elsewhere regarding sacrificial animals:[26] they are to be 'year-old males without defect' taken from 'the sheep or the goats'.[27] The sheep or goats are selected four days prior to their slaughter, perhaps to ensure that they are ritually pure. The sacrificial status of the animals is also reflected in the way they are treated after their slaughter. Special directions are given regarding the handling of the blood, flesh and bones: the blood must be put on the sides and tops of the door-frames of the houses (Ex. 12:7, 22); the meat is to be roasted over the fire and then eaten (Ex. 12:8–10); the victim's bones must not be broken (Ex. 12:46).[28] Taken together, all of these factors suggest that the Passover ritual should be understood as a sacrifice. This is confirmed by the brief comment in 12:27, 'It is the Passover sacrifice to the LORD.'

Although elements of the Passover ceremony resemble other sacrifices, in its entirety it is unique. Since sacrifices in ancient Israel took different forms and fulfilled various functions, it is not unexpected that the Passover should exhibit special characteristics. Moreover, the uniqueness of the occasion recorded in Exodus 12–13 accounts for some of the distinctive elements of the first Passover. Because this Passover occurred prior to the establishment of the Aaronic priesthood (Lv. 8:1–9:24), Moses commands 'all the elders of Israel' to slaughter the Passover victims (Ex. 12:21). Furthermore, no portion of the sacrifice is set aside for priestly consumption as was customary after the exodus;[29] the entire animal is consumed by all those within the house. Similarly, the narrative makes no reference to the central sanctuary or altar which were first instituted after the exodus at Sinai (Ex. 20:24–26; 25:8–27:19). The animals were probably sacrificed either in or close to the homes where the people gathered. The historical context may also explain why the Passover sacrifice took place at 'twilight'[30] whereas other sacrifices were normally offered up during daylight. On account of their exploitation by the Egyptians, the Israelites probably had no opportunity to offer sacrifices during the day. Finally, the timing of the Passover on the fourteenth day of the month coincides with the full moon, which would surely have been the most suitable night for undertaking the activities associated with the Israelites' departure from Egypt.

From the detailed description of the preparations associated with the killing of the Passover victim, there can be little doubt, as noted above, that this constituted a sacrifice. This is underlined by the special use to which the animal's blood is put; it is smeared on the sides and tops of the door-frame of the house (Ex. 12:7, 22). To explain this aspect of the Passover ritual some writers emphasize its apotropaic purpose; it was intended to protect those within from hostile powers without. This explanation is clearly supported by Ex. 12:13, 23 which describes how the destroyer is not permitted to enter those houses marked with blood on the door-frames; the blood apparently protects the Israelites from the plague which kills the Egyptian firstborn. Other scholars suggest that the blood was used to purify the Israelite houses.[31] Apart from other instances of blood being employed in this way, the use of hyssop (Ex. 12:22), associated elsewhere with ritual purification, supports this suggestion.[32] However, since the text does not make explicit the exact purpose of the blood rite, we cannot be completely certain as to its precise function.

Aside from the killing of the lamb or kid and the accompanying blood rite, the eating of the animal was an equally important part of the Passover ritual. This is highlighted by a number of factors. The whole Israelite community was to participate (Ex. 12:47). For each animal slaughtered there had to be an adequate number of people to eat all of its meat; where necessary smaller households joined together (Ex. 12:4). Only those who were circumcised could participate in the meal (Ex. 12:43–45, 48–49). Special instructions were given concerning the cooking of the meat; the entire animal was roasted over a fire, not boiled in water (Ex. 12:9). The meat must be eaten indoors (Ex. 12:46), and it was forbidden to break the bones (Ex. 12:46). Any meat which remained until the morning was burnt (Ex. 12:10). The meticulous nature of these details suggests that the meal had a special significance.

Interestingly, the description of the Passover meal is closely paralleled by the account of the consecration of the Aaronic priests in Exodus 29 and Leviticus 8. Moses was to slaughter a ram and sprinkle some of its blood on Aaron and his sons to consecrate them (Ex. 29:20–21; Lv. 8:23–24, 30). Aaron and his sons were then to cook the ram and eat its meat, along with unleavened bread (cf. Ex. 29:23), at the entrance to the Tent of Meeting (Ex. 29:32; Lv. 8:31). Because the meat was sacred, no-one else was permitted to eat it, and any meat left till the morning was to be burnt up (Ex. 29:33–34; Lv. 8:32). Clearly the slaughter of the ram, together with the sprinkling of its blood and the eating of its meat form the main elements of a consecration ritual.[33]

Although some of the details differ, these same elements underlie the Passover ritual. This suggests that it may have performed a similar function. By participating in the Passover ritual, the Israelites set themselves apart as holy. This conclusion would support the view that the slaughter of the animal atoned for the sin of the people and that the blood smeared on the door-posts purified those within the house. By participating in the Passover the Israelites took an important step towards becoming a holy nation (cf. Ex. 19:6).[34]

Exodus 34:25

The next explicit reference to the Passover comes in Ex.34:25, where it is mentioned briefly in conjunction with the feasts of Unleavened Bread, Harvest and Ingathering (Ex. 34:18–26). This passage comes in the context of the renewal of the divine covenant with the Israelites following their rebellious activity involving the Golden Calf (Ex. 34:1–28; cf. Ex. 32:1–35). Ex. 34:10–26 is probably an abridged version of a covenant document which Moses recorded on this occasion. It resembles closely an earlier covenant document, called 'the Book of the Covenant' (Ex. 24:7), preserved in Ex. 21:1–23:33.[35] Of particular interest is the fact that both texts provide similar instructions regarding the three major pilgrimage feasts of Unleavened Bread, Harvest, and Ingathering.[36] Although the Passover is not named explicitly in Ex. 23:14–19, v. 18 parallels closely 34:25:

Exodus 23:18	*Exodus 34:25*
Do not offer the blood of a sacrifice to me along with anything containing yeast. The fat of my festival offerings must not be kept until morning.	Do not offer the blood of a sacrifice to me along with anything containing yeast, and do not let any of the sacrifice from the Passover Feast remain until morning.[37]

Unfortunately, the concise nature of these regulations has caused commentators to adopt very differing interpretations. Scholarly opinion is divided as to whether or not these verses refer to the Passover.[38] However, there are good reasons for treating both passages as referring to the Passover. Since the word order highlights the importance of unleavened bread, a major element in the Passover (cf. Ex. 12:8, 15, 17–20) but a minor aspect of other sacrifices, Haran rejects the opinion that 23:18a and 34:25a refer to all sacrifices. Furthermore, the requirement that nothing of the sacrifice should be kept or remain until morning did not apply to most sacrifices; it is, however, very reminiscent of the Passover (Exodus 12:10).[39]

As observed above, the first Passover was to be commemorated principally through the week long festival of Unleavened Bread which was preceded by a special commemoration of the Passover night. While the material in Ex. 23:14–19 and 34:18–26 focuses primarily on the three main pilgrimage feasts, it is hardly surprising that the Passover should be mentioned in view of its close association with the Feast of Unleavened Bread. Unfortunately, the brevity of these regulations makes it impossible to reconstruct a detailed picture of the Passover. Nevertheless, they are in keeping with how we might have expected later celebrations of the Passover to be observed on the basis of Exodus 12–13.

Leviticus 23:5

The Passover is listed among 'the appointed feasts of the LORD' in Lv. 23:1–44, where it is mentioned briefly (v. 5) by way of introducing the Feast of Unleavened Bread (vv. 6–8). The chapter as a whole highlights those occasions on which sacred assemblies were held (23:2, 4). Apart from every Sabbath, sacred assemblies were held on the first and seventh days of Unleavened Bread, once during the Feast of Weeks,[40] on the Feast of Trumpets, on the Day of Atonement, and on the first and eighth days of Tabernacles. Significantly, the Passover is not designated a sacred assembly; it is merely stated that it begins at twilight on the fourteenth day of the first month. Furthermore, although details are given regarding some of the sacrifices associated with the appointed feasts, no information is provided about the Passover sacrifice.

Numbers 9:1–14

The first account of the Passover being commemorated after the exodus from Egypt comes in Nu. 9:1–14. This passage is noteworthy because it addresses the problem of those who are unable to celebrate the Passover on the fourteenth day of the *first* month of the year because they are ceremonially unclean. That such a problem should arise indicates that those who observed the Passover were expected to be ritually pure. This was necessary because of the sacredness of the event. To resolve this difficulty the LORD instructs Moses that those who are unable to participate at the usual time may celebrate it on the fourteenth day of the *second* month (v. 11). Apart from the change in date, all other aspects of the commemoration remain the same. It was to be celebrated at twilight (9:3). The people were to eat a lamb or kid together with unleavened bread and bitter herbs (Nu. 9:11; cf. Ex. 12:8). Nothing must be left till the morning and the victim's bones must not be broken (Nu. 9:12; cf. Ex. 12:10, 46).

The Passover sacrifice is described twice as 'the LORD's offering' (Nu. 9:7,13). The Hebrew term used here for 'offering', *qorbān*, refers to that which is brought near. It is frequently used in Leviticus and Numbers of either sacrifices or objects to be used in the sanctuary (cf. Nu. 7:13ff.).[41] This indicates that the Passover sacrifice was to be offered in the sanctuary, and not at home, as happened on the very first Passover. In this regard subsequent Passover commemorations differ markedly from the original event.

Interestingly, the Feast of Unleavened Bread is not mentioned in this passage. This suggests that a distinction was drawn between keeping the Passover and the Feast of Unleavened Bread.[42] While it was possible to celebrate the Passover a month later, it was evidently not always practical to set aside in the second month another entire week to celebrate the Feast of Unleavened Bread. This is supported by the observation that the Israelites begin a three day journey on the twentieth day of the second month (Nu. 10:11, 33), whereas the Feast of Unleavened Bread normally ended on the twenty-first day of the month with a sacred assembly, during which it was forbidden to work.

Numbers 28:16

Nu. 28:1–29:40, which parallels closely Lv. 23:1-44, lists the food for the LORD's offerings made by fire at the appointed times (Nu. 28:2).[43] Significantly, all the sacrifices described in Numbers 28–29 are burnt offerings; that is, the entire offering is consumed by fire. The burning of the victim produces an aroma pleasing to God (cf. Nu. 28:2). As in

Leviticus 23, Passover is mentioned briefly (Nu. 28:16) prior to a fuller discussion of the Feast of Unleavened Bread (Nu. 28:17–25). Although the text focuses on the special daily offering associated with Unleavened Bread, nothing is stated explicitly about the nature of the Passover sacrifice. From the silence of the text, we may deduce that the Passover sacrifice did not fall into the category of offerings made by fire; because its meat is eaten by the worshippers, it is not classified as a burnt offering.

Numbers 33:3

In noting the date of the Israelites' departure from Egypt, Nu. 33:3 alludes only briefly to the Passover and provides no additional information regarding the sacrifice.

Deuteronomy 16:1–8

The last reference to the Passover in the Pentateuch comes in Dt. 16:1–17. This passage, like Ex. 23:14–19 and Ex. 34:18–26, gives details about the three main pilgrimage feasts, Unleavened Bread, Weeks and Tabernacles. Once again the Passover is mentioned in conjunction with the Feast of Unleavened Bread (16:1–8).[44] However, whereas the passages already considered tend to present the Passover and Unleavened Bread as distinctive occasions, they are treated here more as a unity. This does not mean, as many scholars have assumed, that Deuteronomy brings together for the first time two originally unconnected feasts. The apparent separation of the Passover and Unleavened Bread in earlier contexts arises out of the special interests of those passages.[45] Because the author of Deuteronomy is primarily interested in them as a single occasion, he tends to blur the distinctions between the two, especially in vv.1–4a. A careful reading of the text reveals, however, that in spite of this the Passover and the Feast of Unleavened Bread retain their distinctive features.[46]

Another feature of the present passage is the emphasis given to the location at which the Passover and Unleavened Bread will be celebrated. Three times it is made clear that the Passover must be sacrificed and eaten 'at the place the LORD will choose as a dwelling for his Name' (v.2; cf. vv.6, 7). Since the book of Deuteronomy is set against the background of the Israelites' imminent entry into and settlement of the promised land, it is not surprising that something should be said about the venue of the pilgrimage Feast of Unleavened Bread.[47] From this time onwards the people will no longer live in close proximity to the sanctuary.

By treating Passover and Unleavened Bread as a single event the author of Deuteronomy creates a number of apparent discrepancies between his description of these feasts and those recorded elsewhere in the Pentateuch. Unfortunately, more has been made of these differences than is necessary. To a large extent they occur because the deuteronomic legislation is presented in a non-technical or general way.[48]

It is observed that Dt. 16:2 apparently specifies the use of animals from
the flock or herd (*ṣō'n ûḇāqār*) for the Passover sacrifice, whereas
elsewhere this is limited to the flock (*ṣō'n*) alone (Ex. 12:5). Various
solutions have been suggested to account for the deuteronomic legislation.[49] The inclusion of cattle, however, probably relates to sacrifices
which accompany either the Passover or, perhaps more likely, the Feast
of Unleavened Bread; only sheep and goats are used for the Passover
sacrifice itself.[50] Several factors support this interpretation. Firstly, in 2
Ch. 35:7-9 cattle are closely linked with the provision of sheep and goats
for the Passover. Yet, the Hebrew text of 2 Ch. 35:7 makes it clear that
only the sheep and goats constitute the Passover sacrifice; the cattle are
slaughtered, but not as Passover offerings. Secondly, the expression *pesaḥ
lyhwh*, 'Passover to (of) Yahweh', probably designates here the combined
festival of Passover and Unleavened Bread. Verse 2 thus refers to all the
sacrifices made during the seven day festival. This view is supported by
the unique combination of words in the opening phrase of v.2: *weẓāḇaḥtā
pesaḥ lyhwh*, 'sacrifice Passover to the LORD (Yahweh)'. On the one hand,
this is the only example of the expression *pesaḥ lyhwh* being used with a
verb other than *'āśâ* 'to do, perform',[51] and on the other hand, the verbs
'ākal 'to eat', *bāšal* 'to cook', *šāḥaṭ* 'to slaughter' and *zāḇaḥ* 'to sacrifice'
elsewhere always take the object *happesaḥ*, a clear reference to the
Passover victim.[52] Had the author wished to specify only the Passover
victim in v. 2 he would surely have used *happesaḥ*, as in vv.5 and 6, rather
than *pesaḥ lyhwh*. Thirdly, J.B. Segal notes that this is the only occasion
in Deuteronomy where the word order 'flock and herd' is adopted.[53] If
v.2 refers to the combined festival of Passover and Unleavened Bread, this
order reflects accurately the sequence in which the sacrifices were offered.

Another difficulty is noted in verse 3 regarding the length of the
Passover. The text apparently states that the eating of the Passover animal
accompanied the consumption of unleavened bread for seven days. The
interpretation of the verse hinges on the two occurrences of the Hebrew
word *'ālāyw* (the preposition *'al* with the pronominal suffix ending for
'him' or 'it').[54] *'al* has a wide range of meanings,[55] of which two seem
particularly appropriate in the present context. First, it could mean 'in
addition to it', with the antecedent of 'it' being the sacrificial animals.
This has been taken by some scholars to imply that the Passover must
have lasted for the entire period during which unleavened bread was
eaten. However, as we have suggested above, the expression *pesaḥ lyhwh*
is probably used in vv.1-2 as a title for the combined feasts of Passover
and Unleavened Bread. If this is so, v.3 need not imply that the actual
Passover sacrifice was eaten for the entire week.[56] Second, *'ālāyw* might
possibly mean 'in front of him', referring to the LORD (Yahweh).[57] This
proposal removes completely any difficulty over the length of the
Passover. With either of these readings of *'ālāyw* there is no reason to
suppose that the deuteronomic legislation contradicts previous Passover
instructions.

In verse 6 the time of the sacrifice is given as 'in the evening (*bā'āreb*), when the sun goes down'. Elsewhere the expression 'between the evenings' (*bên hā'arbayim*) is used (Ex. 12:6; Lv. 23:5; Nu. 28:4,8). No essential difference is implied by Deuteronomy's adoption of a variant expression for the timing of the sacrifice. The author of Deuteronomy adopts, as is his custom, a less technical equivalent in place of the more specialized expression 'between the evenings'.

According to some scholars, v.7 contradicts what is stated in Ex. 12:9 regarding the cooking of the Passover victim. Whereas Ex. 12:9 clearly prohibits the meat from being boiled, the deuteronomic legislation apparently requires it, the same verb *bāšal* being used on both occasions. However, *bāšal* by itself means 'to cook', not 'to boil'; to specify boiling in Ex. 12:9 it is qualified by the expression 'in water'.[58] There is, therefore, no reason to suppose that Dt. 16:7 required the Passover animal to be boiled rather than roasted. The author of Deuteronomy may have felt it unnecessary to give exact specifications regarding the cooking of the victim, because they were already commonly known and practised.

The meaning of the comment in v.7, 'in the morning return to your tents', has also prompted some discussion. Various writers have taken the term 'tents' to mean 'houses', and consequently have interpreted this instruction as a requirement that the people return to their own homes, wherever these are in Israel, after celebrating the Passover night. But how does one reconcile this with the fact that the male Israelites were expected to be present at the sanctuary during the Feast of Unleavened Bread? Mayes is probably correct when he comments that 'it should be taken literally as a reference to the tent encampments of the pilgrims to the central sanctuary for the celebration of the seven-day festival'.[59] The deuteronomic legislation was probably designed to encourage the people to return to their tents for rest before re-congregating to celebrate together the first day of Unleavened Bread as a holy assembly (cf. Ex. 12:16; Lv. 23:7; Nu. 28:25).

A further problem is raised by the reference to six days in v.8. Many scholars see a direct contradiction between this and the mention of seven days in v.3. However, this difficulty is easily resolved when we note that v.8 echoes the sabbatical section of the deuteronomic decalogue;[60] the festive week is divided into six days, followed by a seventh in which no work is to be undertaken. The verse is structured in this way to highlight the special nature of the closing 'assembly' (*'aṣeret*).[61] It is only by accident that it appears to contradict the statement in v.3 that unleavened bread should be eaten for seven days.

Although many scholars have argued that the deuteronomic record of the Passover differs significantly from descriptions found elsewhere in the Pentateuch, this is not the case.[62] As we have observed, a variety of factors account for the apparent discrepancies observed in the text. While Deuteronomy 16 emphatically confirms our earlier observation that every commemoration of the Passover sacrifice took place at the central

sanctuary and not in the homes of the people, it sheds no new light on the
sacrificial nature of the Passover.

Joshua 5:10–11

Outside the Pentateuch references to the Passover are few. There is a
short notice in Jos. 5:10–11 about the very first celebration of the Passover
in the land of Canaan. After crossing the Jordan on the tenth day of the
first month (4:19), Joshua proceeds to commemorate the Passover on the
fourteenth day of the same month. Although the account is brief, several
points should be noted. Firstly, prior to the celebration of the Passover
Joshua circumcises those Israelites born in the desert during the journey
from Egypt (5:4–7). This is in keeping with the instruction that only those
who were circumcised should participate in the Passover (Ex. 12:44, 48).
Secondly, in spite of suggestions to the contrary, the comment about
eating unleavened bread on the day after the Passover (v. 11) strongly
implies that the Feast of Unleavened Bread was observed on this
occasion.[63] No details are given of the week long festival because the
narrator is chiefly interested in noting that the manna, which formed the
basis of the Israelites' diet in the desert, ceased to be divinely provided;
now that they are in the promised land, the Israelites can enjoy its
bountiful provisions (v.12).

2 Chronicles 30:1–27

Remarkably, the next record of the Passover being celebrated comes
considerably later in 716/5 BC in the first year of the reign of Hezekiah,
king of Judah (2 Ch. 30:1–27). On this occasion the Passover is
commemorated in the second month, which is due to several factors.
First, the temple had to be re-consecrated. Although this was completed
on the sixteenth day of the first month (2 Ch. 29:17), the temple service
was only re-established the next day through the offering of special
sacrifices (29:20–36). It was therefore not possible to commemorate the
Passover on the fourteenth day of the first month. Second, 2 Ch. 30:3
states that the Passover could not be kept at the regular time because (a)
there was an inadequate number of consecrated priests and (b)
insufficient people had gathered in Jerusalem. Consequently, Hezekiah
invites to Jerusalem all the inhabitants of Israel and Judah, from
Beersheba to Dan, to celebrate the Passover in the second month (30:5).
Such was the joy of the occasion that the Feast of Unleavened Bread was
celebrated for an extra week (30:23). Since the time of Solomon there had
been nothing like it in Jerusalem (2 Ch. 30:26).[64]

 A number of points are worth observing in this passage. Firstly, the
celebration of the feast in the second month is reminiscent of the
instruction given in Nu. 9:9–14 that those who are either ceremonially
unclean or unable to attend the sanctuary may observe the Passover on the
fourteenth day of the second month. Secondly, the blood of the Passover

victims is not smeared on the door posts of the houses, as in Egypt, but is sprinkled on or against the altar (2 Ch. 30:16).[65] Moreover, this is done by the priests and not the heads of households (cf Ex. 12:21–22). Thirdly, the holiness of the event is stressed. Although this was a time of great joy (2 Ch. 30:21, 23, 25, 26), it was also a very sacred occasion; those who participated were expected to be ceremonially clean (2 Ch. 30:15, 17; cf. Nu. 9:10). For this reason the Levites kill the Passover victims on behalf of those who are ritually unclean (2 Ch. 30:17). Similarly, Hezekiah intercedes for those who eat the Passover without having purified themselves (2 Ch. 30:18–20). This emphasis upon the holiness of the occasion is reminiscent of the first Passover; it was intended to create a holy nation.

2 Kings 23:21–23 and 2 Chronicles 35:1–19

There are two accounts of the Passover being commemorated in the eighteenth year of king Josiah; a brief description in 2 Ki. 23:21–23, and a much fuller one in 2 Ch. 35:1–19. Both passages record the Passover celebrations held following the discovery in the temple of the Book of the Law or Covenant (2 Ki. 22:8, 11; 23:2, 21): 'Not since the days of the judges who led Israel, nor throughout the days of the kings of Israel and the kings of Judah, had any such Passover been observed' (2 Ki. 23:22).[66] As was customary, the Feast of Unleavened Bread was observed for the seven days after the Passover (2 Ch. 35:17).

As in 2 Chronicles 30, the role of the priests and in particular the Levites is highlighted in 2 Chronicles 35. Although no-one is described as ceremonially unclean, verses 6 and 11 imply that the Levites killed all of the Passover victims. This represents an innovation regarding the slaughter of the Passover animals; apart from the exceptional instance in 2 Ch. 30:17, the sheep or goats had previously been slaughtered by the heads of the households. By requiring the Levites to kill the animals, Josiah was concerned to ensure the ritual purity of those involved in offering the Passover sacrifices.

As in Dt. 16:1–4a, the present passage sometimes blurs the distinction between the Passover and the Feast of Unleavened Bread. This is so as regards the mention of cattle in vv.7–9, 12. These did not constitute the Passover sacrifice itself, but most likely relate to the 'holy offerings' (*qᵒdāšîm*) mentioned in v. 13. Whereas the Passover animals were roasted,[67] the 'holy offerings' were cooked in pots, cauldrons and pans, probably during the Feast of Unleavened Bread.[68]

Ezekiel 45:21–24

The Passover and the Feast of Unleavened Bread are mentioned briefly (45:21–24) in Ezekiel's vision of the restoration of temple worship in the New Israel (Ezk. 40:1–48:35). They are introduced in the context of the offerings which the 'prince' will make at the festivals, the New Moons and the Sabbaths to atone for the house of Israel (45:13–46:15; see especially 45:17). Little is said about the Passover itself, with most of 45:21–24 centring on the Feast of Unleavened Bread.[69] Much of this passage resembles Nu. 28:17–22 and deals with the burnt offerings and purifications offerings made during the Feast of Unleavened Bread. Verse 22, however, relates to the Passover night, and describes the offering of a bull as a purification offering for the prince and all the people of the land; this is clearly in addition to the usual Passover sacrifices. Since this section of Ezekiel's vision concentrates on the special offerings presented by the 'prince' it offers no further information regarding the actual Passover sacrifice itself.

Ezra 6:19–22

The final reference to the Passover comes in Ezr. 6:19–22, which records the Passover being celebrated by the Jewish exiles following the completion and dedication of the temple in Jerusalem in 515 BC. After observing the Passover, the people joyfully celebrated the Feast of Unleavened Bread for seven days (v.22). Once again various features of the text stress the sacredness of the Passover. The ritual purity of the priests and Levites is noted. As in 2 Chronicles 35, the Levites sacrifice the Passover animals on behalf of all the people, including the priests (Ezr. 6:20). Finally, apart from the returned exiles, only those who separated themselves from the unclean practices of their Gentile neighbours may participate in the Passover commemoration.

III.   THE THEOLOGICAL SIGNIFICANCE OF THE PASSOVER

The exodus from Egypt is clearly presented within the Old Testament as one of the most important events in the history of God's relationship with Israel. Although many modern scholars tend to dismiss its historical reality, it is clear that this tradition was deeply ingrained in Israelite thought. We find, for example, that the expression 'out of Egypt' is used with reference to the exodus approximately 135 times throughout the Old Testament. Since the Passover lies at the very heart of the exodus story, it is hardly surprising that it is associated with several important theological ideas.

First, the deliverance of the Israelites from slavery in Egypt is presented as an act of God's faithfulness. Through it he fulfilled his earlier promise to Abraham that, although his descendants would be 'enslaved and ill-treated four hundred years,' God would afterwards bring them out with great possessions (Gn. 15:13–14; cf. Ex. 2:24; 3:7–10, 17; 6:5–8; 13:3–5, 11).

Second, the Exodus narrative emphasizes that the initiative in rescuing the Israelites from Egypt rested with the LORD. Although there are brief references to the Israelites crying out for help and God hearing (e.g. 2:23–24; 3:7), the narrative consistently implies that the LORD was not coerced into helping by the people's actions, but acted freely, motivated in part at least by a feeling of compassion for them and a desire for justice (3:7; 4:31). Nowhere does the text suggest that the people persuaded God to act on their behalf by the offering of sacrifices or the performance of meritorious deeds; their deliverance from Egypt is portrayed as an act of sovereign grace.

Third, throughout the Exodus account special attention is focused on the power of God to deliver the Israelites from Egypt. This idea is encapsulated in the references to God's 'mighty hand' (13:3,9,14,16; cf. 3:19; 6:1; 32:11) or 'outstretched arm' (6:6). The power of the LORD is contrasted favourably with that of the Egyptian Pharaoh.

Fourth, the concept of atonement, while not mentioned specifically, underlies the offering of the Passover sacrifice. Whereas on previous occasions the LORD had distinguished between the Israelites and the Egyptians without requiring any special ritual, on the occasion of the Passover the Israelites had of necessity to mark their houses with sacrificial blood. Obviously the blood of the sacrifice played a significant part in preventing the death of the male firstborn. Implicit in this is the idea that the Israelites were inherently no different from the male firstborn of the Egyptians. Without the atoning blood of the sacrifice they too would have been struck dead by the 'destroyer'.

Fifth, redemption is another important theological idea associated with the Passover. It is mentioned first in Ex. 6:6 where it is used in the context of the release of slaves (cf. 21:8). The concept reappears in 13:14–16 where it is linked to the future redemption of the male firstborn in commemoration of the Passover. In this context two aspects are prominent: (a) as a consequence of the Passover all the firstborn of the Israelites, both human and animal, owe their lives to the LORD; they belong uniquely to him and this has to be acknowledged in a special way; (b) since all the male firstborn belonged to the LORD, this required that each life be offered up to the LORD in sacrifice. However, in the case of human beings and non-sacrificial animals it was possible to offer a substitute. This is apparent from the brief remark about the redemption of every firstborn donkey in 13:13: if the donkey is redeemed it lives; otherwise it must be put to death. Here redemption involves the offering of a substitute sacrifice.

Sixth, a further dimension to the Passover account is the sanctification of the people. Not only does the blood of the Passover sacrifice protect the male firstborn from death, but the eating of the sacrificial meat sanctifies all who consume it. The Passover marks the setting apart of the Israelites as a 'holy nation'.

In the light of these observations, the present biblical account is clearly much richer in theological ideas than the alternative reconstructions proposed by recent writers (e.g. to express gratitude for fruitful flocks and herds; to guarantee the prosperity of livestock; to protect those within from hostile powers without). In spite of the ingenuity underlying them, modern hypotheses concerning the origin and development of the Passover fail to account for the inclusion of all the theological ideas which are now an integral part of the biblical tradition. Furthermore, it is difficult to explain how, and also why, relatively simple theological concepts derived from the domestic concerns of nomads evolved into much more sophisticated ideas associated with a national feast of a sedentary population. If the Passover tradition, as we now know it, does not derive from an actual exodus of slaves from Egypt, we still lack a satisfactory explanation for the origin and development of the different theological ideas associated with it.

IV. CONCLUSION

Although the OT does not provide a complete and detailed accountof the Passover's origin, development and history for the entire biblical period of over one thousand years, it does reveal a consistent picture, with only minor modifications being introduced through time. We observed, however, that the original Passover had certain unique features not found in later commemorations, and that although instituted in Egypt the Feast of Unleavened Bread was inaugurated only on the first anniversary of the Israelites' departure from Egypt. On the basis of the biblical evidence we see no reason to follow the modern view that the Passover and the Feast of Unleavened Bread had separate origins completely unassociated with the Israelite exodus from Egypt.

On account of similarities with the ritual for the consecration of the Aaronic priests in Exodus 29, there is good reason to believe that a major purpose of the original Passover was the consecration of the Israelites as a holy nation (cf. Ex. 19:6). By offering the Passover sacrifice, smearing its blood on their doors, and eating its meat the Israelites set themselves apart as holy; they become the people of God.[70] Consequently, they are delivered from the destructive power of the Destroyer who slew the firstborn of the Egyptians. The importance of this original consecration is highlighted in later commemorations by the requirement that all the participants in the Passover be ceremonially clean.

NOTES

1. *Prolegomena to the History of Israel* (Edinburgh: A. and C. Black, 1885.)
2. Wellhausen, op. cit. 85, n.1, emends the expression *ḥāg happāsaḥ* 'feast of the passover' in Ex. 34:25, to *ḥaggî* 'my feast' on the basis of Ex. 23:18.
3. For a brief critique of the view that the book of Deuteronomy was composed in the time of Josiah, see G.J. Wenham, 'The date of Deuteronomy: linch-pin of Old Testament

criticism', *Themelios* 10 (1985) 15–20; 11 (1985) 15–18; cf. J.G. McConville, *Grace in the End: a Study of Deuteronomic Theology* (Carlisle: Paternoster, 1993).

4. E.g. the precise dating of the Passover; more exact specifications regarding the offerings.

5. The inadequacy of this reconstruction is highlighted by M. Haran, 'The Passover Sacrifice', *Studies in the Religion of Ancient Israel* (VTSup 22) (Leiden: Brill, 1972) 94–95; cf. R. de Vaux, *Ancient Israel: its life and institutions* (London: Darton, Longman & Todd, 1965²) 489.

6. *Sacrifice in the Old Testament: its theory and practice* (Oxford: Clarendon, 1925) 337–382.

7. Gray, op. cit. 368, observes that in Ex. 12:9 and 12:46 it is forbidden to eat the victim raw, or to break any of its bones. He concludes, 'A legal prohibition is commonly directed against what is, or has been, actual practice. It has therefore been inferred that at one time the Paschal victim was eaten raw, and that the bones, having been broken and pounded for the purpose, were eaten as well as the flesh.'

8. de Vaux, *Ancient Israel*, 484–493. He appears to follow L. Rost's comparative study of the customs of nomadic Arabs, 'Weidewechsel und altisraelitischer Festkalender', *ZDPV* 66 (1943) 205–216; reprinted in L. Rost, *Das kleine Credo und andere Studien zum AT* (Heidelberg: Quelle & Meyer, 1965) 101–112. The relevance of Rost's study has been queried by B.N. Wambacq, 'Les origines de la *Pesah* israélite' *Bib* 57 (1976) 206–224. In particular he notes that the blood rite among nomadic Arabs concerns their arrival and settlement in a new location, whereas the Passover ritual in Ex. 12 focuses on the Israelites' departure from Egypt.

9. R. de Vaux, op. cit. 489; cf. N.M. Sarna, *Exploring Exodus: the Heritage of Biblical Israel* (New York: Schocken, 1986) 88. The suggestion that various features of the Passover indicate that it was originally a nomadic festival is rejected by I. Engnell, *Critical Essays on the Old Testament* (London: SPCK, 1970) 190. He writes: 'The command to put the blood on the door-posts and lintel does not fit a nomadic situation, because it assumes a settled community with more permanent types of houses . . . The fact that the Passover was originally a lunar festival proves nothing: lunar calendars were used in the civilized country of Canaan, and they were used in Babylon from time immemorial. The fact that a lamb or a kid was used in this festival is no proof that it has to be nomadic. These sacred victims or sacrificial animals played a prominent rôle in Canaan, as well as in Ras Shamra and Babylon.'

10. J. Van Seters, 'The Place of the Yahwist in the History of Passover and Massot' *ZAW* 95 (1983) 169–70.

11. J. Halbe, 'Erwägungen zu Ursprung und Wesen des Massotfestes' *ZAW* 87 (1975) 325–334. Among the reasons listed by Halbe, the following are the most convincing: (a) the month of Abib (March–April) is too early for a harvest festival; (b) it is strange that a harvest celebration should be marked by the eating of unleavened bread; (c) a seven-day festival is hardly likely to have occurred at the beginning of the harvest; (d) a special reason, the exodus from Egypt, has to be provided for celebrating the Feast of Unleavened Bread; this is not so for the true harvest feasts of Harvest (Weeks) and Ingathering (Tabernacles/Booths).

12. S.R. Driver, *Introduction to the Literature of the Old Testament* (Edinburgh: T. & T. Clark, 1913⁹) 28, assigns 12:1–20, 28, 37a, 40–51; 13:1–2 to P; 12:29–30 to J; 12:31–36, 37b–39, 42a to E; and 12:21–27; 13: 3–16 to JE.

13. J. Van Seters, op. cit. 180–181.

14. This proposal raises a number of problems. The smearing of blood on the door posts is mentioned only in connection with the original Passover night in Egypt. There is no hint that the blood was used in this way during subsequent commemorations of the Passover. In view of the uniqueness of the original occasion, the Exodus narrative hardly provides a suitable etiology for justifying the adoption of this practice on future occasions. Furthermore, would the Priestly Writer have supported a practice which involved the offering of sacrifices by non-priests? Finally, Van Seters offers no evidence of it having

been practised in the exilic or post-exilic period, and no explanation as to why it ceased, presumably soon afterwards, to be observed.

15. E.g. J. Van Seters, *Abraham in History and Tradition* (New Haven: Yale University Press, 1974); Y.T. Raddai and H. Shore, *Genesis: an Authorship Study in Computer Assisted Statistical Linguistics* (AnBib 103) (Rome: Biblical Institute Press, 1985); R.N. Whybray, *The Making of the Pentateuch: A Methodological Study* (JSOTS 53) (Sheffield: SAP, 1987).

16. E.g. R. Rendtorff, *The Problem of the process of transmission in the Pentateuch* (JSOTS 89) (Sheffield, SAP, 1990), ET of *Das überlieferungsgeschichtliche Problem des Pentateuch* (BZAW 147) (Berlin: de Gruyter, 1976); A. Hurvitz, *A Linguistic Study of the Relationship between the Priestly Source and the Book of Ezekiel: A New Approach to an Old Problem* (Paris: Gabalda, 1982). Rendtorff (169) comments: 'We possess hardly any reliable criteria for the dating of pentateuchal literature. Every dating of the pentateuchal "sources" rests on purely hypothetical assumptions, which ultimately only have any standing through the consensus of scholars.'

17. The source analysis of the flood narrative illustrates this possibility. Although the Yahwistic material contains no reference to the building of the ark, it clearly presupposes that one was constructed. If the present account is the product of J and P material having been combined, the editor has adopted the P version of the ark's construction in preference to that of J.

18. As Haran, 'The Passover Sacrifice', 88, observes, 'The J passage (Exod. xii 21–27) in no way contradicts the description given in P . . . Both refer to the same happening, only neither of them embraces all the details, which means that they actually complement each other.' Such is the unity of the present narrative that Van Seters assigns all of Ex. 12:1–28 to P.

19. Only two passages mention the Passover without making any reference to unleavened bread: Num. 33:3, a brief chronological remark, and 2 Ki. 23:21–23, a short description of the Passover celebrated by Josiah. Passover and the Feast of Unleavened Bread are linked in Ex. 12:1–13:16; 23:15–18; 34:18–25; Lv. 23:5–6; Dt. 16:1–16; 2 Ch. 30:1–21; 35:1–19; Ezr. 6:19–22. Passover and the eating of unleavened bread are associated in Ex. 12:1–13:16; 23:18; 34:25; Nu. 9:2–14; 28:16–17; Dt. 16:1–8; Jos. 5:10–11; Ezk. 45:21.

20. 'The Passover Sacrifice', 96–101.

21. Cf. J.G. McConville, *Law and Theology in Deuteronomy* (JSOTS 33) (Sheffield: JSOT Press, 1984) 99–123. See below our discussion of Dt. 16:1–8.

22. Among all the references to the Passover in the Pentateuch, only in Lv. 23:5–6 is there no mention of the exodus. Apart from Ex. 12:1–13:16, the two events are linked together in Ex. 23:15; 34:18; Nu. 9:1; 33:3; Dt. 16:1, 3, 6.

23. H.-J. Kraus, *Worship in Israel: A Cultic History of the Old Testament* (Oxford: Blackwell, 1966) 45–46; cf. J.B. Segal, *The Hebrew Passover from the earliest times to AD 70* (London Oriental Series 12) (London: Oxford University Press, 1963) 95–101.

24. Apart from the week set aside for the Feast of Unleavened Bread, the exodus from Egypt was also commemorated through the consecration of every firstborn male (13:2, 11–16). This, however, is not directly associated with the Passover sacrifice.

25. There are various ways of understanding the chronology of the Passover and the Feast of Unleavened Bread in Ex. 12:18, depending upon the starting time of the calendar day. According to de Vaux, *Ancient Israel*, 180–181, in the post-exilic period the Jewish calendar was based on the day beginning and ending with sunset. Many scholars suppose that this system of dating underlies the present passage. For this to work, however, it is necessary to assume that the 'evening' comes prior to sunset and not after it (cf. R.T. Beckwith, 'The day, its divisions and its limits, in biblical thought' *Ev Q* 43 (1971) 218–227). Alternatively, the dating formulae adopted in all the Pentateuchal Passover texts may reflect the pre-exilic system in which the day begins with sunrise, with 'evening' falling, more naturally, after sunset.

26. Cf. Ex. 29:1; Lv. 1:3, 10; 3:1, 6–7; 9:3.

27. Ex. 12:5. The Hebrew term *śeh* refers to either a lamb or a kid. Male animals, like male human beings, were less liable to ritual uncleanness. The youthfulness of the animal may also have guaranteed the purity of the sacrifice.

28. In his Gospel John implies that Jesus fulfils the role of the Passover victim by observing that his bones were not broken at the time of his crucifixion (Jn. 19:36).

29. This applied to all sacrifices, apart from those which were completely consumed by fire upon the altar.

30. Ex. 12:6 (cf. Lv. 23:5; Nu. 28:4, 8) uses the technical expression *bên hā'arbayim* 'between the evenings'. The precise meaning of this phrase is not known. It probably refers to the time between the sun's disappearance below the horizon and the onset of total darkness (cf. Dt. 16:3; Ex. 30:8; see C.F. Keil, *Manual of Biblical Archaeology* (Edinburgh: T. & T. Clark, 1888) vol. 2, 21–22).

31. Cf. Wambacq, 'Les origines', 321–26; Van Seters, 'The Place of the Yahwist in the History of Passover and Massot', 180–181.

32. Hyssop may have been used because it is an aspergillum (i.e. it prevents the blood from congealing). It is often associated with ceremonial purification (Lv. 14:4, 6, 49, 51, 52 (the purification of lepers); Nu. 19:6, 18; Ps. 51:7; Heb. 9:19).

33. Ex. 29:33 states, 'They are to eat these offerings by which atonement was made for their ordination and consecration.'

34. The concept of holiness, rarely mentioned in Genesis, appears frequently in Exodus.

35. The covenant document recorded in Ex. 21:1–23:33 is much fuller than that preserved in Ex. 34:10–26. Many commentators wrongly suppose that this document begins in Ex. 20:22. Ex. 20:22–26 consists, however, of instructions, not laws, and therefore is placed before the formal introduction to the covenant legislation (21:1).

36. A comparison of Ex. 23:14–19 and 34:18–26 reveals a number of close parallels: 'Three times a year all your men are to appear before the Sovereign LORD, the God of Israel' (34:23; cf. 23:14, 17). 'No-one is to appear before me empty-handed' (23:15; 34:20). 'Bring the best of the firstfruits of your soil to the house of the LORD your God. Do not cook a young goat in its mother's milk' (23:19; 34:26). As we might expect in a document of this kind, the legislation is very concise. This unfortunately creates difficulties regarding the interpretation of the text.

37. The Hebrew text is not quite as similar as the NIV translation suggests.

38. According to Haran, 'The Passover Sacrifice', 95–96, A. Dillmann, S.R. Driver, U. Cassuto, and M. Noth view 23:18 as referring to any ordinary sacrifice. Driver and Noth maintain that only the second part of 34:25 relates to the Passover, whereas H. Holzinger, B. Baentsch, G. Beer and K. Galling believe that all of 34:25 refers to it. De Vaux sees both verses as referring to the Passover, but finds evidence of Deuteronomic editing. The Mekhilta and the Babylonian Talmud (Pes., Talmud 63a) understand Ex. 23:18 as Passover legislation.

39. The only other offering which comes close to meeting these requirements is the thanksgiving (or confession) offering outlined in Lv. 7:12–15 (cf. 22:29–30). However, it is explicitly stated that this should be accompanied by 'cakes of bread made with yeast' (7:13).

40. On the day which later became known as Pentecost.

41. The term *qorbān* comes 78 times in Leviticus and Numbers but only twice elsewhere (Ezk. 20:28; 40:43). Ne. 10:35 and 13:31 have *qurbān*.

42. In 2 Ch. 30:1–27 the Feast of Unleavened Bread is celebrated in the second month. However, it had not been celebrated at all in the first month.

43. These instructions apply to the following offerings: daily, Sabbath, monthly, Unleavened Bread, the Day of Firstfruits (associated with the feast of Weeks), Trumpets, Day of Atonement, Tabernacles.

44. Although Dt. 16:1–8 makes several references to the eating of unleavened bread (vv. 3, 8), the designation Feast of Unleavened Bread comes only later in 16:16. For this reason the term *pesaḥ* 'Passover' in v.1 (and perhaps v.2) probably specifies not merely the

first night, as elsewhere in the Pentateuch, but rather the entire week (cf. Keil, *Biblical Archaeology*, vol.2, 31). In vv. 4 and 6, *happesaḥ* clearly refers to the passover victim.

45. Exodus 12–13 distinguishes carefully between the first Passover night and the week set aside for future celebrations of the feast of Unleavened Bread. The Passover is mentioned only briefly in Leviticus 23 and Numbers 28; unlike Unleavened Bread, it is not classified as a sacred assembly, the particular interest of Leviticus 23, nor does it involve an offering consumed totally by fire, the main concern of Numbers 28–29. Special factors also explain why Numbers 9 concentrates solely on the Passover and ignores Unleavened Bread. See Segal, *The Hebrew Passover*, 203.

46. The proposal of J. Halbe, 'Passa-Massot im deuteronomischen Festkalender: Komposition, Entstehung und Programm von Dtn 16:1–8', *ZAW* 87 (1975) 153, that vv. 1–7 form a chiastic pattern with elements of the Passover and Unleavened Bread balancing each other fails to capture the true structure of the passage. Verses 1–4a give an overview of the combined feast. Verses 4b–7 relate explicitly to the events of the Passover night. This is apparent from the time references: 'on the evening of the first day until the morning' (v. 4); 'in the evening, when the sun goes down' (v. 6); 'in the morning' (v. 7). Verse 8 focuses solely on the Feast of Unleavened Bread.

47. The same point is echoed in vv. 11 and 15 with regard to the feasts of Weeks and Tabernacles respectively. Verse 16 reaffirms this emphatically for all three feasts.

48. McConville, *Law and Theology*, highlights well this trend with regard to the cultic legislation in Deuteronomy.

49. Segal, *The Hebrew Passover* 205, concludes that the term *bāqār* came to be included in the text due to a scribal error. P.C. Craigie, *The Book of Deuteronomy* (NICOT) (London: Hodder & Stoughton, 1976) 242, suggests that it relates to a 'broadening of the original prescription' to include cattle.

50. C.F. Keil, *The Pentateuch* (Edinburgh: T. & T. Clark, 1864) vol. 3, 374–375, argues that the cattle relate to the sacrifices made during the Feast of Unleavened Bread; cf. McConville, *Law and Theology* 116. This is also the position adopted in the Targum Onkelos on Deuteronomy, Siphre on Dt. 16:2, and Mek. on Ex. 12:5. The NIV translation mistakenly implies that v. 3 refers to only one animal being sacrificed. A more literal translation of the Hebrew would be, 'Sacrifice Passover to the LORD your God small cattle (i.e. sheep and goats) and cattle in the place which the LORD will choose as a dwelling place for his name.'

51. Cf. Ex. 12:48; Lv. 23:5; Nu. 9:10, 14; 28:16; Dt. 16:1; 2 Ki. 23:21; 2 Ch. 30:1, 5; 35:1.

52. Ex. 12:21; Dt. 16:5, 6; Jos. 5:11; Ezr. 6:20; 2 Ch. 30:15, 18; 35: 1, 6, 11, 13. Deuteronomy 16 is the only place where the verb *zābaḥ* is used in conjunction with the Passover sacrifice. It is more usual for the verb *šaḥaṭ* to be used (cf. Ex. 12:21; Ezr. 6:20; 2 Ch. 30:15; 2 Ch. 35: 1, 6, 11).

53. Segal, *The Hebrew Passover* 205, draws attention to the fact that in Deuteronomy this is the only instance of the flock (*ṣō'n*) being mentioned before the herd (*bāqār*). Dt. 15:19, for example, refers to the firstborn of your herds and flocks (cf. 12:17, 21; 14:23, 26; 32: 14). Outside Deuteronomy it is quite usual to find the order 'flock and herd' (e.g., Gn. 12:16; 13:5; 20:14; 21:27; 24:35; 26:14).

54. The NIV does not draw attention to the presence of *'ālāyw* after both occurrences of the verb 'to eat'.

55. Cf. W.L. Holladay, *A Concise Hebrew and Aramaic Lexicon of the Old Testament* (Leiden: Brill, 1971) 272–273.

56. Verses 4b–7 clearly indicate that the actual Passover celebration took place only on the first evening.

57. P.C. Craigie, *Deuteronomy* 242, suggests that *'ālāyw* should be translated 'in his presence', following M. Dahood, 'Review of *The Torah. A new translation of the Holy Scriptures according to the Masoretic text*' *Bib* 45 (1964) 283.

58. The NIV translation of *bāšal* as 'roast' is too specific. Most writers now seem to accept that *bāšal* means 'to cook' (cf. J.A. Thompson, *Deuteronomy* (TOTC) (London:

IVP,1974) 195–196; Craigie, *Deuteronomy* 244, n. 9; A.D.H. Mayes, *Deuteronomy* (NCB) (London: Marshall, Morgan & Scott, 1979) 259; McConville, *Law and Theology* 117–118. According to Thompson, 195, n.1, the Akkadian verb *bašālu* means to cook by roasting or boiling (cf. *CAD*, B, 135–136).

59. A.D.H. Mayes, *Deuteronomy* 259.

60. Dt. 5:12–15; cf. C.M. Carmichael, *The Laws of Deuteronomy* (Ithaca and London: Cornell University Press, 1974) 93–94; McConville, *Law and Theology* 118–119.

61. In Ex. 12:16, Lv. 23:8 and Nu. 28:25, it is known as a 'holy assembly' (*miqrā' qōdeš*); in Ex. 13:6 it is called a 'feast' (*ḥaḡ*). The last day of the feast of Tabernacles is also referred to as an 'assembly' (*'aṣeret*), which the NIV translates as 'closing assembly' (Lv. 23:36).

62. Segal, *The Hebrew Passover* 206, comments, 'These discrepancies between Deuteronomy and the other Passover documents are capable of comparatively easy solution.'

63. Halbe, 'Erwägung zu Ursprung und Wesen des Massotfestes,' 332, maintains that the Joshua text knows nothing of a seven day festival; cf. T.C. Butler, *Joshua* (WBC 7) (Waco, Texas: Word, 1983) 56.

64. This is possibly a reference back to Solomon's dedication of the temple and the celebrations which accompanied it (1 Ki. 8:65–66; 2 Ch. 7:1–10). Although this took place in the seventh month, at the time of the feast of Tabernacles, the text implies that the celebrations lasted for two weeks instead of one (1 Ki. 8:65; 2 Ch. 7:9).

65. Although the altar is not specifically mentioned, it would appear to be the most likely object on which the blood would have been sprinkled.

66. The Chronicler gives a similar assessment (2 Ch. 35:18). 'The Passover has not been observed like this in Israel since the days of the prophet Samuel; and none of the kings of Israel had ever celebrated such a Passover as did Josiah, with the priests, the Levites and all Judah and Israel who were there with the people of Jerusalem.' The magnitude of this Passover commemoration can be judged on the basis of the number of animals sacrificed. At least 37,600 sheep/goats and 3,800 cattle were offered up during the festival (2 Ch. 35:7–9). This is almost double the number sacrificed at the Passover in the first year of Hezekiah: 17,000 sheep/goats and 2,000 cattle (2 Ch. 30:24).

67. Note the use of the verb *bāšal* 'to cook' followed by the expression *bā'ēš* 'with fire' (2 Ch. 35:13). See above (p. 13) for a fuller discussion of the verb *bāšal*.

68. The Hebrew text of v.13 does not imply that the roasting of the Passover victims and the boiling of the holy offerings took place simultaneously.

69. The designation 'Feast of Unleavened Bread' is not used here for the seven day festival, although the eating of unleavened bread is mentioned in v.21.

70. This idea probably lies behind the comments found in 1 Peter chaps. 1–2. Although the reference to 'a lamb without blemish and defect' (1:19) need not necessarily designate the Passover sacrifice, the context in which it comes has many links with the exodus story (see especially, 1 Pet. 2:9–10). Note in particular the emphasis upon holiness (1 Pet. 1:15–16; 2:5, 9).

FOR FURTHER READING

A. Bible Dictionaries

B.M. Bokser, 'Unleavened Bread and Passover, Feasts of', *The Anchor Bible Dictionary*, vol. 6, 755–765.

J.C. Rylaarsdam, 'Passover and Feast of Unleavened Bread', *Interpreter's Dictionary of the Bible*, vol. 3, 663–668.

R.A. Stewart, 'Passover', *Illustrated Bible Dictionary*, vol. 3, 1157–1158.

M.R. Wilson, 'Passover', *The International Standard Bible Encyclopedia*, vol. 3, 675–679.

B.   Other works

B.S. Childs, *Exodus* (London: SCM, 1974) 178–214.

M. Haran, 'The Passover Sacrifice', *Studies in the Religion of Ancient Israel* (VTSup 22) (Leiden: Brill, 1972) 86–116.

J.G. McConville, *Law and Theology in Deuteronomy* (JSOTS 33) (Sheffield: JSOT Press, 1984) 99–123.

J.B. Segal, *The Hebrew Passover from the earliest times to* AD 70 (London Oriental Series 12) (London: Oxford University Press, 1963)

J. Van Seters, 'The Place of the Yahwist in the History of Passover and Massot' *ZAW* 95 (1983) 167–182.

R. de Vaux, *Ancient Israel: its life and institutions* (London: Darton, Longman & Todd, 1965²) 484–493.

J. Wellhausen, *Prolegomena to the History of Israel* (Edinburgh: A. and C. Black, 1885) 83–120.

2

The Levitical Sacrificial System

PHILIP P. JENSON

I. INTRODUCTION

The description of sacrifice in Leviticus forms part of the divine instruction to Israel about worship extending from Exodus 25 to Numbers 10.
Although the rituals are set out in great detail, the interpretation of many
aspects of the Levitical sacrificial system remains uncertain. In part, this
is because the material stems from a priestly circle which was all too
familiar with sacrifice, and which did not feel the need to question or
explain it. But it is also due to the enormous cultural distance between a
world where sacrifice is a living language, and a society in which the word
'sacrifice' has taken on a very different set of meanings.[1] Some translations, such as 'mercy seat' (others 'cover') or 'atone' (others 'expiate' or
'purge'),[2] can seriously mislead us as we seek to read these complex texts.
   In the search to understand sacrifice in Leviticus, three main
approaches can be discerned. German scholars (e.g. Rendtorff; Janowski)
have explored historical–critical questions about the historical development of sacrifice. Jewish scholars, above all Jacob Milgrom, have studied
carefully the nuances of sacrificial terminology.[3] Since understanding
other cultures is a central concern of anthropologists, their insights too
have proved valuable in setting issues of interpretation and understanding
in a wider context.
   This chapter will not attempt to survey theories of the historical
development of sacrifice. Following a brief introduction to the different
kinds of sacrifice (II), one type of sacrifice will be discussed in more detail
(III). In practice a priestly ritual involved several sacrifices, and the Day
of Atonement illustrates how sacrifices can be fine-tuned to fulfil the
specific purposes of a ritual (IV).[4]

II. THE DIFFERENT KINDS OF SACRIFICE

In order to give an overview of the mass of detailed laws found in
Leviticus 1–7 and elsewhere, Table 1 lists the five main types of sacrifice.

Offering	*Material*	*Action*	*Offerer*	*Priest*
'ôlâ burnt offering whole offering holocaust Lv. 1:1–17; 6:8–13	herd or flock or bird (dove or pigeon) male animal without blemish	completely burned	brings offering places hand on head slays, skins, cuts in pieces	throws blood against altar places pieces on fire washes entrails and legs receives the offering

ḥaṭṭā't
purification
offering
sin offering
 	
Lv. 4:1–35;
6:24–30; cf.
Nu. 15:22–31
	1 priest: bull
	2 congregation:
	    young bull
	3 ruler: male goat
	4 individual: female
	    goat or sheep
	5 poor: dove or
	    pigeon
		fatty
		portions
		burned
		remainder
		eaten by
		priests
		(3,4,5) or
		burned
		(1,2)
			1,3–5: brings
			    offering
			2: elders do so for
			    congregation
				burns fat etc.
				1–2 burns rest
				outside camp
				3–5: eats flesh
				pours rest of
				blood out at the
				base of the altar

'āšām reparation offering guilt offering Lv. 5:14–6:7; 7:1–10	ram	(as for purification offering)	makes restitution then as for purification offering	burns fat etc. eats flesh throws blood on the altar
minḥâ grain offering cereal offering Lev. 2:1–16; 6:14–23	fine flour, cakes, wafers, first fruits with oil, frankincense, salt no leaven or honey	token (memorial portion) burned	brings offering takes handful	burns handful priests and sacrificer eat remainder
šelāmîm peace offering shared offering completion offering communion sacrifice gift of greeting Lv. 3:1–17; 7:11–36	from herd or flock male or female without blemish	fatty portions burned remainder eaten	brings offering places hand on head slays, skins, cuts in pieces	throws blood on altar burns fatty portions eats breast and right thigh

Table 1 The different types of sacrifice described in Leviticus 1–7

The details of the different kinds of sacrifice may be analysed from several perspectives.

1. The material of sacrifice

Most sacrifices involve the slaughter of an animal and the manipulation of its blood in some way.[5] The chief exception is the grain offering, which was occasionally offered alone (Nu. 5:15), but generally accompanied blood sacrifices (Lv. 23:13; Nu. 15:1–12).

2. The eating of the sacrifice

Only the peace offering could be eaten by the offerer (and his family), once the fat was burnt and the priest had received his portion. The rules for the priest differed, and he was allowed to eat other types of sacrifice (except for the burnt offering) as long as it was not offered on his own behalf (Nu. 18:8–10).

3. The order of sacrifices

Although Leviticus 1–7 describes distinct types of sacrifice, several were usually combined in one ritual. Further, the sacrifices were not performed in the order listed in Leviticus 1–5, which is a didactic order oriented to the priest's point of view (burnt offering, grain offering, peace offering, purification offering, reparation offering). Passages describing the practice of the ritual (descriptive texts) show that the normal order was purification offering, burnt offering (with grain offering), peace offering (e.g. Lv. 9:15–22; Nu. 6:16–17).[6]

4. The procedure of sacrifice

A sacrificial ritual comprised several stages, typically (i) the offerer approaches the sanctuary with the animal to be sacrificed (ii) lays his or her hand on it (iii) slaughters it (iv) the priest performs a blood ritual (sprinkling, pouring out, applying) (v) the priest prepares and burns the sacrifice on the altar (vi) the flesh may be eaten and the remains are disposed of. The detailed rules for the final three stages vary widely according to what kind of sacrifice is being offered for what reason. Thus the thank offering (Lv. 7:12), the votive offering (Lv. 7:16), the freewill offering (Lv. 7:16), and the ordination offering (Lv. 8:22–29) are all peace offerings, but were offered in different circumstances, have special names, and have slightly different procedures. Similarly the ritual for the purification offering described in Leviticus 4 differs from that of Leviticus 5:1–13.

The meaning of the different types of sacrifice continues to be actively discussed. One reason for this is that all the sacrifices have much in common, so that there may be a substantial overlap of meaning and function, as well as each sacrifice having a distinctive function. Another difficulty is that the sacrificial texts have been transmitted and redacted over a lengthy period, and the interpretation of a sacrifice or ritual can change in the course of time. So the final form of Leviticus may witness to more than one level of interpretation. While the assumption of coherence is a good starting point, there may be occasions when a hypothesis of historical change is the best way to explain difficulties.[7]

1. The burnt offering ('ôlâ)

Several factors suggest that the burnt offering is the most important sacrifice. For example, it is the most prominent sacrifice at the Israelite festivals (Nu. 28–29), it has a pre-eminent position in the prescriptive lists (e.g. Lv. 1–7), only male animals could be offered, and it is completely burnt (i.e. the priest cannot benefit from its flesh). What, however, is its purpose?

There are two main explanations which seek to do justice to the range of occasions on which it was offered, and the interpretations suggested in the texts. One is that it was the premier *expiatory* or *atoning* sacrifice.[8] According to this understanding, the death of the sacrificial animal (symbolized by the shedding of blood, Lv. 17:11) substitutes for the offerer and thereby ransoms his life, which was forfeit because of his sin against God. In accord with this understanding, *kipper* ('atone') can be derived from the Hebrew *kōper*, which means ransom in certain legal texts (e.g. Ex. 21:30; 30:12; Nu. 35:31–32). The laying on of hands (Lv. 1:4) identifies the substitute, whose death (v.5) takes place instead of the sinner and results in acceptance (vv.3–4), represented by the pleasing odour (v.9). Outside Leviticus there are various texts where the burnt offering deals with sin (Gn. 8:20–21; Jb. 1:5).

However, there is less evidence than we would expect for the association of the burnt offering and atonement in the Levitical writings. When atonement is associated with both a burnt offering and a purification offering (e.g. Lv. 5:9–10; 9:7; 12:6–8), it could refer to the latter alone. Further, Nu. 15:3 suggests that the burnt offering could be a votive or freewill offering, whereas Israelites were required to offer atoning sacrifices in order to deal with their impurity or sin. It also raises the question how the burnt offering is distinct from the other atoning sacrifices.[9] The substitutionary interpretation of the laying on of hands and the ransom understanding of *kipper* have also been challenged.

An alternative explanation is that the burnt offering represents a *gift* to God. The laying on of hands identifies the gift as that of the offerer's,[10] no return is expected (whether atonement or eating the flesh[11]), and the gift evokes a positive response by God. Further, the burnt offering can serve as the fulfilment of a votive or freewill offering as well the peace offering (Lv. 22:17–19; Nu. 15:1–16). As for the texts outside the Levitical writings, it is possible that 'burnt offering' described all kinds of sacrifices which were dedicated totally to God, in contrast to the peace offering. In the case of the priests, the contrast would be between the sacrifice dealing with sin, which is more accurately described as a 'purification offering', and the priestly burnt offering that excluded atonement.

One difficulty which faces both theories is that they use sophisticated ideas whose relation to the priestly vocabulary is at best indirect. According to context, 'gift' can take on overtones of bribe, contract (*do ut des*), honour, homage, tribute, thanksgiving, or a combination of these. Similarly 'expiation', 'atonement' and 'substitution' are loaded theological terms. This means that great care must be taken in defining the language used. It is also possible to combine both ideas. For example, the burnt offering may have been a general gift sacrifice to begin with, but was later assimilated to the other blood sacrifices with which atonement is associated. The main evidence for the association of atonement with the burnt offering (Lv. 1:4; 16:24) could derive from a later systematizing tendency which associated atonement with any manipulation of the blood.[12]

2. The purification offering (*ḥaṭṭā'ṯ*)

The older translation ('sin offering') focuses on the role that this sacrifice plays in the forgiveness of sin according to Leviticus 4 (vv. 3, 14 etc.). But Milgrom has collected a good deal of evidence which suggests that this is not the best place to start. On many occasions a *ḥaṭṭā'ṯ* is to be offered not because of personal sin, but because the person has sustained a major impurity, and so it is better called a purification offering.[13] As such it is closely integrated with the rest of the priestly purity system. From various laws it is clear that there are two grades of impurity, a lesser kind which cannot be passed on to someone or something else, and a more serious degree in which impurity is communicated to those who come into contact with the affected person or object.[14] Major impurities derive from childbirth (Lv. 12:6, 8), skin disease (14:19, 22, 31), discharges (15:15, 30) and contact with a corpse (Nu. 6:11; 19:1–22). Purification from the latter usually requires a wait of seven days, followed by purification rituals and a purification offering or its equivalent.[15] The lesser grade of impurity requires only simple water purification (bathing, washing clothes) and waiting until evening.

The concern for purity and impurity is largely foreign to Western culture, which tends to emphasize the categories of sin and guilt. But anthropologists have shown that impurity plays an extremely important role in many traditional cultures.[16] In such societies, impurity is not an abstract or secondary concept, but a powerful vehicle of social and religious realities. The maintenance of a stable society requires a careful limitation of impurity and regular purification. This is what we find in Leviticus, particularly since impurity is incompatible with holiness, and holiness is a necessary requirement if God is to dwell in the Tabernacle at the centre of the camp (Ex. 25:8).

It remains true that a purification offering is required for 'inadvertent sin' (Lv. 4:2 etc.), which is distinguished from deliberate sin ('with a high hand', Nu. 15:30–31), for which no atonement is available. It has proved difficult to define precisely the relation between sin and impurity. They are distinct but overlapping concepts. Impurity can result from physical conditions for which a person is not responsible (e.g. Lv. 12, childbirth). But the purity laws can be the occasion for conscious or unconscious transgression, and it is not always clear whether the problem is simple impurity, an inadvertent neglect of the purity laws, or a deliberate transgression of them. If we begin from the idea of impurity, then 'inadvertent sin' could be due to an infringement of the impurity laws (cf. Lv. 5:2–3). Major impurities can defile the sanctuary (Lv. 15:31), and it is an offence not to be purified (Nu. 19:20). If we begin from the concept of sin, then impurity may be understood as a way to express cultically the offence against God and society, and purification is the equivalent of forgiveness. However, it may also be the case that we are working with categories that are too sharply defined and so demanding too much precision from the texts.[17]

3. The reparation offering (*'āšām*)

Most scholars now prefer the translation 'reparation offering' to 'guilt offering', since financial compensation is its distinctive feature (Lv. 5:14–26).[18] In addition to the sacrifice, reparation (the amount plus a fifth) must be rendered to the party defrauded (5:14–16; 6:1–7; Nu. 5:5–10).[19] Economic offences belong to the sphere of civil law, but they are also sins and a matter of divine concern. It is possible to extend this interpretation to sacrifices where there is no overt financial reference. A Nazirite who has been defiled has had to delay the payment of his vow and so must offer a reparation offering (Nu. 6:9–12), and similarly someone who has had a skin disease has forgone a number of sacrifices and offerings (Lv. 14:12–14). The sacrifice thus compensates God for what he is owed and repays the offerer's cultic debt.

4. The peace offering (*šelāmîm*)

The distinctiveness of the peace offering is evident in the final stage of the sacrificial ritual. Since it was not an atoning sacrifice, it could be eaten by the offerer as well as the priest. Whereas the distinctiveness of the burnt offering lies in the complete burning of the animal, the purification offering in the blood manipulation, and the reparation offering in the additional reparation, the peace offering is unique in the way in which the parts of the sacrifice are distributed.

The usual translations as 'peace' or 'communion' or 'fellowship' offering suggest the communion or fellowship that exists amongst participants in a meal.[20] The fat which is burnt can even be called 'food' for God (Lv. 3:11; cf. 21:6). In recent discussion the notion of a 'communion' sacrifice has come in for a certain amount of justified criticism. Some of the earlier impetus for the communion theory derived from anthropological theories which have since been modified or abandoned (e.g. totemism). Nor is there necessarily an etymological or semantic connection between $\check{s}^e l\bar{a}m\hat{i}m$ and $\check{s}\bar{a}l\hat{o}m$, peace. The texts do not stress the communion aspect (contrast Ex. 12:8–10; 24:11), and the consumption of the sacrifice happens after the sacrifice has been performed. Scholars have made several alternative suggestions, including that it represents a gift that brings about 'agreement' or 'reconciliation',[21] or that it is simply a 'completion offering', since it is the last of a series of sacrifices.[22]

Despite this uncertainty, the importance of the sacrifice as an occasion for the common enjoyment of a meal before God should not be underestimated. It is likely that festivals and family trips to the sanctuary (cf. 1 Sa. 1:21) were the only occasions when meat was eaten, and the importance of this opportunity to feast and rejoice in God's goodness is evident.[23] It is not necessary to understand the meal and communion aspect in a crude or literal way. The Israelites were as aware as anyone that God did not physically eat food, but eating is a rich symbolic resource for theological reflection.[24]

The peace offering is also the final sacrifice in a series (cf. the translation 'completion offering'). Once the purification offering has dealt with any fault that might hinder celebration and feasting, and God has been honoured with a burnt offering, a peace offering is an appropriate expression of harmonious relation with God, the ultimate goal of worship (cf. Ex. 24:9–11).

III.   THE INTERPRETATION OF SACRIFICE

1. A General Theory of Sacrifice?

The previous section has explored the distinctive character and meaning of the individual sacrifices, but where should we start in trying to understand the purpose and meaning of sacrifice in general? Older theories sometimes sought to explain all kinds of sacrifice in terms of one key meaning. De Vaux recognized the partial validity of these suggestions by suggesting that there are three key ideas to sacrifice: communion, gift, and expiation.[25] As we have seen above, it is often difficult to relate a general idea exclusively to a particular kind of sacrifice because of the overlap between sacrificial rituals. A burnt offering as well as a peace offering may well express communion between God and an offerer. Perhaps because blood is closely linked with atonement, the blood of the burnt offering could also have been regarded as atoning.

There is, however, an alternative approach which may prove useful in looking at the whole of the Levitical system of worship, and the rest of the chapter will pursue this perspective.[26] Sacrifice can initiate a state of affairs (e.g. priestly status, Lv. 8–9), it can correct a state of affairs (e.g. sin, impurity), and it can maintain and strengthen a relationship (the peace offering). It can be argued that the central concern of the priestly writings is the creation, maintenance and restoration of an ordered world.[27] The concern with purity and impurity is in part a concern for maintaining boundaries which must not be transgressed. Otherwise, there will be a descent into chaos, disaster and death.

From this perspective, sacrifice has a crucial role in maintaining order and restoring the equilibrium when that order is disturbed. Both sin and impurity can be understood as generating disorder, a broad category which can apply to the personal and the impersonal, the unavoidable and the deliberate, the individual and the corporate. This is therefore one way to do justice to the range of faults for which sacrifices are prescribed. It also makes some sense of the substantial overlap between the concepts of sin and impurity.

2. Grading and Sacrifice in Leviticus 4

We often think in terms of strictly distinct binary categories. A person, place or action is either holy or profane. However, the priestly system of worship is more nuanced, and sets out various grades or levels of holiness and impurity. The grades of holiness can be seen most clearly in the architecture of the Tabernacle. The Holy of Holies, the Holy Place, and the Court are clearly divided by walls and entrances, and the innermost area is the holiest and the one most closely associated with the presence of God (e.g. Lv. 16:2).[28] The grading of various aspects of priestly worship are correlated closely with each other, depending on the character of the problem being dealt with. The use of space, the persons involved, the procedure carried out, and the time that it is done can all be significant factors in the structure and movement of the overall ritual.

The fruitfulness of this approach to sacrifice may be illustrated from Leviticus 4. This chapter consists of five sections, each of which describes a particular case of the purification offering. Some of the details are summarized in the table below.

Several kinds of grading are evident here. The rituals in the holy place are described first, and the nearer the blood comes to the centre of the sanctuary, the more effective is the purification. The inner ritual ('the major blood rite') is also more complex, comprising a sevenfold sprinkling as well as application to the horns of the incense altar. In the other three cases ('the minor blood rite'), the blood is applied only to the horns of the main altar and the sacrificial meat may be eaten by the offering priest. The ritual of the purification offering on the Day of Atonement can be integrated with the scheme, since the ritual on that day

A. Major blood rite takes place in the Holy Place					
Lv. 4	Offender	Animal	Blood sprinkled	Applied to	Food for
3–12	anointed priest	bull	7x in front of the	horns of the incense	no-one
13–21	congregation	bull	veil	altar	no-one

B. Minor blood rite takes place in the Court of the Tabernacle					
Lv. 4	Offender	Animal	Blood sprinkled	Applied to	Food for
22–26	leader	f goat		horns of the altar of	priests
27–31	anyone	f goat		burnt offering	priests
32–35	anyone	m lamb			priests

Table 2 The ritual of the purification offering according to Leviticus 4

is the most potent purification of all. The high priest, takes the blood into the holy of Holies, the highest grade of space, sprinkles it on the surface of the cover, and then sprinkles it before the cover seven times (Lv. 16:14–15).

The spatial grading is correlated with the personal dimension. The major blood rite is performed for the anointed priest and for the congregation, while the leader and the ordinary person are atoned for by the blood ritual in the outer court. The defilement of the anointed priest is so serious because he is the religious head of the community and represents the people, who are bound up in his guilt (Lv. 4:3). The sacrificial code thus reflects and reinforces the hierarchical order of society reflected in other priestly texts.

The nature of the sacrificial animal is another important element of the sacrificial code. In the two most important cases, bulls are offered, while the fourth and fifth are distinguished only by the alternative sacrifices which a common person may offer, a female goat or a female sheep. The grade of the animal depends principally on its cost (the bull is the most expensive, a member of the flock the least) and its gender (a male has a higher sacrificial status than the female). Such observations remain largely unaffected by the interpretations given to particular aspects of the sacrifice and provide an important way in which a great number of disparate rituals are integrated and unified.

IV. THE DAY OF ATONEMENT

One of the dangers of concentrating on Leviticus 1–7 is that the diversity and flexibility of sacrificial practice is underestimated. The ritual of the Day of Atonement illustrates how the principle of grading can be developed to illuminate a unique and puzzling ritual. As set out in Leviticus 16, the heart of the ritual comprises two distinct actions. One of these is a special form of the purification offering, while the other is the famous scapegoat ritual. These two parts are often regarded as distinct, and having different origins.[29] But whatever the history of the ritual, an analysis of the present ritual in its several dimensions reveals that the two parts complement one another in a remarkable way.

The two parts of the ritual introduce two unique movements in space. Only once in the year is the blood of the purification offering brought into the heart of the Tabernacle, the Holy of Holies, and sprinkled on and before the cover of the ark (vv.14–15). The second movement is even more irregular, since the second goat, assigned by lot 'for Azazel' (v.8), is driven out into the wilderness. It is difficult to avoid the conclusion that this contrary spatial movement comprises a deliberate structural contrast. Space has a quality as well as a quantity in the priestly writings, and the two goats eventually encompass the extreme reaches of significant space in the priestly worldview. The blood of one goat reaches to the heart of holy space, whereas the other is driven out to where major impurities have their proper place (cf. Nu. 5:1–3). At no other time of the year are these spaces employed in priestly rituals.

This extreme polar structure is also reflected in the personal dimension, if Azazel is correctly understood as the name of a demon.[30] The blood of one goat is brought into God's presence (v.2), while the scapegoat is driven into the wilderness, the home of demons (cf. Lv. 17:7). While it is unlikely that Azazel is conceived as having any independent power, the unusual reference would stress in the strongest possible way that the scapegoat represents the polar opposite of God's holy presence in the Holy of Holies.

In some way, it appears that this movement restores harmony between God and Israel. At the beginning the two goats are indistinguishable, and are both designated 'for the purification offering' (v.5). At the conclusion, they mark the extreme spatial and personal boundaries which delineate the priestly world. The movement of the goats represents, or even effects, the re-establishment of the normative world order, thus allowing normal offerings to be resumed. The remarkably comprehensive blood manipulation should also be noted. The blood is sprinkled on every part of the holy domain, beginning at the Holy of Holies (v.16), then the Tent of Meeting (v.16),[31] and finally the altar of Burnt Offering (vv.18–19).

The human side of the personal dimension also displays unique elements which have a fitting ritual logic. The central ritual is carried out by the High Priest, but he has a peculiar double role. He acts as the priestly representative of the people, but also needs to atone for himself and his own household (v.6). This double status is reflected in the character of his garments, which are not his usual resplendent outfit (Ex. 28), but of simple linen (Lv. 16:4). The clothing code perhaps signifies the levelling of all hierarchical distinctions in a common membership of a people who need to be purified. Only when atonement has been successfully performed is the normal hierarchical order reestablished and the distinctive high priestly garments once again donned (v.24).

Perhaps the most difficult question about the ritual logic is about the function of the two parts. The purpose of the blood ritual (v.16) and the scapegoat (v.21) are stated as follows:

> Thus he shall make atonement for the sanctuary, because of the uncleannesses of the people of Israel, and because of their transgressions, all their sins . . . and confess over it all the iniquities of the people of Israel, and all their transgressions, all their sins . . . (vv.16, 21, NRSV)

These refer to the two main classes of fault in the priestly system, impurity and sin (sins, iniquities, transgressions). But what kind of sin and impurity is the object of the ritual, and is there any difference between the function of the blood and scapegoat rituals? It seems unlikely that the priests would worry about minor impurities, since they could be purified without any recourse to the cult and were not contagious. But identifying the particular source of major impurity which needed to be purified is not easy. Deliberate refusal to be purified from a major impurity resulted in death not purification (e.g. Nu. 19:13), so it is possible that the Day of Atonement dealt with the effects of such unpurified impurity on the sanctuary. However, it seems more likely that the purpose of the ritual is comprehensive and should not be defined so narrowly. The Day of Atonement was the appointed time when all the serious impurities accumulated throughout the year were dealt with. The ordered world of the cult could be compromised by an unchecked multiplication of impure people and places, but on the Day of Atonement the appropriate boundaries were re-established and the sanctuary purified from every possible defilement.

The other focus of the ritual is sin. If this refers to the deliberate neglect of the purity laws, there is an overlap of the concepts of sin and impurity. This partial overlap between sin and impurity could explain the close association of uncleannesses and sins in v.16, and the way in which the scapegoat ritual is associated with atonement in v.10. But it is also true that certain sins which do not have a direct bearing on the purity system can be described using the language of impurity.[32] While the exact relation between sin and impurity is never spelled out, it seems appropriate to have some sort of ritual which deals with the cultic aspects of sin, however these are perceived, and this is what happens on the Day of Atonement.

Similar difficulties are found when it is asked what the relation is between the two parts of the ceremony. One possible explanation would be that the purification offering dealt with impurities and the scapegoat with sins. However, the text refers once to atonement in connection with the scapegoat (v.10), and both v.16 and v.21 include 'sin' words.[33] Another explanation would be that the rites are continuous in their action. For example, Kiuchi has argued that the scapegoat completes what the purification offering could not do. The atonement system in Lv. 4:1–12 is defective because a priest cannot atone for his own sin and so no forgiveness is recorded, a lack remedied in Leviticus 16. Normally atonement comprises two parts, the purification of the sanctuary and the bearing of guilt, which is removed by the burning of the flesh of the purification offering. In Leviticus 16, the expulsion of the scapegoat into the wilderness is the symbolic equivalent of burning the purification offering outside the camp.[34] A third possibility is that the two parts of the ritual fulfil the same function from different points of view.[35] This would do justice to the comprehensive character of the texts and the structural relation between the two parts of the ritual.

The Day of Atonement also has a unique place in the calendar of festivals. Indeed, strictly speaking it is not a festival, for on this day the Israelites were commanded to 'afflict themselves' (Lv. 16:29; 23:27–32; Nu. 29:7). The problem of sin and impurity plays a minor role in the other festivals, and at most is alluded to in the prescription of a goat for a single purification offering. The negative aspect of Israel's life with God becomes dominant only on the Day of Atonement. In the list of sacrifices in Numbers 29, the scapegoat is explicitly called the purification offering of atonement (v.11). Its date near the beginning the seventh month (the tenth day) also means that it is a fitting contrast to the important Festival of Booths. A successful atonement ensured a purified sanctuary and the assurance that the large number of sacrifices offered at Booths would be accepted. Furthermore the affliction, which probably involved fasting, would suitably set off and heighten the subsequent rejoicing and feasting.

V.   LEVITICUS IN THE CONTEXT OF THE BIBLE

It is clear that the authors of the Levitical texts have a more detailed acquaintance with the sacrificial system than is evident elsewhere in the Bible. The presentation is characterized by a clear distinction between several types of sacrifice and an attempt to construct a coherent practice and theology centred around the sanctuary and its service. At the same time, the paucity of conscious reflection on the meaning of sacrifice means that great care must be taken not to read later concepts back into the texts or impose an explanatory system that is too rigid.

A particular emphasis of this chapter has been that order, grading and hierarchy are central organizing principles in the Levitical system. In this way the cult seeks to integrate all aspects of Israel's life and bring them under God's rule. Sacrifice plays a role in that enterprise by summing up and reflecting the values and hierarchies found in other areas of life. It also performs the essential task of restoring the order of things when it is compromised by fault of some kind. As such, it preserves and enhances Israel's life before God, which is constantly threatened by the disorder and death associated with impurity and sin.

In terms of the wider biblical context, the Levitical understanding of sacrifice is a distinctive and positive contribution. Though the patriarchs performed sacrifices from time to time, Leviticus describes a comprehensive system appropriate for a people and nation with considerable resources and a wide variety of needs. It is thus an essential part of the lawgiving at Sinai, setting out the religious dimension of Israel's life, and providing the means for individuals and people to deal with their faults and respond wholeheartedly to God. The Tabernacle and its sacrificial service is thus a gracious gift from God which allows a liberated people to worship and serve God in purity and holiness. The magnitude of this gift is emphasized in the exodus narrative by contrast with Pharaoh's restrictions and his prohibition of sacrifice (e.g. Ex. 8:25–32; 10:24–29).

The tone of the Levitical writings is positive and confident that this task of worship and ordering can be carried out successfully within the priestly system. There is little evidence of the false consciousness and misuse of the cult which the prophets depict so vividly. Although the history of Israel shows clearly that sacrifice could be subverted and used to legitimate injustice and oppression (see Chap. 3), these truths qualify rather than undermine the Levitical perspective. Ezekiel, who is both priest and prophet, displays the same priestly concerns for order and system in his portrayal of the restored temple system (Ezk. 40–48).

From a historical–critical point of view, many scholars consider that the priestly texts received their final form in the exile. It is questionable whether the priestly sacrificial system was ever regarded as a detailed plan for the people on their return. Rather, the principles at work abide as pattern and inspiration for anyone concerned to worship God in rich diversity and explicit detail. Israel's relation to God at her birth expressed through sacrifice is a pattern for future rebirths and renewals, though in a way that must take into account changes in cultural and historical context.

It is therefore understandable that later reflection on Levitical sacrifice in a different cultural context proceeded in a number of different directions. The NT as a whole is not aware of or interested in the fine technical distinctions between types of sacrifice which are important in the Levitical system. The main exception is the Epistle to the Hebrews, where the radical way in which the author has taken up priestly concepts of grading and sacrifice displays a fundamental and comprehensive approach to the challenge of interpreting the Levitical system in the context of the rest of the OT, and the coming of Christ.

In fact, the Sinai covenant with its sacrifices was already portrayed as temporary and inadequate in the OT (Heb. 10:1–18, quoting Ps. 40:6–8), endlessly repetitive and so powerless to deal decisively with sin (7:27; 8:7–13 quoting Je. 31:31–34; 9:25–26). Therefore a completely new way had to be found, involving a priest who was not subject to the limitations of the Aaronic high priesthood (the priesthood after the order of Melchizedek), a new covenant, and a better sacrifice. Precisely through a careful consideration of the details of the sacrificial procedure the author is able to expound the uniqueness of the offering of Christ by means of a subtle *a fortiori* argument.

Thus in Hebrews 9 the author summarizes the spatial architecture of the Tabernacle, particularly stressing the distinction between the outer tent, the Holy Place, and the Holy of Holies that lies behind a second curtain (vv.1–5). In the Levitical system, the graver the sin, the more potent the sacrifice required and the nearer it had to be brought to the presence of God by the one most conformed to the holiness of God, the high priest. In all these features the death of Christ is shown to be the supreme sacrifice. For the earthly Holy of Holies was a mere copy of the heavenly sanctuary (cf. Ex. 25:40), which is where Christ entered upon his death, into the very presence of God (Heb. 4:14; 8:5; 9:11, 24). Nor is he unqualified for this task, since he is the promised high priest after the order of Melchizedek (5:5–6; 7:1–28; cf. Ps. 110:4). Rather than taking the blood of goats and calves, he brings his own precious blood, supremely powerful to purify from sin (9:12–14; 10:11–14). And because of the ultimate value of this self-offering, he does not need to offer a sacrifice every day, or even once a year, but once for all (9:12), thereby establishing a better covenant than that of Sinai (9:15–22).

The important thing to note is that the power of the author's argument assumes the validity, albeit limited and imperfect, of the Sinai order of worship. The basic parameters of discourse remain the same (Tabernacle, priesthood, sacrifice, time), but the work of Christ transcends and intensifies them in order to open up a new way of purification and forgiveness (1:3; 9:14). This brings to an end the old order of sin and death, and establishes a new age of holiness and holy worship (10:14; 12:18–24). The power and persuasiveness of the argument can be appreciated only if we treasure and respect the remarkable achievement of his mentors and teachers, the priestly writers of Exodus and Leviticus.

NOTES

1. For the connotations of 'sacrifice' see G. Ashby, *Sacrifice: Its Nature and Purpose* (London: SCM, 1988) 1–4.

2. Both these terms have the same root in the Hebrew (*kpr*), the meaning of which is disputed (see below).

3. Some of the different translations are listed in Table 1. Milgrom has now summarised much of his previous work in his magisterial commentary on Leviticus 1–16 (*Leviticus 1–16: A New Translation with Introduction and Commentary* (AB) (New York: Doubleday, 1991), where detailed information about practically every aspect of sacrifice may be found, together with further bibliography.

4. Compare the wide variety of forms a eucharist or mass can take in different contexts.

5. An exception which proves the rule is Lv. 5:11–13, where fine flour can substitute for an animal if the offerer is too poor. The need to make atonement takes precedence over the good of offering a blood sacrifice.

6. A.F. Rainey, 'The Order of Sacrifices in Old Testament Ritual Texts', *Bib 51* (1970) 485–498.

7. J.W. Rogerson, 'Sacrifice in the Old Testament: Problems of Method and Approach', in M.F.C. Bourdillon and M. Fortes (ed.), *Sacrifice* (New York: Academic Press, 1980) 45–60, especially 45, 56.

8. E.g. G.J. Wenham, *The Book of Leviticus* (NICOT) (Grand Rapids: Eerdmans, 1979) 57–63; Milgrom, *Leviticus* 175–177. 'Expiate' generally refers to the means by which sins are dealt with. 'Atone' has such a wide range of meaning that it can mean practically anything or nothing—a useful feature for the translation of a disputed term! Another explanatory term found is 'propitiation', the appeasing of an offended person (i.e. God, on account of sin). B.A. Levine, *In the Presence of the Lord* (SJLA 5) (Leiden: Brill, 1974) 74–77) also refers to the 'apotropaic' function of sacrifice, the means by which an evil influence or force is averted (e.g. impurity conceived as a demonic force; cf. J. Milgrom, *Studies in Cultic Theology and Terminology* (SJLA 36) (Leiden: Brill, 1983) 75–84). However, there is little evidence in Leviticus that sacrifice is understood in terms of these last two concepts.

9. Wenham, *Leviticus* 111, distinguishes between the burnt offering for broad sins and other sacrifices for more specific sins, but the texts give little support for this interpretation.

10. See D.P. Wright, 'The Gesture of Hand Placement in the Hebrew Bible and in Hittite Literature', *JAOS* 106 (1986) 433–446.

11. R. de Vaux, *Ancient Israel: Its Life and Institutions* (London: Darton Longman & Todd, 1961) 452–453.

12. J.R. Porter, *Leviticus* (CBC) (Cambridge: CUP, 1976) 20.

13. Milgrom, *Studies* 67–84.

14. See D.P. Wright, *The Disposal of Impurity* (SBLDS 101) (Atlanta, Georgia: SBL, 1987). The degree of contact (touch, in the same room) will depend on the impurity.

15.n In this context, *kipper* may well mean 'purge' (Milgrom, *Leviticus* 1–16, 1079–1081).

16. Mary Douglas' brilliant and positive volume *Purity and Danger* (London: Routledge & Kegan Paul, 1966) remains a classic treatment of themes relevant to understanding the priestly worldview.

17. B.A. Levine, *Leviticus* (JPS Torah Commentary) (Philadelphia: Jewish Publication Society, 1989) 19, considers that the legal and ritual contexts have been blended in Leviticus, so that the purification offering both purifies and removes guilt. Compare the coalescence of sin and impurity ideas in texts such as Isaiah 6 and Psalm 51, and in the NT.

18. A great deal of confusion arises because of the different meanings of the word translated 'reparation offering' (J. Milgrom, *Cult and Conscience* (SJLA 18) (Leiden: Brill, 1976) 1–12). According to context, it could refer to a sacrifice of reparation (Lv. 5:14–26), the penalty for guilt (for which a purification offering is prescribed, Lv. 5:6) or the state of guilt (4:13, 22, 27; 5:2–5).

19. The exception in Lv. 5:17–19 may be because defrauding is suspected, but no specific sum can be determined.

20. The classic statement of the theory is generally attributed to W. Robertson Smith, *Lectures on the Religion of the Semites: The Fundamental Institutions* (Edinburgh, A. and C. Black, 1889).

21. Porter, *Leviticus* 29–30.

22. R. Rendtorff, *Studien zur Geschichte des Opfers im alten Israel* (WMANT 24) (Neukirchen-Vluyn: Neukirchener Verlag, 1967) 133. However, in his *Leviticus* (BKAT) (Neukirchen-Vluyn: Neukirchener Verlag, 1990), Vol 3.2, Rendtorff translates 'communion offering' ('Gemeinschafts-Schlachtopfer').

23. Levine, *Leviticus* 14, suggests that the sacrifice was 'a sacred gift of greeting' within the context of a sacred meal.

24. Y. Kaufmann, *The Religion of Israel* (Chicago: University of Chicago Press, 1960) 111–112. Subtle expositions of symbolic behaviour by anthropologists have made it unlikely that 'primitive' rituals are as crude as is sometimes assumed. Compare the meal quality of the Christian Holy Communion.

25. De Vaux, *Ancient Israel* 451–454. The NT often stresses the relation of sin and sacrifice, the gift theory is generally associated with G.B. Gray, *Sacrifice in the Old Testament: Its Theory and Practice* (Oxford: Clarendon Press, 1925), and the communion theory with W.R. Smith, *Lectures*.
26. For a fuller exploration of this approach, see P.P. Jenson, *Graded Holiness: A Key to the Priestly Conception of the World* (JSOTS 106) (Sheffield: JSOT Press, 1992).
27. F.H. Gorman, *The Ideology of Ritual: Space, Time and Status in the Priestly Theology* (JSOTS 91) (Sheffield: JSOT Press, 1990).
28. See M. Haran, *Temples and Temple-Service in Ancient Israel* (Oxford: Clarendon Press, 1978) and Wright, *Disposal* 232–243.
29. E.g. De Vaux, *Ancient Israel* 507–510.
30. H. Tawil, 'Azazel, The Prince of the Steppe: A Comparative Study', *ZAW* 92 (1980) 43–59.
31. Ex. 30:10 includes the incense altar in the purification ritual.
32. T. Frymer-Kensky, 'Pollution, Purification, and Purgation in Biblical Israel', in C.L. Meyers and M. O'Connor (ed.), *The Word of the Lord Shall Go Forth: Essays in Honor of David Noel Freedman in Celebration of His Sixtieth Birthday* (Winona Lake, IN: ASOR/ Eisenbrauns, 1983) 399–414; D.P. Wright, 'The Spectrum of Priestly Impurity', in G.A. Anderson and S.M. Olyan (ed.), *Priesthood and Cult in Ancient Israel* (JSOTS 125) (Sheffield: JSOT Press, 1991) 150–181.
33. Milgrom, *Studies* 81, follows the Mishnah (Sheb., Mishnah 1:6) and attempts to distinguish pollutions deriving from wanton sins (v.16) from iniquities (v.21), but this seems forced.
34. N. Kiuchi, *The Purification Offering in the Priestly Literature* (JSOTS 56) (Sheffield: JSOT Press, 1987) 148–159. However, the linking of these texts remains hypothetical. Nor is it evident that the burning of the purification offering can bear the theological and exegetical weight Kiuchi sets upon it.
35. Kiuchi's objections (*Purification Offering* 146–148) to this view are mainly based on a strict interpretation of the order in which the two rituals in Leviticus 16 are performed, but a complex ritual need not have a strict chronological logic.

FOR FURTHER READING

G.A. Anderson, 'Sacrifice and Sacrificial Offerings (OT)', *Anchor Bible Dictionary*, vol.5 (1992) 871–886.
G. Ashby, *Sacrifice: Its Nature and Purpose* (London: SCM, 1988).
M.F.C. Bourdillon and M. Fortes (ed.), *Sacrifice* (New York: Academic Press, 1980).
F.H. Gorman, *The Ideology of Ritual: Space, Time and Status in the Priestly Theology* (JSOTS 91; Sheffield, JSOT Press, 1990).
J.E. Hartley, *Leviticus* (WBC) (Waco: Word, 1992).
N. Kiuchi, *The Purification Offering in the Priestly Literature: Its Meaning and Function* (JSOTS 36) (Sheffield: JSOT Press, 1987).
P.P. Jenson, *Graded Holiness: A Key to the Priestly Conception of the World* (JSOTS 106) (Sheffield, JSOT Press, 1992).
J. Milgrom, *Studies in Cultic Theology and Terminology* (SJLA 36) (Leiden: Brill, 1983).
J. Milgrom, *Leviticus 1–16: A New Translation with Introduction and Commentary* (AB) (New York: Doubleday, 1991).
R. de Vaux, *Ancient Israel: Its Life and Institutions* (London: Darton Longman & Todd, 1961).
G.J. Wenham, *The Book of Leviticus* (NICOT) (Grand Rapids: Eerdmans, 1979).

3

Sacrifice in the Psalms

NIGEL B. COURTMAN

We will examine the significance of sacrifice in the Psalms under three headings. 'The Purpose of Sacrifice' will explore the motives with which sacrifices are offered. This is an appropriate starting point because the motives are the most readily discernible aspect of sacrifice in the Psalms. This section will involve a survey of all the relevant texts. Under the second heading, 'The Value of Sacrifice', we will examine a small group of psalms which call into question the absolute value of sacrifices. These psalms make an important contribution to our understanding of the true significance of sacrifice. Finally, under the heading, 'The Meaning of Sacrifice', we will examine certain key ideas associated with the inherent meaning of sacrifice, and explore their particular relevance to the Psalms.

I. THE PURPOSE OF SACRIFICE

Broadly speaking, three distinct motives may be discerned in the offering of sacrifices in the Psalms: to give thanks, to bring a petition, and to offer worship. Of these, the motives of thanksgiving and petition are quite specific, corresponding to the situations of distress and deliverance regularly depicted in the psalms of thanksgiving and lament. The motive of offering worship is rather more general, and corresponds loosely to the purpose of the hymnic psalms, that is, to offer praise to God. This last group of sacrifices may be further subdivided into three: those offered as God's due, those which express joy, and those which speak of devotion.

1. Thanksgiving

To give thanks to God for a specific occasion of deliverance is the chief motive of sacrifice in the Psalms. The idea appears in some eleven psalms, all of which are either laments in which the note of assurance predominates, or psalms of thanksgiving.[1] They are also all either psalms of the individual or psalms in which the individual comes to the fore. The sacrifices themselves arise out of situations of distress or deliverance which are typical of such psalms, and are offered by the individual in public worship. Thus the purpose of the sacrifices and the nature of the psalms are very closely related. In the case of the laments, the reference to sacrifice invariably occurs in the thanksgiving section, usually at the close of the psalm: by his sacrifice the psalmist indicates his sense of assurance of God's salvation, whether it has arrived or is still to come.[2] In the psalms of thanksgiving, the individual's thanksgiving always takes place in a communal context,[3] often accompanied by spoken testimony.[4]

Great joy surrounds the sacrifices offered in the psalms of lament, reflecting the confident mood of these psalms. This is true even when, as in Psalms 27 and 54, the psalmist has yet to be delivered and the sacrifice is promised in anticipation of salvation. In neither of these psalms is mention made of a vow or a votive offering, nor does the psalmist's promise to God contain any petitionary element: the promise of sacrifice is unconditional for the psalmist is already convinced that God will indeed help him. In the light of such certainty, sacrifice is freely offered in gratitude and praise, as for example in Psalm 27:

> And I will sacrifice in his tabernacle joyful sacrifices;
> I will sing and make music to Yahweh (v.6b).

Likewise, at the conclusion of Psalm 54, the psalmist promises:

> With a freewill offering I will sacrifice to you;
> I will praise your name, O Yahweh, for it is good (v.6[8]).

The rather unusual term 'joyful sacrifices' (Ps. 27:6; literally, 'sacrifices of rejoicing'), is essentially an alternative expression for the thank-offering. By it the psalmist emphasizes that his offering of praise to God arises out of his own volition and out of the great joy which God's act of salvation has inspired.

When deliverance has already been experienced, as in Psalms 22, 56 and 61, then the sense of joy is even more immediate. In each case, the psalmist is fulfilling sacrificial vows he made to support his plea for divine assistance when he was in trouble. His prayer has been answered, ('For you, O God, have heard my vows', Ps. 61:5[6]), so now he must keep his promise. Any sense of obligation, however, is far outweighed by his gratitude, and by the generosity with which he offers his sacrifice and praises:

> Then will I sing praise to your name continually
> as I fulfil my vows day after day (Ps. 61:8[9]).

Elsewhere, though, the fulfilling of a vow is acknowledged as an obligation before God:

> Your vows, O God, are upon me;
> I will present thank-offerings to you (Ps. 56:12[13]).

In Psalm 22, fulfilment of the vows is accompanied by praise, followed by a sacrificial meal in which the poor participate (vv.25–26[26–27]). In this way, the one who has received God's mercy is able to share his experience with others. By offering sacrifice in payment of a vow, therefore, the psalmists express praise and gratitude to God for their deliverance.

A similar picture of joy and abundance emerges from the psalms of thanksgiving.[5] When the psalmists have experienced God's deliverance, sacrifices of thanksgiving are offered in the temple because of what God has done for them. Again these may be, as in Psalms 66 and 116, the fulfilment of sacrificial vows made when the psalmist was in distress. On at least one occasion, the psalmist even goes beyond the strict requirements of a votive offering by presenting burnt offerings (Ps. 66:13–15): the high cost and quality of these offerings clearly indicate his willingness and generosity. The same psalmist's testimony to what God has done lends further support to the depth of praise and personal thanksgiving signified by such sacrifices (Ps. 66:16–20). As in the lament psalms, greater emphasis is placed on the psalmist's eagerness to show gratitude than on any sense of duty about fulfilling his vow. He is especially concerned to give credit to God:

> How shall I repay to Yahweh
> all his goodness to me? . . .
> To you I will sacrifice a thank-offering
> and on the name of Yahweh I will call (Ps. 116:12, 17).

Another example of thanksgiving by sacrifice occurs in Psalm 107, though on this occasion without reference to the paying of vows. The basic pattern of the psalm is built around the testimonies of God's deliverance for four separate groups of people, and each of the psalm's four main stanzas concludes in the same way:

> Let them thank Yahweh for his mercy,
> and his wonderful deeds to men (vv.8, 15, 21, 31).

To this refrain is added in v.22:

> And let them sacrifice thank-offerings,
> and recount his deeds in joyful song.

In three other psalms, Psalms 40, 51 and 69, sacrifices are contemplated apparently as an expression of thanksgiving for a specific occasion of deliverance. Each of them stresses the importance of giving testimony to God's deeds in public worship. Since, however, the sacrifices are not in fact offered, these psalms will merit special attention later on.

The primary purpose of sacrifice then, in these eleven psalms, is to give joyful thanks to Yahweh for a particular act of deliverance. The usual sacrifice for this purpose is the thank-offering, which may or may not be offered in fulfilment of a vow. In various ways the psalmists indicate their eagerness to sacrifice generously, and to celebrate with great joy as they bear testimony to the saving deeds of Yahweh.

2. Petition

In contrast to the substantial and significant group of psalms just described, a petitionary motive is associated with sacrifice only rarely. The clearest example occurs in Psalm 20, which is a prayer of intercession for the king's victory in battle:

> May he send you help from the sanctuary . . .
> May he remember all your sacrifices
> and accept your burnt offerings.
> May he give you all your heart's desire
> and make all your plans succeed (vv.2–4[3–5]).

Rather than describing the king's regular sacrifices, these verses probably refer to one particular occasion. Since acceptance is regarded as a precondition of victory, these sacrifices clearly have petitionary significance.[6]

In Psalm 141 by contrast, the precise nature of the psalmist's attitude toward sacrifice is less clear, and we shall defer a more detailed consideration of this psalm. Suffice it to say here that in praying for deliverance from sin and from the malice of the wicked, the psalmist draws a parallel between his prayer on the one hand and sacrifice and incense on the other. He appears therefore to attribute to the latter a petitionary significance. It may be, however, that the comparison is limited to the idea of both prayer and sacrifice ascending to God and so coming to his attention.

An even more doubtful case of petitionary sacrifice appears in Ps. 5:3[4]. The psalmist pleads for deliverance from malicious attack:

> O Yahweh, in the morning you hear my voice,
> in the morning I arrange (. . .) for you, and watch.

Since in some contexts, the verb 'to arrange' is used of preparing a sacrifice, the meaning here could be that the psalmist is presenting a morning sacrifice as a petition to God (as RSV,NEB,REB). However, the same verb can also refer to preparing a case in a dispute, and this interpretation seems preferable in the present context (cf. NIV, GNB). The following verb 'to watch', which is used of waiting for a revelation or a judgment, tends to support this idea. The psalmist then is simply presenting his complaint to God.

3. Homage

In a number of psalms, sacrifice takes on the significance of praise which is offered to God as his due. Unlike the psalms of thanksgiving, which testify to God's gracious intervention on a specific occasion, the majority of these psalms are hymnic compositions describing in general terms the greatness of God and his works.[7] They emphasize that sacrifice, like praise, is due to God alone.

Psalm 96 celebrates Yahweh's kingship over all the world, and calls on all nations to worship him. In this context the call to 'bring an offering and come into his courts' (v.8) suggests that sacrifices and other gifts are a prerequisite of access to the divine presence, and represent an act of homage and submission to the king before whom the nations must tremble and bow down (v.9). As part of this act of homage, vows and votive offerings may also be brought. This is the case in Psalms 65 and 76, where the vows seem to be mentioned in the context of sacrifice. In neither psalm, however, does the petitionary aspect of a vow have any relevance, nor are the offerings occasioned by any specific cause of thanksgiving. The votive offering is simply a vehicle of the praise that is God's due:

> Before you silence is praise, O God in Zion;
> and to you are vows fulfilled (Ps. 65:1[2]).[8]

Similarly in Psalm 76, which celebrates Yahweh's defence of Jerusalem and his rule in heaven and earth, the psalmist encourages rightful worship:

> Vow and fulfil to Yahweh your God, all those around him;
> let them bring gifts to the one who is to be feared (v. 11[12]).

This is not a command to make a vow, since the making of a vow is a purely voluntary act. Rather, the psalm stresses that when promises are made, it is to Yahweh that they must be paid. The presentation of gifts to an awesome God reinforces the idea that the votive offerings themselves are presented as an act of homage to God.

Two further psalms belong here. Ps. 22:29 describes a sacrificial feasting by the nations in an eschatological setting. The hymnic character of the passage suggests that these sacrifices are offered chiefly to honour Yahweh. Secondly, a hymn–like prayer occurs in Ps. 119:108: 'Accept, O Yahweh, the freewill offerings of my mouth'. Here the sacrificial term is clearly a metaphor for praise, and the psalm's formal nature indicates that such praise is quite general.

In these five psalms, then, and especially in Psalms 65, 76 and 96, sacrifices are offered in praise of Yahweh as an expression of the homage and submission due to him. The 'gift offering' (Ps. 96:8) is particularly appropriate as a means of offering homage, and even the special nature of vows and freewill offerings, as a means of giving thanks on a particular occasion, can be subordinated to this wider purpose.

4. Joyful Worship

In a few psalms, sacrifices evoke the pure joy of worship in the sanctuary. Two of these are processional psalms, where the altar functions as the very focus of sacrificial worship. On one occasion, a psalmist undergoes an act of ritual purification as he prepares to approach the altar:

> I wash my hands in innocence,
> and I will go about your altar, O Yahweh (Ps. 26:6).

His mood is clearly one of joyful anticipation, as he speaks of love for God's house and praise for what God has done. A very similar atmosphere is evoked in Ps. 118, as first the psalmist enters the temple gates (vv.19–20), before approaching the altar itself:

> Lead the festal procession with dense foliage
> right up to the horns of the altar (v.27).

Since both Jewish tradition and the psalm's own language (v.27) suggest that his psalm was originally associated with the Feast of Tabernacles, it is likely to have been accompanied by sacrifices in abundance, offered in joyful thanks for harvest.

In Psalms 42–43, however, the psalmist in exile can only express a wistful longing to be present at such a celebration:

> Then will I go to the altar of God,
> to God, my joy and delight;
> And I will praise you with the harp,
> O God, my God (Ps. 43:4).

Here again one notes that the altar represents not only the very centre of worship but also the focal point of God's presence. In such a context, sacrifice expresses both real communion with God and the opportunity to offer joyful praise.

5. Devotion

There remain three psalms where sacrifices offered to a particular deity are seen as a mark of loyalty to that deity. Indeed, they mark off the worshipper of one deity from another in a quite distinctive way.

In Psalms 16 and 106, pagan deities are the object of devotion. In the former case, the psalmist repents of his earlier ways:

> I will not pour out their libations of blood,
> nor will I take up their names on my lips (Ps. 16:4b).

He expresses his confidence in Yahweh by affirming his dissociation from pagan worship. It has even been conjectured that this is the prayer of a Canaanite convert to Yahwism. In Psalm 106, the whole Israelite community confesses to having been guilty in former days of such sins, of which they now repent. Those whose predecessors 'yoked themselves to Baal of Peor' (v.28) and who 'served their idols' (v.36) acknowledge that by their sacrifices they worshipped 'lifeless gods' (v.28) and participated in the sacrificial murder of children (vv.37–38).

The positive counterpart to this misplaced devotion is found in Psalm 4. Here the psalmist affirms his trust in Yahweh, and encourages those who are in danger of apostasy to follow his example: 'Offer righteous sacrifices, and trust in Yahweh' (v.5[6]). These 'righteous sacrifices' should be thought of as offered in the right spirit and disposition toward Yahweh, rather than according to the correct ritual. The context suggests that they indicate a religious orientation toward Yahweh (cf. vv.4, 5b). They signify a right and integral relationship with him, and express trust in the one true God.[9]

6. The Purpose of Sacrifice: Summary

Psalm 50 is unique among the psalms in dealing explicitly with sacrificial motives. It is therefore a convenient focus for summarizing what has been learnt from the other psalms (a detailed discussion of this psalm is found in Section II).

The most frequent motive for sacrifice is to give thanks to God for a deliverance he has already accomplished. Such sacrifices are offered in a spirit of generosity and with great joy, and are intended above all to give the credit to God. Often the sacrifice had been previously promised when the offerer was still in trouble. In fact, such a procedure is recommended in Ps. 50:14–15, since God is honoured when people express their dependence on him in this way, acknowledging his power to save. It is because of the testimony and honour they bring to God that the practice of offering sacrifices of thanksgiving is particularly commended in Psalm 50 (cf. vv.14, 23).

One or two petitionary sacrifices are found in the Psalms. Ps. 50:8–13, however, draws attention to the dangers inherent in such sacrifices, which might be offered with a view to influencing God in one's favour. This may explain why they are so rarely found.

The remaining sacrifices in the Psalms reflect the purpose of offering worship to Yahweh in a more general way. In particular, they demonstrate the need to recognize God's sovereignty by bringing him a worthy offering; they express the tremendous joy that is to be experienced in God's presence; and they indicate the depth of devotion the worshipper gives to his God. The last of these finds particular expression in Psalm 50: in the covenant sacrifices which seal the relationship between Yahweh and his worshipping people (v.5), and in the requirement to integrate appropriate attitudes to sacrificial worship with the practice of covenant law in daily life.

II.   THE VALUE OF SACRIFICE

Despite the widespread importance clearly attached to sacrifice in the Psalms, certain psalms seem to maintain a very different attitude. In Psalms 40, 50, 51, 69 and 141, the very value of sacrifice itself is open to question. We begin with Psalm 50, where the subject of sacrifice is dealt with in a direct and comprehensive manner.

1. Psalm 50

At first sight, this psalm seems to cast doubt on the necessity for any kind of sacrifice at all:

> I have no need of a bull from your stall
> or of goats from your pens, . . .
> Do I eat the flesh of bulls
> or drink the blood of goats? (Ps. 50:9,13).

This view seems to be confirmed by the intervening verses. If a person makes his offering with the aim of putting God in man's debt, his sacrifices are worthless, because there is nothing in this world that God does not already own (vv.10–11).[10] Further, even the very idea that God needs sacrifices for food, widespread in the ancient Near East, is absurd (vv.12–13). Man can therefore never use sacrifice for his own ends.

But it is plain from the rest of the psalm that it is the abuse of sacrifice, rather than its absolute worth, that is so emphatically condemned. God himself, for example, has entered into a covenant with his people by sacrifice, and he is revealing himself to them now in order to renew that covenant:

> Gather to me my devotees
> who enter into my covenant with sacrifice (v.5).[11]

Indeed, he goes on to encourage them to offer the right kind of sacrifice in response:

> Sacrifice to God a thank-offering,
> and fulfil your vows to the Most High.

> Call on me in time of trouble:
> I will deliver you so that you may honour me (vv.14–15).

God is honoured in the sequence of petition, deliverance, and thanksgiving; and this is true whether or not a vow is involved. By making an appeal for help, man acknowledges his dependence on God; by the act of deliverance God affirms his power to save; and by his sacrifice man testifies publicly to the power of God. Far from sacrifice being devalued, the thank-offering is particularly commended as a means of giving honour to God (cf. also v.23). The people who are criticized are those who present their offerings without moral integrity, as if mere ritual could cover up or atone for such things as slander, theft, or adultery (vv.16–21). Only to the person 'who is set in the way', says the Lord, 'will I show him the salvation of God' (v.23).

The contrast is therefore between a right and wrong use of sacrifice. Of itself, sacrifice is meaningless, possibly even harmful. But when it is offered with the aim of bringing glory and honour to God, it acquires positive value and meaning. The thank-offering is singled out as the sacrifice which most clearly fulfils this aim.

2. Psalm 141

Here the psalmist makes his plea to God in distinctive language:

> Let my prayer be established (as) incense before you,
> the lifting of my hands (as) an evening offering (v.2).

Clearly some kind of relationship is envisaged between the psalmist's prayer, symbolized by uplifted hands, and the daily offering of sacrifice with incense in the temple, though contrasting explanations of this relationship have been offered. It has been proposed either that prayer is an inferior substitute for sacrifice, perhaps because of some physical limitation, or that prayer reflects a more spiritual approach that has progressed beyond mere ceremonial.[12] But there is no clear evidence that prayer is viewed as a substitute here, and other parts of the OT confirm the continuing importance of sacrifice in the post–exilic period.[13] It is much more likely that a direct comparison is being made. Just as the smoke and incense ascend to heaven every morning and evening, so the psalmist trusts that his prayers will come regularly before God. Although we do not know for certain whether he was actually present at the altar, it is apparent that this psalmist upholds physical sacrifice as a helpful model of man's approach to the divine presence.

3. Psalm 69

After a long prayer of lament, Psalm 69 concludes on a note of thanksgiving:

I will praise the name of God in song,
and magnify him with thanksgiving;
This will please Yahweh more than a bull–ox
having horns and cloven hooves (vv.30–31[31–32]).

The key question here is why song should apparently give greater
pleasure to God than sacrifice. It cannot be that a song is more personal,
for singing was one of the most distinctive features of corporate temple
worship.[14] Nor does a song especially represent the worshipper's inner
disposition, for both singing and sacrifice are outward acts of worship.[15]
The difference seems therefore to lie in the fact that whereas sacrifice
offers only silent praise, a song declares God's praises in an intelligible
manner to all who listen.

Far from attempting to do away with sacrifice altogether, it is quite
possible that this psalm would have been accompanied by thank-
offerings. The point is, however, that even the most costly sacrifices have
their limitations. Their material aspects are subordinate to a deeper
meaning, which is made explicit only by verbal means. Though sacrifice
and singing are both essential to public worship, only the latter can
actually declare the greatness of God's name (cf. v.30).

4. Psalm 40

As this psalmist looks back to a specific instance of answered prayer
(vv.1–10 [2–11]), he recalls that what God had required of him was
obedient trust rather than any special offering:

You did not desire sacrifice or offering
– You made me understand it! –[16]
You did not ask for burnt offering or sin offering (v.6[7])

He had expressed himself ready to do God's will, as it was contained in
God's written word:

So I said, 'See! I have come;
it is written for me in the roll of a scroll.
I have desired to do your will, O my God,
and your teaching is in my inmost parts' (vv.7–8 [8–9]).[17]

Although the sacrificial reference in verse 6[7] is quite comprehensive,
this need not imply 'the axiomatic repudiation of the whole sacrificial
cult'.[18] If we have interpreted the overall structure of the psalm correctly,
it would appear once more that the sacrifices envisaged are intended as
sacrifices of thanksgiving, expressing gratitude for deliverance. It is not
impossible that the burnt offering[19] and sin offering[20] should be related to
this purpose. All such sacrifices, however, are subordinate to the
intention of dedicating one's life to the will of God.

5. Psalm 51

The most emphatic rejection of sacrifice anywhere in the Psalms seems to occur in the following lines:

> For you would not delight in sacrifice, were I to bring it;
> a burnt offering you would not accept.
> The sacrifices of God are a broken spirit;
> a broken and crushed heart, O God, you will not
> despise (Ps. 51:16–17 [18–19]).

To understand these lines, however, it is essential to consider their context. Because of the penitential nature of the psalm it might be assumed that the sacrifices contemplated are intended to be expiatory.[21] This, however, creates a difficulty in the sequence of vv.13–17[15–19], where a votive offering would then be followed by an expiatory one.[22] The confession of sin and prayers for forgiveness end at v.12[14], while from v.13[15] onwards the psalmist turns to the outcome of his deliverance. The usual response to deliverance, as we have seen frequently in the Psalms, is to offer both sacrifices of thanksgiving and verbal testimony. Since the verbal testimony here is in evidence in vv.13–15 [15–17], it seems most reasonable to conclude that the sacrifices of vv.16–17 [18–19] are in fact sacrifices of thanksgiving.[23]

Moreover, the psalmist is making an individual statement concerning God's will for him in particular circumstances, rather than a general assertion about the value or otherwise of sacrifice. More important than any blood offering is the psalmist's deep contrition: the sacrifice of his self–will in surrender to God. This does not mean that contrition itself is an act of thanksgiving. True thanksgiving is the result of contrition, demonstrated in a turning away from sin and in a determination to lead other sinners back to God (v.13[15]).

In the closing verses, the individual's prayer for himself passes over into intercession for the nation. When Israel too has been restored to favour,

> Then will you delight in righteous sacrifices,
> burnt offering and whole offering;
> Then bulls will ascend upon your altar (v.19[21]).

Despite the views of many interpreters who regard vv.18– 19 [20–21] as a post-exilic supplement,[24] there is a close relationship between these verses and the rest of the psalm.[25] The 'righteous sacrifices', for example, are to be closely identified with the 'sacrifices of God' (v.17[19]). Although now they are no longer metaphorical but literal, they are offered as thanksgiving sacrifices for sin that has been dealt with, whether on behalf of an individual or a nation, in gratitude for a restored relationship with God.

So this psalm also looks for no ultimate rejection of sacrifice. In fact, sacrifices are valued as a symbol of thanksgiving and of one's right standing before God. More important, however, than the physical act of sacrifice is a true self-offering in penitence and thanksgiving.

6. The Value of Sacrifice: Summary

Despite the fact that sacrifice played a vital role in worship alongside the psalms, it had its limitations. On its own, it was a mute witness, and the mere presentation of material things had no intrinsic value. It was therefore a symbol, whose true value was measured by the purposes and motives with which the worshipper made his offering.

On the basic level, sacrifice might symbolize the regular elements of cultic worship (Ps. 141:2). It was particularly valued as a means of offering thanks to God, supremely as a symbol of the worshipper's own self-offering of thanks. On such occasions, physical sacrifice might be suspended altogether, either to allow a specific verbal testimony to be more clearly heard (Ps. 69:30–31 [31–32]) or to enable a worshipper to ensure that his inner desires were right before God (Ps. 40:6–8 [7–9]; 51:16–17 [18–19]). Having confirmed the motives of his heart, he could then fully express his renewed faith by physical acts of sacrifice (Ps. 51:18–19 [20–21]; cf. Ps. 50:14, 23).

III. THE MEANING OF SACRIFICE

We have seen that sacrifices in the Psalms may be offered for a variety of motives, and that the value of sacrifice is dependent on a proper relationship between motive and offering. These motives must now be compared with the inherent meaning of sacrifice, especially the three main concepts widely held to lie behind OT sacrifices. These are, firstly, sacrifice as a gift to God, usually linked with the burnt offering and the cereal offering; secondly, the notion of communion, usually especially related to the peace or fellowship offerings; and finally, the idea of atonement, which is particularly associated with the sin and guilt offerings.

1. Gift

The idea of sacrifice offered to God as a gift is most clearly presented in Ps.96:8: 'Bring an offering and come into his courts'. The Hebrew word for 'offering' (*minḥā*) includes secular ideas such as 'gift' or 'tribute', and seems to include here the notion of the tribute offered to a king in recognition of God's sovereignty and majesty. It therefore expresses the worshipper's homage and submission, though the precise form of the sacrifice remains unclear.

There is, of course, some danger in regarding one's sacrifice as a gift to God. This is spelled out in Psalm 50, where the idea that man could somehow gain credit with God, so as to expect some return for his outlay, is strongly condemned. All gifts made to God in a very real sense already belong to him. The same difficulty is also possible in connection with the petitionary offerings of Psalms 20 and 141. In both of these psalms, however, the sacrifices function as an appeal to God rather than as part of a contract with him. This is clearly the case in Psalm 141, since sacrifice is compared with prayer, which can scarcely be considered a gift in the strict sense. It is also true in Psalm 20, where acceptance of the king's sacrifices and the battle's victorious outcome remain undecided. Such sacrifices may further an appeal to God, but are not to be regarded as attempts to buy his favour.

Votive offerings also appear in Psalms 65 and 76 in a role similar to that of the gift in Psalm 96. Their normal function as vows, however, has dropped out of sight. In fact, as in most cases where vows are involved (Pss. 22, 56, 61, 66, 116), the idea of obligation is replaced by an overwhelming sense of gratitude. Such offerings are willing gifts, not the result of a routine dutifully fulfilled.

A desire to express gratitude is a common feature of all the various sacrifices of thanksgiving, whose chief function is as a public memorial to honour God for what he has done. Indeed, it is primarily the thanksgiving and honour, rather than the sacrifice itself, that constitutes the gift to God.

2. Communion

The sacrificial notion of communion is commonly associated with the peace or fellowship offerings, when worshippers shared a sacrificial meal. In the light of Lv. 7:11–18, this would include the various votive, thanksgiving, and freewill offerings mentioned in the psalms, with the possible exception of Ps. 66:13[14] where a vow is fulfilled with a burnt offering. Only in Ps. 22:26[27] (cf. v.29[30]) is specific mention made of such a meal, where the poor are invited to join in celebrating God's salvation. Fellowship with one's fellow men as well as with God is therefore involved, as in all the references in the Psalms to sacrifices of thanksgiving.

Communion as expressed by a sense of loyalty to a particular deity occurs in Pss. 4:5[6]; 16:4 and 106:28, though again it is not associated with any one type of sacrifice. More importantly, the covenant itself is sealed by sacrifice (Ps. 50:5), so that to be in communion with God is to have one's entire life directed by the revealed nature of God. A close parallel is found in Psalm 4, where to offer the right kind of sacrifices means to refrain from sin and to approach God in humility and trust. The covenant relationship is therefore to be maintained through sacrificial meals. As these were celebrated in the presence of God, his people shared not only in a particular occasion of thanksgiving but also in their own covenant commitment to God and to each other.

The theme of communion with God in temple worship is central to Psalms 26, 42–43 and 118. In most cases such communion with God is probably associated with the peace offerings, though no specific type of sacrifice is mentioned in any of these psalms. Here it is the altar on which sacrifice is offered which serves as the focal point for worship and the presence of God.

Three aspects of communion therefore emerge from its association with sacrifice in the Psalms. It involves commitment to and covenant with a particular deity, indicated both by the physical act of sacrifice and by the spirit in which it is offered. It includes the participation of God's people together in God's gift of salvation, in an expression of deep gratitude to God. It focuses on worship in the presence of God, symbolized above all by sacrifice on God's altar.

3. Atonement

The lack of any clear reference to sacrificial atonement in the Psalter is remarkable. The one explicit mention of expiatory sacrifice which does occur is purely formal, where it is simply listed as one of four different types of sacrifice (Ps. 40:6). Furthermore, the primary emphasis of the context is on sacrifices of thanksgiving, suggesting either that forgiveness of sin is only one of several reasons for thanksgiving or that the significance of the sin offering was not confined to atonement. Conversely, where sin is clearly acknowledged as the cause of Israel's difficulties, as in Ps. 107:11, 17, no atoning rite is mentioned. This is true even in Psalm 51, where the reference to sacrifice (vv.16–17 [18–19]) occurs in the context of thanksgiving. The mention of purificatory rites in verse 7 seems to be metaphorical rather than literal.

Sacrifice and atonement do occur side by side in the opening verses of Psalm 65, but here too there is no explicit connection between them:

> Before you silence is praise, O God in Zion,
> and to you are vows fulfilled.
> O hearer of prayer, to you all flesh will come.
> When the weight of our sins overwhelms us,
> it is you who atone for our transgressions (Ps. 65:1–3 [2–4]).

The means of atonement seems not to be important to the author of this hymn of praise, only that God himself is the source of his forgiveness. God alone receives praise and sacrifice, God alone answers prayer, and God alone atones for sin. It is striking therefore, that in those psalms in which a major concern with the forgiveness of sin includes some reference to sacrifice (Pss. 51; 65), the latter has to do with thanksgiving or homage rather than with atonement.

All this clearly indicates that for the psalmists, sacrifice was not regarded as an automatic means of atonement. The primary significance of sacrifice for them lay outside the realm of atonement and, conversely, atonement was largely achieved by means other than sacrifice (eg. Ps. 25, 32, 51, 103, 130). In particular, due weight must be given to the roles of prayer, confession, contrition, and even instruction (cf. Ps. 25:8–9; 32:8–9).[26]

It should not be concluded, however, that the psalmists recognized no atoning role for sacrifice. For example, a prayer for deliverance from sin is compared with the regular twice daily offerings (Ps. 141:2). Ps. 76:10–11 speaks of votive offerings to a God of wrath, who may therefore need to be propitiated. Expiatory rites may have been performed by pilgrims as they entered the temple (Ps. 26:6). But the connection between sacrifice and atonement is never explicit. On the one hand, the psalmists confess their sin, pray for forgiveness, and await God's pleasure. On the other, they give thanks to God for a forgiveness already made freely available. The first approach stresses God's sovereignty and man's dependence, while the second lays emphasis on God's forgiving nature. Both approaches point to God himself as the only true source of atonement. By attributing atonement to the direct action of God, these psalmists remain consistent with the theme of the whole Psalter, the 'Book of Praises', which is to give all honour to God.

4 The Meaning of Sacrifice: Summary

The idea of sacrifice as a gift, offered to God as his due and as an expression of honour and thanksgiving, is widespread in the Psalms. The notion that such a gift can be used to influence God, however, is strongly condemned (Ps. 50:8–13). With regard to communion, sacrifice symbolizes a covenant commitment to a particular deity, the thankful participation with God's people in his salvation, and the focal point of worship in the presence of God. Sacrifice, however, can never be divorced from the spirit in which it is offered, and it is never automatic in its effects. With regard to atonement, therefore, the psalmists stress the sovereignty of God, whose nature it is to forgive those who thankfully acknowledge their dependence upon him.

IV. THE SIGNIFICANCE OF SACRIFICE: CONCLUSION

It is evident from the majority of psalms that sacrifice is instinctively accepted as a regular feature of OT worship. It is also clear that the psalmists are far more interested in the significance of sacrifice than in its material aspects. This is particularly true of those psalms which seem to question the value of sacrifice, where it is more important first to make sure that one's heart is in tune with the underlying aim of sacrifice, than merely to offer the sacrifice itself.

It is also true that the psalmists are more concerned with the specific purposes for which sacrifices are offered than with any supposed inherent meanings associated with the particular types of sacrifice. The most prominent motive is that of giving public testimony to God's deliverance from a variety of distressing situations, but others include presenting petitions, giving due recognition of God's sovereignty, worshipping in God's presence, and confessing devotion and loyalty to Yahweh.

In fact, it is impossible to tie down specific meanings to individual types of sacrifice. The meaning of any sacrificial act must be interpreted in the light of the motive with which it is offered rather than any significance artificially attributed to a particular kind of sacrifice. The element of gift, for example, is present in the idea of tribute offered in due homage to God's sovereign majesty as well as in the frequent expressions of thanksgiving. The notion of communion is also associated with sacrifices of thanksgiving, as well as with worshipping in God's presence and indicating one's devotion to him. Atonement, however, scarcely figures in the sacrifices of the Psalms, because the hope of forgiveness is centred on the nature and action of God rather than on what might appear to be the human aspects of sacrifice.

Ultimately, of course, the significance of all types of sacrifice in the Psalms is determined by the nature of God and of his relationship to his people. Communion, therefore, is encounter with the divine overlord; gift is the offering of what is his due; while atonement is a gift from God which cannot be elicited either by sacrifice or by prayer. The sacrificial cult, however, does provide the means by which people can approach God, and through which God bestows his gifts. If true sacrifice testifies to God's glory, it also witnesses to man's response in devotion and ultimately in self-offering. It is not surprising therefore that it is the sacrifice of thanksgiving which is particularly favoured by the psalmists. When combined with a life of integrity, such sacrifices render true honour to God.

NOTES

1. Psalms 22, 27, 40, 51, 54, 56, 61, 69 (laments), 66, 107, 115 (thanksgivings). On these Psalm types, see H. Gunkel and J. Begrich, *Einleitung in die Psalmen* (Göttingen: Vandenhoeck & Ruprecht, 1966[2]), 172–292; C. Westermann, *The Praise of God in the Psalms* (ET) (London: Epworth, 1966) 64–81, 102–116.

2. It is often difficult to decide in the laments whether the psalmist has already experienced salvation or still awaits it, and proposals are sometimes conjectural. See, for example, A. Szörényi in D.J.A. Clines, *Tyn. B* 18 (1967) 107–108.

3. See A. Weiser, *The Psalms* (OTL) (London: SCM, 1962) 468–469, 685, 719; cf. S. Mowinckel, *The Psalms in Israel's Worship* (Oxford: Blackwell, 1962) vol. 2, 31.

4. Such testimony is encouraged in Ps. 107:22, and actually given in Ps. 66:16–20.

5. Pss. 66, 107, 116.
6. For similar examples outside the Psalter, cf. e.g. 1 Sa. 7:7–9; 13:9–12.
7. On the distinction between Hymns (or Descriptive Praises) and Thanksgivings (or Declarative Praises), cf. Gunkel and Begrich, *Einleitung* 32–94, 265–292; Westermann, *Praise of God* 25–35, 102–116.
8. Most EVV follow LXX, 'A hymn (of praise) becomes you . . .', which presupposes a slightly different Hebrew text. MT, however, reads 'silence' (and also in Pss. 22:2; 39:2; 62:1), which makes excellent sense if taken metaphorically to mean a 'quiet confidence' in God. Cf. Ps. 62:1 and F. Delitzsch, *Psalms* (Grand Rapids: Eerdmans, 1871), vol. 2, 226.
9. Cf. the occurrence of an identical phrase with similar meaning in Dt. 33:19.
10. See chap. 6, Section II(2) for detailed evidence of this practice.
11. Both at the original ratification ceremony of the Sinai covenant (Ex. 24:3–8) and at its renewal (Ps. 50), sacrifice plays an important role in sealing the relationship between God and his people.
12. Cf. A.F. Kirkpatrick, *Psalms* (Cambridge: Cambridge University Press, 1921) 797; M. Dahood, *Psalms* (AB) (Garden City: Doubleday, 1965) vol. 3, 309; Weiser, *Psalms* 811; W.O.E. Oesterley, *The Psalms* (London: SPCK, 1939) vol. 2, 561.
13. E.g. Ezr. 3:6; 6.17; 2 Ch. 7:12.
14. Cf. Mowinckel, *Psalms in Israel's Worship*, vol. 2, 25.
15. Cf. L. Jacquet, *Les Psaumes et le Coeur de l'Homme* (Belgium: Duculot, 1975–79) vol. 2, 387; H.C. Leupold, *Exposition of the Psalms* (Welwyn: Evangelical Press, 1974) 508.
16. This line has been variously translated and interpreted from ancient times, although the Hebrew MSS contain no variants. Literally it may be translated, 'Ears you dug for me', apparently based on the idea that God formed the cavities of his ears (cf. C.A. Briggs, *Psalms* (ICC) (Edinburgh: T. & T. Clark, 1906) vol. 1, 355). Metaphorically this may mean that he was given the capacity to hear and understand the import of God's will. See also J. Calvin, *Commentary on the Book of Psalms* (Edinburgh, 1845–49, vol. 2, 99).
17. For 'See! I have come' as an expression of loyalty, cf. 2 Sa. 19:20; for the scroll, cf. 2 Ki. 22:8–13.
18. Weiser, *Psalms* 338.
19. See Ps. 66:13–15 where a burnt offering fulfils a vow.
20. The sin offering in this context may acknowledge either the offerer's general sinfulness or the fact that sin was a factor in the distress from which he has been delivered (see v. 12[13]).
21. E.g. R.J. Thompson, *Penitence and Sacrifice in Early Israel Outside the Levitical Law* (Leiden: Brill, 1963) 150, 156; J.H. Eaton, *Psalms* (Torch) (London: SCM, 1967) 142; A.A. Anderson, *The Book of Psalms* (NCB) (London: Oliphants, 1972) 401.
22. As Eaton, ibid., acknowledges.
23. H.J. Kraus, *Psalmen* (BKAT 15) (Neukirchen-Vluyn: Neukirchener Verlag, 1978⁵) 547; Jacquet, *Psaumes*, vol. 2, 181; Weiser, *Psalms* 409.
24. E.g. E.R. Dalglish, *Psalm Fifty-One in the Light of Ancient Near Eastern Patternism* (Leiden: Brill, 1962) 204–206.
25. Cf. e.g. Dahood, *Psalms*, vol. 2, 2; Eaton, *Psalms* 142.
26. Cf. H. McKeating, 'Divine forgiveness in the Psalms' *SJT* 18 (1965) 78–81; Mowinckel, *Psalms in Israel's Worship*, vol. 2, 13.

FOR FURTHER READING

General works on the Psalms:

L.C. Allen, *Psalms 101–150* (WBC) (Waco: Word, 1983).
A.A. Anderson, *The Book of Psalms* (NCB) (London: Oliphants, 1972)

P.C. Craigie, *Psalms 1–50* (WBC) (Waco: Word, 1983).
M. Dahood, *Psalms*, 3 vols. (AB) (New York: Doubleday, 1966– 1970).
H.J. Kraus, *Theology of the Psalms* (Minneapolis: Augsburg, 1979, 1986).
S. Mowinckel, *The Psalms in Israel's Worship*, 2 vols. (Oxford: Blackwell, 1962).
L. Sabourin, *The Psalms: Their Origin and Meaning* (New York: Alba House, 1974).
M.E. Tate, *Psalms 51–100* (WBC) (Waco: Word, 1990).
A. Weiser, *The Psalms* (OTL) (London: SCM, 1962).

Specialist works:

L.C. Allen, 'Structure and Meaning in Psalm 50', *VE* XIV (1984) 17–37.
J.W. Bos, 'Oh, When the Saints: A Consideration of the Meaning of Psalm 50', *JSOT* 24 (1982) 65–77.
S. Daiches, 'The Meaning of "Sacrifices" in the Psalms', *Essays in Honour of the Very Rev. Dr. J.H. Hertz* (London: 1944).
H. McKeating, 'Divine Forgiveness in the Psalms', *SJT* 18 (1965) 69–83.
R.J. Thompson, *Penitence and Sacrifice in Early Israel Outside the Levitical Law* (Leiden: Brill, 1963).

4

Sacrifice in the Prophets

ERNEST C. LUCAS

I. THE PRE-EXILIC PROPHETS

There are fashions in OT studies, as in most things. Certainly the 20th century has seen a change in the way that most OT scholars view the relationship between the prophets and priests in ancient Israel. Writing in 1904, Kautzsch summed up the legacy of the nineteenth century on this subject when he said,

> The gulf between the religion of the Prophets and that of the Priests' Code has been described as one that cannot be bridged.[1]

He goes on to endorse that view. Skinner, in his influential book *Prophecy and Religion*,[2] devotes a whole chapter to 'the two religions of Israel'. He brings out the implications of this view for our topic of sacrifice when he says that the prophets (he means the pre-exilic ones) held up to their contemporaries

> the ideal of a religion wholly based on moral fellowship between God and man, and in which sacrificial worship was at best an irrelevance, and at worst an offence.

As late as 1961, Pfeiffer could describe the cult as

> the heathen element of the religion of Israel derived from the religion of Canaan and attacked by the prophets.[3]

From the late 1930s onwards, this view came under increasing criticism.[4] As a result, in the 1960s we find Von Rad saying,

> We have also abandoned the whole idea of a religion of the prophets as a religion of the spirit opposed to the cultic religion of the priests.[5]

Clements wrote in similar vein,

Some scholars have claimed that these pre-exilic prophets were giving expression to a total rejection of all cult in the interest of a more spiritual religion. This view has necessarily undergone considerable criticism and some modification in the light of a closer examination of the evidence contained in the Old Testament. In its radical form we must abandon it.[6]

A more recent review of the situation shows how decisively the old dichotomy has been abandoned, for according to Ashby, 'the anti-sacrificial strain seems to have died out of contemporary Old Testament scholarship'. In order not to be the slaves of fashion, however, we need to follow Clements' hint and closely examine the evidence in the OT to see whether the new consensus is justified. Central to the debate are the handful of passages which we must consider in some detail.[7]

Primacy of consideration must go to Am. 5:25 and Je. 7:21–23. Both might be taken as saying that sacrifice played no part in Israel's religion during the wilderness period, and so has no real place in it at all. This carries with it the implication that the wilderness period was regarded as a time of special faithfulness in Israel's relationship with God. Now, as Mays recognizes,

> There is no way to reconcile this view with the extant Pentateuchal tradition which knows nothing of a period of Israel's beginnings when sacrifice was not offered.[8]

Faced with this contradiction, scholars who believe that these prophets were rejecting sacrifice outright have adopted one of two stances. First, there is the view articulated by Mowvley,

> Lv. 1–9 certainly provides regulations for elaborate sacrifice and as it now stands this applies to the wilderness period. However, these chapters are most commonly regarded as coming from the exilic or post-exilic period in which case they would be unknown to the prophets.[9]

Now, without going to the major issues of the dating of the supposed Pentateuchal sources, one can say that even if the so called 'P' material is exilic or later in its present form, this does not preclude the probability that it enshrines traditions and laws of sacrifice that are pre-exilic, even Mosaic, in date. Moreover, the so-called 'J' and 'E' material, held by most scholars to predate the eighth century prophets, knows of the murmurings in the wilderness and sacrifices dating to the time of Moses.[10] On balance, then, it seems unlikely that Amos and Jeremiah were totally ignorant of the traditions which by the early post-exilic period at the very latest were accepted as a major component of Israel's sacred history and traditions.

Secondly, Wolff links Am. 5:25–26 and Je. 7:21–23 (both of which he attributes to deuteronomistic editors rather than the prophets themselves) with 'in a sense esoterically, preserved traditions that were otherwise little known' which presented the wilderness as the time of absolute faithfulness.[11] He finds evidence of this little-known, esoteric tradition in Dt. 32:10; Ho. 9:10; Je. 2:2–3. Now the first point to make is that both Amos and Jeremiah are posing a question to the people at large, and it would be strange if either the prophets or their editors based the questions on esoteric traditions which the people were hardly expected to know about! The second is that it is by no means clear that the esoteric tradition to which Wolff appeals is evidenced by the passages quoted. Dt. 32:10 says nothing about Israel's spiritual state in the wilderness:

> He found him in a desert land,
> and in the howling waste of the wilderness;
> he encircled him, he cared for him,
> he kept him as the apple of his eye.

It simply stresses the goodness of God in taking her from the wilderness to the Promised Land with its plenty. There is nothing in Ho. 9:10 ('Like grapes in the wilderness I found Israel . . . But they came to Baal Peor . . . and consecrated themselves to Baal') or Je. 2:2–3 ('I remember the devotion of your youth . . . how you followed me in the wilderness') that goes beyond an emphatic stress on Israel's *relative* innocence and faithfulness to Yahweh prior to her contact with the Baal cult when she reached Baal Peor. Even in the golden calf incident it is Yahweh who is invoked. The sin there is not worshipping another god, but making an image to represent Yahweh.

If we reject both the view that the pre-exilic prophets were (for whatever reason) ignorant of the tradition that Moses instituted the sacrificial system in the wilderness and the idea that they were consciously following a minority variant tradition, what can we say about these two passages? Rowley discussed them at some length in dialogue with Cadoux and Snaith in 1946/47.[12] What follows is heavily indebted to this discussion, and to a much earlier discussion of Am. 5:25 by Macdonald,[13] as well as commentaries on these passages.

Amos 5:25

If this verse is to taken literalistically as meaning:

> Was it sacrifices and offerings you brought to me forty years in the wilderness,
> O house of Israel?

we must surely conclude that, if any credence is to be given to the OT evidence, Amos' hearers would have answered with an emphatic 'Yes!'. That there is nothing in the form of the question to preclude this is shown by the similarly formulated question in 1 Sa. 2:27, where the Hebrew text reads:

Did I reveal myself to the house of your father when they were in Egypt subject
to the house of Pharaoh?.

Here the expected answer is clearly 'Yes'.[14] Where then is there a
challenge in Amos' question? Clearly one is intended. It is here that
Macdonald helps us by drawing attention to the unusual word order of
Amos' question. The object of the verb comes first in the sentence, so
giving it emphasis, i.e. 'Was it sacrifices and offerings you brought me
. . .?'. This amounts to saying, 'Was it *only* sacrifices and offerings you
brought me . . .?'. In addition, the verb used here for 'bringing' (hiph.
ngš) is only rarely used of offering sacrifices (normally expressed by the
hiph. of either *bw'* or *qrb*), and is more often used of 'drawing near' to God
in worship. Its use here might be intended to remind the people that what
is important is not the offering *per se* but the attitude of worship it is meant
to express. Therefore, the looked for response to the question is, 'We
brought more than just sacrifices, we brought true worship.' True
worship is the giving of oneself to God and is reflected in the obedience of
the totality of his demands. This is just the point of the preceding verses in
Am. 5:21–24. Here God rejects the people's sacrifices not because
sacrifice is wrong, but because it is meaningless unless accompanied by
obedience to God's moral commands. Without this sacrifice becomes just
an empty ritual.

Jeremiah 7:21–23

This passage is a little less problematic than Am. 5:25. Nicholson
reluctantly recognises that the understanding of it

> usually accepted by commentators today is that it does not deny the validity of
> sacrifice or that it was offered from the earliest days of Israel's history but seeks
> to place the emphasis in Israel's religion on obedience to God's law: it declares
> 'obedience *rather than* sacrifice' but not 'obedience and no sacrifice'.[15]

There seem to be four main reasons for this:
(i) A fairly literalistic translation of v. 21 reads,

> for in the day that I brought them out of the land of Egypt, I did not speak to
> your fathers or command them concerning burnt offerings and sacrifices.

However, as we have seen, to understand it as denying that sacrifices were
ordained in the wilderness is to create more problems than it solves.

(ii) As Thompson among others argues, Jeremiah can be understood as
making the point that, historically speaking, obedience to God was the
primary covenant demand.[16] The sacrificial cult was only one aspect of
that obedience. In fact, in the account of the making of the covenant in
Exodus 19–24 the primary emphasis is on God's moral demands. A
sacrificial cult is presupposed in places (e.g. Ex. 22:20; 23:18), but the
details of the Tabernacle and the sacrificial system were not given until
after the covenant making ceremony at which the people said, ' All that

the Lord has spoken we will do, and we will be obedient' (Ex. 24:7). Jeremiah's hearers can be justly accused of having given sacrifices a prominence in Yahweh worship which is not justifiable on historical grounds, let alone on spiritual ones. This interpretation is strengthened if the phrase *'al-dibᵉrê* (Je. 7:21) is given its usual sense of 'for the sake of, because of' rather than 'concerning'.[17] Then God is saying that he did not speak to the people in the wilderness in order to ask for sacrifices, but to ask for acceptance of the covenant and the obedience that it required.

(iii) It is a feature of Hebrew speech to use absolute, even hyperbolic, language where English uses comparison,[18] as for example in Lk. 14:26 with reference to hating one's family. This is particularly the case in negations.[19] It is therefore possible to understand Jeremiah as saying here (speaking of God), 'I did not speak . . . concerning burnt offerings and sacrifices *only*. But, *more importantly*, this command I gave . . .'

(iv) Such a reading of the passage is consistent with the preceding context, on which the pronouncement of vv. 21–23 is based. This accuses the people of moral evils (note how v.9a echoes the second part of the Decalogue) and apostasy but says nothing about sacrifices being evil *per se*. It is also consistent with Je. 6:19–20, where God rejects the people's burnt offerings and sacrifices as they are offered by disobedient, law-breaking worshippers.

Milgrom has proposed a novel interpretation of Je. 7:21–23 which has been endorsed by Holladay.[20] He points out that Jeremiah rebukes the people rather than the priests, and specifies only two sacrifices—the *'ôlâ* and the *zebaḥ*. Now, he says, in the Priestly Code the combination of these two sacrifices occurs only in the context of individual voluntary sacrifices.[21] The *zebaḥ* never appears in any cultic calendar of public sacrifices. Even in non-Priestly sources the combination of *'ôlâ* and *zebaḥ* appears only as offerings of the individual worshipper.[22] Milgrom concludes that Jeremiah is urging the people to renounce their individual offerings because their ritual piety is vitiated by the immoral behaviour. What he says about the covenant in the wilderness is true because these sacrifices were not mandatory but voluntary and the maintenance of the covenant did not depend on them. This interpretation is interesting and may be correct. However, further study is probably needed to establish the validity of the distinction on which it is based. In addition, it should in any case be taken along with point (iv) above. Individual voluntary sacrifices, if that is what is in mind, are not rejected *per se*.

In summary, it seems that both Am. 5:25 and Je. 7:21–23 are asserting in strong terms a view of animal sacrifice which says that it was given by God as a means of expressing devotion to him. He also gave the moral law. Devotion to him is to be expressed by keeping that as well. Failure to obey the moral law breaks the covenant and renders the offering of material sacrifices null and void as an act of worship of Yahweh.

This view of sacrifice is also expressed in three other key passages in the pre-exilic prophets, which themselves cause some controversy.

Hosea 6:6

> For I desire steadfast love and not sacrifice,
> the knowledge of God, rather than burnt offerings.

The rendering of the second half of the verse as a comparative would certainly be the natural way of understanding it if it stood on it is own. The fact that it was a negative statement means that it is just possible that it could be taken in a privative sense, 'without burnt offerings', as Wolff argues.[23] However Rowley's comment is judicious:

> That the preposition might have this meaning is indubitable, but that it is not the natural rendering is clear from the fact that the Septuagint, Vulgate, Peshitta, and the standard versions in modern language render by the comparative. The rendering *without* has been adopted only by the school of writers that was antecedently persuaded that the prophets rejected all sacrifice. A rendering which rests on a theory can offer no support to it. The alternative rendering is perfectly natural and does not rest on any theory about the prophets.[24]

The comparative rendering of the second half of the verse does not contradict the first half, but serves to complement the hyperbole and draw out its meaning. Such a reading of Ho. 6:6 makes it a parallel to the classic statement in 1 Sa. 15:22–23 that obedience is better than sacrifice. It also accords with Ho. 8:13 where, as the context shows, Yahweh has 'no delight' in the people's sacrifices because they have no interest in obeying his laws.

Isaiah 1: 10–17

Heaton says of this passage:

> Isaiah is quite explicit in declaring that sacrifice is a ludicrous way of worshipping the transcendent King . . . It is strange that so many commentators are able to interpret such vituperative language as being no more than a demand that sacrifice should be offered only by moral persons with the right intention.[25]

The reason why so many commentators do interpret it that way is that it is the natural way to understand it in view of the fact that prayer is condemned alongside sacrifice and the climax of the oracle is a call to moral living and social justice:

> Bring no more vain offerings; incense is an abomination to me . . .
> Your new moons and your appointed feasts my soul hates . . .
> When you spread forth your hands, I will hide my eyes from you;
> Even though you make many prayers, I will not listen;
> Your hands are full of blood . . .

Cease to do evil, learn to do good;
Seek justice, correct oppression.

Heaton's attempt to make verse 15 mean that God rejects the people's prayer because it has sunk to the level of sacrifice reads a novel[26] and elsewhere unattested sense into what would naturally be taken as an example of a well established idiomatic way of referring to crimes of violence, viz. 'hands full of blood'.[27]

Micah 6:6–8

This short passage is the response of an imaginary Judean worshipper to God's indictment of his people in vv. 1–5. Modern commentators generally agree that it takes the form of a request for a priestly 'torah',[28] in this case a ruling on what kind of sacrifice is acceptable to Yahweh. It is notable that the verb used in v. 7 of Yahweh being pleased ($r\d{s}h$) is that used in Lv. 1:4; 22:23–27 of sacrifices being acceptable.

In response to God's claim that his people have grown tired of him (v.3), the worshipper's questions get more and more desperate as he moves from the quality of the offering ('Shall I come before him with burnt offerings, with calves a year old', v.6b) to its quantity ('thousands of rams . . . ten thousands rivers of oil', v.7a), to the (for the orthodox Yahwist) unthinkable supreme sacrifice ('shall I give my first-born for my transgression?', v.7b; is Isaac in mind?). The reply in v. 8 shifts the focus from the thing offered to the quality of life of the offerer. God does want a human sacrifice of a kind—the life of willing obedience to his covenant requirements, 'do justice . . . love kindness . . . walk humbly with your God.'

Whilst it is not impossible to see in the verse an almost total devaluing of sacrifice, Allen is probably right when he says,

> it would be unfair to conclude that Micah replaces the forms of religion with social ethics, for God's covenant with Israel traditionally included a strong cultic emphasis as an integral part. So a careful walk with God would find partial fulfilment in the observance of ritual laws. The message of the Master is here foreshadowed: 'first be reconciled to your brother, and then come and offer your gift' (Matt. 5:24).[29]

Conclusion

The general conclusion to be drawn from this study of these key texts is that the pre-exilic prophets did not reject sacrifices as something alien to Yahweh worship. Rather, they rejected as unacceptable to Yahweh sacrifices offered by people who were living in disobedience to the covenant law.

Würthwein provides support for this conclusion in a form critical study which includes passages we have considered, together with some others.[30] He argues that these passages are in the form of the 'cultic answer' which worshippers expected when they brought offerings to the Temple.

However, instead of expressing acceptance and promising blessing for the offerer, they express rejection and warn of coming evil because of the sinfulness of the offerer. They are criticisms of cultic abuses from within the cult, not rejection of the cult *per se* by those who stand completely apart from it. Würthwein points out that the demand for moral obedience on the part of the worshipper is not something unique to the writing prophets. Some of the Psalms, such as 15 and 24, show that it was part of 'priestly' religion too. The prophets were not making radically new demands.

The emphasis of the pre-exilic prophets on obedience to Yahweh as his fundamental requirement, with sacrifice as only one expression of it, did give sacrifice less significance that it had in popular religion. This may have helped in the time prophesied in Ho. 3:4 when the people had to 'dwell many days . . . without sacrifice'. Although this was an act of judgement, in the light of the prophetic teaching about sacrifice, this was not the shattering blow to true Yahwistic religion that it would have been if sacrifice had been allowed the position many Israelites wanted to give it as the only, or primary, means of expressing worship of Yahweh and obedience to him.

II. THE EXILIC PROPHETS

Ezekiel is something of an enigma to those who hold that the pre-exilic prophets were opposed in principle to the sacrificial cult. Instead of sharing in such opposition, Ezekiel regards the sacrificial cult as having an important role to play in the relationship between God and his people. In his vision in chapters 8–11, he sees Yahweh gradually withdrawing from the temple at Jerusalem. This is not because he rejects the cult *per se*, but because of the sinfulness of the nation. They are guilty of idolatry (8:10), violence (8:17), injustice (9:9) and neglect of the covenant ordinances (11:12). Ezekiel's vision of the restoration of Israel centres on a rebuilt Temple and a reorganized sacrificial cult. Then Yahweh will once again be able to dwell in the midst of his people and bless them.

If the conclusion we came to above is correct, we can see that Ezekiel stands in the same stream as the pre-exilic writing prophets. He too is critical of the cult of his day, even to the point of saying, like them but in a different way, that Yahweh rejects it because the worshippers have broken the covenant. Like them he stresses the importance of obedience to the covenant laws as the fundamental basis of Yahweh worship (18:1–32; 36:26–27). It is only in this context that the sacrificial cult becomes a meaningful thing.

Isaiah 40–55 is clearly addressed to the late exilic situation and so requires consideration here. There is very little mention of the Temple and its cult. This is partly because, unlike Ezekiel, the emphasis is on God's act of deliverance and not on the conditions to which it will lead.

However, 44:28 and 52:11–12 do contain an expectation that the Temple will be rebuilt and the worship there restored.

Is. 43:22–24 calls for special consideration because it refers explicitly to the sacrificial cult, though scholars disagree about its exact import. Those who take Am. 5:25 and Je. 7:22 as denying that sacrifices had any place in the Yahweh cult tend to see v. 23b as repeating this denial, 'I have not burdened you with offerings, or wearied you with frankincense'. However, according to Whybray, who seems to want to adopt such a reading, v. 23 must be read in the light of v. 24b, which parallels it closely in form and in the verbs used, 'but you have burdened me with your sins, you have wearied me with your iniquities'.[31] It then becomes clear that Yahweh is not complaining that the people have not offered sacrifices at all, nor that they have offered sacrifices when he did not want them. Rather, he is saying that

> these sacrifices had not been offered *to him*: that is their worship had never reached him, because it had been offered by a people incapable, through its sinfulness, of acceptable worship'.

This interpretation assumes that the oracle looks back to the pre-exilic period. Knight rejects this view.[32] He argues that this must apply to the situation c. 540 BC. At this time the people could not offer sacrifices. Therefore he argues, the point being made is that even when Yahweh did not demand material sacrifices of his people, because they could not offer them, they failed to live in communion with him by putting their faith and trust in him (v. 22a). As a result, says Knight, they failed to learn the lesson that they could make sacrifices of another kind, the kind that the Servant would make.

This is an attractive interpretation theologically, but it seems a bit forced. Moreover, it breaks down if vv. 22–23 are taken as part of a single oracle with vv. 24–28. Westermann,[33] followed by Whybray,[34] argues that vv. 22–28 have the form of a Trial Speech in which Yahweh defends himself against the charge that he has treated Israel unfairly in view of all the sacrifices they offered to him. Yahweh's response is that the sacrifices were not really offered to him because they were the insincere worship of a sinful people. This certainly makes good sense of these verses, whereas either vv. 22–23 or vv. 24–28 on their own seem to lack coherence. The blanket condemnation of pre-exilic worship must not be taken literalistically, any more than the totally black pictures of Israel's history in Ezekiel 16 and 23 should be taken literalistically. A measure of hyperbole is used to make the point.

III.   THE POST-EXILIC PROPHETS

Ezekiel looked for a restoration of the Temple and its cult. It was the ministries of the two prophets Haggai and Zechariah which led to this becoming a reality. For them the rebuilding of the temple was an important step of obedience to Yahweh. Only when it had been rebuilt would the people fully enjoy the blessing of God. However, this did not mean any departure from the earlier prophetic position that 'obedience is better than sacrifice'. This is made clear in Zechariah 7 and 8 and in Hg. 2:10–19.

Haggai 2:10–19 has been much discussed. Scholars differ over the meaning of v.14,

> 'So it is with this people, and with this nation before me', says the Lord; 'and so with every work of their hands; and what they offer here is unclean.'

Who are 'this people . . . this nation', and why are their offerings 'unclean'? There are three main positions.[35]

Some argue that the people/nation concerned are the inhabitants of Samaria, who were eager to take part in the rebuilding of the Temple and to participate in the cult there. There are good reasons for rejecting this view. First, there is no clear evidence that Samarians did offer to help in 520 BC. Ezr. 3:8–4:3 refers to such an offer in 536 BC, and there are no good grounds for suggesting, as some do, that the passage in Ezra really refers to Haggai's time. Secondly, in Hg. 1:2, 'this people' clearly refers to the Jews in Jerusalem. In fact, as Hildebrand shows, in the prophets in general 'this people' nearly always refers to the people of Yahweh, usually with a nuance of reproach.[36]

Those who understand 'this people . . . this nation' as the Jews differ over whether the origin of the uncleanness is primarily cultic (the altar built in 536 BC being unclean because of the ruined state of the Temple) or moral (the people were living in disobedience, having put their own interests before those of Yahweh). In the light of what is said in Haggai 1, the moral issue seems to be the primary one. As Verhoef concludes,

> Disobedience is the main reason for God's displeasure in their sacrifices. Salvation and blessing can only be expected when the Lord receives and retains the place of honour in the midst of the people. In this respect Haggai is in full accord with the criticism of the pre-exilic prophets concerning a sacrificial system and practice which does not comply with the covenant relationship with the Lord.

Malachi is as strong in his denunciation of the cult of his day as any of his pre-exilic predecessors. He declares that God would rather they shut up the Temple and stopped offering sacrifices than go on as they were (1:10). Like Hosea and Ezekiel, he denounces specific cult abuses. However, there is also a strong condemnation of moral failure as well. Yahweh rejects offerings both because they are ritually unclean (1:7) and because of the sinfulness of the offerers (2:13–16).

Mal. 1:11 is a well known *crux interpretum*, though we do not have the space to discuss it in detail.[37]

> From the rising of the sun to its setting my name is great among the nations, and in every place incense is offered to my name, and a pure offering; for my name is great among the nations, says the Lord of hosts.

There are two main questions. The first concerns the identity of the people making the offerings. Are they Gentiles in general, Jewish proselytes or the Jews of the dispersion? The universality of the geographical reference 'from the rising of the sun to its setting', counts against the latter two suggestions since in Malachi's time neither Jews of the dispersion nor proselytes could be said to be so widespread. Also, orthodox Jews would not be offering material sacrifices away from the Jerusalem Temple. On the other hand, nowhere else in OT prophecy do we find the idea that the worship of the Gentiles as such is acceptable to Yahweh. What Malachi says of marriage to foreigners in 2:10–12 does nothing to suggest that he would take a radically new view on this point. What we do find in the other prophets is the belief that one day all the nations will come to worship Yahweh in an acceptable way. Usually this is seen in terms of their making a pilgrimage to Jerusalem (e.g. Is. 2:2–4; Zc. 8:20–23; 14:16), though Zp. 2:11 speaks of the nations worshipping 'each in its place'.

This leads us to the second question. Is Malachi speaking about the present or the future? The only verb in the sentence is found in the phrase *muqṭār muggāš lišᵛemî*, usually translated 'incense is offered to my name'. However, *muggāš* is a Hoph'al participle and the tense is flexible. It could mean, as Baldwin argues, 'is about to be offered', giving the verse an eschatological slant.[38] This eschatological interpretation of the verse is the most satisfactory one. Verhoef arrives at it by a different exegetical route and concludes,

> The inclusion of all nations in the kingdom of God was an integral part of prophecy, but the idea of the sanctification of the whole world to become one great Zion from the rising to the setting of the sun is found only in this text, and partly also in Isa. 19:19 and Zeph. 2:11.

Isaiah 56–66 is considered here because it seems to address the returned exiles in Judea. On the whole these chapters assume the restoration of the Temple and its sacrificial cult. This is especially clear in chapter 56, which takes up the theme of Gentiles coming to worship in Jerusalem. It declares that the cult there is open to all, regardless of nationality, who are willing to keep the covenant. Here, by implication, there is reiteration of the theme that sacrifice without that obedience to the covenant which evidences faithfulness to Yahweh is unacceptable to him.

Is. 66:1–4 seems to stand out as an anomaly amongst the post-exilic prophecies because it apparently rejects the rebuilding of the Temple in 515 BC.[39] One way of avoiding such a conclusion is the suggestion that the object of attack is the desire of the Samaritans to build a temple.[40] However, this is purely hypothetical since there is nothing in the text itself to suggest it.

Jones argues that the oracle should be understood in the light of the early post-exilic situation when the Temple was still in ruins.[41] Verses 1 and 2 are a word of comfort to the people. The absence of the Temple in no way prevents Yahweh from making his presence known to his people. He is not tied to any house made by men. The meaning of vv. 3–4 is that because the sacrificial cult is not possible at the Temple it is not permissible anywhere. Therefore to practise sacrifice is to perpetuate a serious, wilful act of disobedience. While this interpretation of vv. 1–2 is plausible, that of vv. 3–4 seems forced.

Westermann[42] and Herbert[43] point to the obvious echoes of 2 Sa. 7:4–7; 1 Ki. 8:27–30 and various Psalms in vv. 1–2. They conclude that these verses stand in the tradition of prophetic warnings against a reliance on the Temple alone as a basis of security and salvation (cf. Je. 7:1–15). There is here no more a total rejection of the Temple than there is in Solomon's words in his prayer of dedication of the Temple. There may, however, be a word of warning to those who put all their hopes for the arrival of the new age of salvation on the rebuilding of the Temple in 515 BC. Both scholars point out that the problem with vv. 3–4 is that the language is very condensed and that in translating v. 3ab, link words have to be added. Though the English versions differ over what these should be,[44] Westermann and Herbert argue that since it is known that in the early Persian period the Phoenicians sacrificed humans and ate dogs, and swine flesh was forbidden for Jews, the polemic is aimed at syncretistic worship. Such worship is also condemned in Is. 65:1–7. Of the various possible interpretations of this difficult oracle this one seems to have the firmest exegetical base.

IV.   WORSHIP, SACRIFICE AND MORALITY

Having considered the texts that have been central to the debate about the place of sacrifice in the thinking and message of the prophets, we can now conclude that in all periods from the eighth century onwards, the prophets were to a greater or lesser extent critical of the sacrificial cult. However, they did not reject material sacrifices *per se* as having no place in the worship of Yahweh. Rather, they stressed that the sacrifices had their proper significance only in the context of the covenant. To understand this we need to consider briefly the purpose of the cult within the covenant community.

Here we cannot enter into the debate about the history of the concept of 'covenant' within Israel.[45] What is clear is that the prophets understood that there was a special relationship between Israel and Yahweh. We see this in the earliest of the prophets whose words have been preserved. Amos expresses this understanding in 3:2, where he says in the name of Yahweh,

> You only have I known of all the families of the earth;
> therefore I will punish you for all your iniquities.

As Am. 2:9–11 shows, this relationship is rooted in the events of the exodus, wilderness wanderings and entry into Canaan. Hosea speaks of this relationship as being like a marriage (Ho. 2) or the relationship of a parent and an adopted child (Ho. 11:1–9).

At the heart of this special relationship was the privilege of having Yahweh 'dwell' with his people. His very presence brought them blessing. This is clearly expressed by Ezekiel, perhaps reflecting his priestly background. So in chapters 8–11 he writes about an extended vision in which he sees the presence of Yahweh, symbolized by the shekinah glory, departing from the temple and city of Jerusalem because of the idolatry and moral sin of the priests and people. The high point of the promise of restoration is,

> I will bless them and multiply them, and will set my sanctuary in the midst of them for ever. My dwelling place shall be with them; and I will be their God and they will be my people (37:26–27).

This is expressed pictorially in chapters 40–48 in the vision of the rebuilt temple from which flows the river of life-giving water. This theme is taken up in Hg. 1:8; 2:9 as the prophet exhorts the people to take up once again the stalled task of rebuilding the temple.

The purpose of the institution of the cult was to establish the presence of Yahweh and mediate it to his people. In this sacrifice played a part. The history of sacrifice in Israel is another major area of debate on which we cannot embark.[46] It does seem clear, however, that the sacrifice offered to Yahweh had three main aspects. Some (whole burnt offerings, freewill offerings) were expressions of pure devotion and homage. Others (communion or peace offerings) were a way of enjoying fellowship with Yahweh, since part of the sacrifice was eaten at the sanctuary in his presence. Still others (sin and guilt offerings) made atonement for all forms of wrong.

What the prophets stress is that the special relationship between Yahweh and Israel involved more than punctilious observance of the ritual of the cult. It was meant to be a way of life which involved obedience to certain moral stipulations. Thus we find Hosea indicting the people on the basis of what seems very like a summary of the second half of the Ten Commandments (Ho. 4:1–2). Micah says that what Yahweh requires of his people is 'to do justice, and to love kindness and walk humbly with your God' (6:8).

This view did not originate with the prophets, since we find them condemning the priests for failing to teach the people the torah, i.e. to instruct them about how to live in the way that Yahweh required (Ho. 4:6; Mi. 3:1; Mal. 2:1–9).

There are four expressions the prophets use time and again to express what Yahweh looks for and fails to find in his people. They are justice, righteousness, steadfast love and faithfulness. Key texts in this regard are Ho. 2:19; Am. 5:24; Is. 1:26; 5:7,26; Mi. 6:8. It is clear that for the prophets the expression of these qualities in personal and communal life was the indispensable prerequisite for meaningful public religion. This is because the homage expressed by sacrifices was meant to be a symbol of a life of homage to Yahweh, and the homage he looked for was obedience to the moral laws which he had given to his people. They were grounded in his character, and so should characterize his people's attitude towards him and towards one another.

Sacrifice, at its best, was an expression of homage and obedience to Yahweh. It was an expression which he ordained. Such homage and dedication, if genuine, would be shown by a life lived in daily obedience to his moral requirements as well as the ritual ones. In other words, it was the way of life of the person who offered the sacrifice that Yahweh looked at, not merely the sacrifice itself.

It is against this background that we must finally come to Isaiah 53. We cannot give detailed consideration to this important chapter here.[47] The major point to be noticed is the reference in v. 10 to the servant making himself 'an offering for sin'. Whybray says of this,

> nowhere else in the O.T. is it stated that a man's life can be a guilt offering, whether in a literal or metaphorical sense, and the idea would appear to be entirely foreign to O.T. thought.[48]

He therefore thinks it 'unwise to press the significance of this statement'. However, in the light of what we have concluded about the prophetic understanding of sacrifice, it is arguable that Is. 53:10 does not present an idea that is entirely foreign to the OT thought. Rather it is a natural development of it. It takes up the view that the real sacrifice that pleases God is the life of the offerer and goes on to contemplate the possibility that that life, given over totally to the obedient service of God, may be accepted by him as an offering on behalf of other people.[49] Although we have disagreed with Knight's exegesis of Is. 43:22–24, he may well be right in making the point that the exilic experience might have helped in the development of such an idea about the value of sacrificial obedience. In fulfilling the prophetic expectations of the servant, Jesus fulfilled all that the prophets taught about sacrifice.

NOTES

1. E. Kautzsch, *Hastings' Dictionary of the Bible* vol. 5 (Edinburgh: T. & T. Clark, 1904) 723a.

2. J. Skinner, *Prophecy and Religion* (Cambridge: Cambridge University Press, 1922) 182, note.

3. R.H. Pfeiffer, *Religion in the Old Testament* (London: A. & C. Black, 1961), 191.

4. E.g. A.C. Welch, *Prophet and Priest in the Old Testament* (London: SCM, 1936); W.O.E. Oesterley, *Sacrifices in Ancient Israel* (London: Hodder & Stoughton, 1937).

5. G. von Rad, *Old Testament Theology* (London: SCM, 1965) vol.2, 4.

6. R.E. Clements, *Prophecy and Covenant* (London: SCM, 1965) 95.

7. G. Ashby, *Sacrifice: Its Nature and Purpose* (London: SCM, 1988) 47.

8. J.L. Mays, *Amos* (OTL) (London: SCM, 1969) 11.

9. H. Mowvley, *Guide to Old Testament Prophecy* (Guildford: Lutterworth, 1979) 79, n.81.

10. E.g. the 'Ritual Decalogue' of Ex. 34:12–26 (J): Ex. 32–33 (J): Ex. 15:20–27 (E); Ex. 20–23 (E).

11. H.W. Wolff, *Joel and Amos* (Hermeneia) (Philadelphia: Fortress, 1977) 264–265; H.W. Wolff, *Hosea* (Hermeneia) (Philadelphia: Fortress, 1974) 164.

12. H.H. Rowley, *BJRL* 29 (1946) 340ff.; C.J. Cadoux, *Exp Tim* 58 (1946/47) 43–46; H.H. Rowley, *Exp Tim* 58 (1946/47) 69–71; N.H. Snaith, *Exp Tim* 58 (1946/47), 152–153; H.H. Rowley, *Exp Tim* 58 (1946/47) 305–307.

13. D.B. Macdonald, 'O.T. Notes 2. Amos v 25', *JBL* 18 (1899) 214–215.

14. J.A. Moyter, *The Day of the Lion* (London: IVP, 1974) 134, n.4.

15. E.W. Nicholson, *Jeremiah 1–25* (CBC) (Cambridge: Cambridge University Press, 1973) 81.

16. J.A. Thompson, *Jeremiah* (NICOT) (Grand Rapids: Eerdmans, 1980) 287–288.

17. Cf. *BDB* 184 (*dābār* §IV.8).

18. C. Lattey, 'The Prophets and Sacrifices: A study in biblical relativity', *JTS* 42 (1941) 155–165.

19. H. Kruse, 'Die "dialektische Negation" als semitische Idiom', *VT* 4 (1954) 385–400; R.de Vaux, *Ancient Israel* (London: Darton Longman & Todd, 1965²) 454–455.

20. J. Milgrom, 'Concerning Jeremiah's repudiation of sacrifice', *ZAW* 89 (1977) 273–275; W.L. Holladay, *Jeremiah* (Hermeneia) (Philadelphia: Fortress, 1986), vol.1, 262.

21. Lv. 17:8; 22:17ff.; Nu. 15:1ff. The *zebaḥ* in Lv. 23:37 refers to the Pentecost offering brought by the individual (vv.19–20) and is not part of the regular public offering for that day.

22. Cf. Ex. 18:12: Dt. 12:11: Jos. 22:26–28: 1 Sa. 15:22: 2 Ki. 5:17; 10:24; Is. 56:7.

23. Wolff, *Hosea* 120–121.

24. H.H. Rowley, *The Unity of the Bible* (London: Carey Kingsgate, 1953) 40, n.1. Both *BDB* 582 (*min* § 6a) and A.B. Davidson, *Hebrew Syntax* (Edinburgh: T. & T. Clark, 1901³) §34 rem.2, take Ho. 6:6b as comparative. GKC §119w takes it as privative.

25. E.W. Heaton, *The Hebrew Kingdoms* (New Clarendon Bible) (Oxford: Oxford University Press, 1968) 324.

26. E.C.B. Maclaurin, *The Origin of the Hebrew Sacrificial System* (Sydney: 1948) 13, seems to have been the first person to suggest this interpretation, as part of his attempt to show that sacrifice was not original to Israel's religion and was totally rejected by the pre-exilic prophets.

27. See *BDB* 196–197 (*dām* §2d,f). Note in particular Is. 59:3; Ezk. 23:45.

28. On this literary form, see G.von Rad, *Old TestamentTheology* (London: SCM, 1962), Vol.1, 244–248, and the literature cited there.

29. L.C. Allen, *Joel, Obadiah, Jonah and Micah* (NICOT) (Grand Rapids: Eerdmans, 1976) 324. See also 249–250.

30. E.Würthwein, 'Kultpolemik oder Kultbescheid?', in E. Würthwein & O. Kaiser, *Tradition und Situation* (Göttingen: Vandenhoeck & Ruprecht, 1963) 115–131.

31. R.N. Whybray, *Isaiah 40–66* (London: Oliphants, 1975) 91–92.

32. G.A.F. Knight, *Servant Theology: A Commentary on the Book of Isaiah 40–55* (ITC) (Edinburgh: Handsel, 1984) 68–70.

33. C. Westermann, *Isaiah 40–66* (OTL) (London: SCM, 1969) 130–133.

34. R.N. Whybray, *Isaiah 40–66* (NCB) (London: Oliphants, 1975) 91–92.

35. P.A. Verhoef, *The Books of Haggai and Malachi* (NICOT) (Grand Rapids: Eerdmans, 1987) 110–137, provides a detailed discussion of the differing interpretations of this oracle, with bibliographical references.

36. D.R. Hildebrand, 'Temple Ritual: a Paradigm for Moral holiness in Haggai ii 10–19', *ZAW* 100 (1988) 217–244.

37. Verhoef, *Haggai and Malachi* 222–232, provides a detailed discussion with bibliographical references. See also chap.10, Sect. II(1).

38. J.G.Baldwin, *Haggai, Zechariah, Malachi* (TOTC) (London: IVP, 1972) 228–229.

39. So for example, J.L. Mackenzie, *Second Isaiah* (AB) (New York: Doubleday, 1968); G.A.F Knight, *The New Israel: A Commentary on the Book of Isaiah 56–66* (ITC) (Edinburgh: Handsel, 1985).

40. B. Duhm, *Das Buch Jesaja* (Göttingen, 1922).

41. D.R Jones, *Isaiah 56–66 and Joel* (Torch) (London: SCM, 1964).

42. C. Westermann, *Isaiah 40–66* (OTL) (London: SCM, 1969) 411–414.

43. A.S. Herbert, *Isaiah 40–66* (CBC) (Cambridge: Cambridge University Press, 1975).

44. (i) 'whoever . . . is like one who . . .' (NRSV, cf. NIV, RSV, REB); (ii) 'to . . . or to . . .' (NEB, cf. GNB); (iii) 'some . . . some . . . ' (JB).

45. E.C. Lucas, 'Covenant, Treaty and Prophecy', *Themelios* 8 (1982) 19–23, provides an introduction to the debate.

46. H.H. Rowley, 'The Forms and Meaning of Sacrifice', in H.H. Rowley, *Worship in Ancient Israel* (London: SPCK, 1967) 111–143, provides a useful, if dated, discussion of the matter.

47. See the discussions of this chapter in e.g. S. Mowinckel, *He That Cometh* (Oxford: Blackwell, 1956) 187–260; H.H. Rowley, *The Servant of the Lord* (London: Lutterworth, 1952) 1–88; C.R. North, *The Suffering Servant in Deutero-Isaiah* (Oxford: Oxford University Press, 1956[2]); R.N. Whybray, *Thanksgiving for a Liberated Prophet* (JSOTS 4) (Sheffield: JSOT Press, 1978).

48. R.N. Whybray, *Isaiah 40–66* (NCB) (London: Oliphants, 1975), 179.

49. H.L. Ginsberg, 'The Oldest Interpretation of the Suffering Servant,' *VT* 3 (1953) 400–404, has argued that this idea, derived from Is. 53, is applied to the *maskîlîm* in Dn. 11:35; 12:2–3. The link, he suggests, is the word *yaśkîl* in Is. 52:13.

FOR FURTHER READING

G. Ashby, *Sacrifice: its nature and purpose* (London: SCM, 1988), chap.3.

R.E. Clements, *Prophecy and covenant* (London: SCM, 1965), chap.5.

H. Mowvley, *Guide to Old Testament prophecy* (Lutterworth: Guildford, 1979), chap.11.

H.H. Rowley, *The unity of the Bible* (London: Carey Kingsgate, 1961), chap.2.

5

The Theology of Old Testament Sacrifice

GORDON J. WENHAM

Today theology is a byword for irrelevance. Among theologians sacrifice is usually relegated to the fringe of their consciousness. So to write about the theology of sacrifice is to court the charge of the ultimate in academic timewasting. But the modern instinctive rejection of the value of sacrifice and ritual is quite misguided. A study of the sacrificial system illuminates some of the most fundamental principles of biblical faith.

In this short essay I want to explore four issues. First, why is sacrifice important to an understanding of OT theology? Second, how should it be interpreted in general? Third, what is the function of some of the sacrifices? Fourth, what theological principles are expressed through the sacrificial system?

I. THE IMPORTANCE OF SACRIFICE

First, why is sacrifice with its associated rituals so important that the Pentateuch devotes about half its space to expounding it? Social anthropologists have alerted biblical scholars to the importance of ritual. For them the key to a society's deepest values is its ritual system. Writing in 1954 Monica Wilson said, 'Rituals reveal values at their deepest level . . . men express in ritual what moves them most.' Ritual reveals 'the value of the group. I see in the study of rituals the key to an understanding of the essential constitution of human society.'[1]

Let me explain what she means. We resort to ritual when we want to express our deepest feelings. Consider the rituals used in greeting people in our society — a nod, a handshake, a kiss, or a hug. One gesture is appropriate when the milkman calls for his money, another for your aunt, yet another for your wife. We express our relationships to other people through these ritualized greetings. Indeed the more moved we are emotionally, the more ritual we employ. Think of baptisms, weddings

and funerals. On such occasions people dress up to look their best. The
giving of flowers, and the consumption of food and drink is conspicuous.
That we have rituals on some occasions, e.g. a twenty-first birthday party
or seventieth birthday party, indicates that we regard reaching twenty-
one or seventy as significant milestones, but few people would want to
make such a splash on their twenty-second or seventy-first birthdays.
People express in ritual what moves them most.

Monica Wilson claims that ritual does not merely express personal
individual feelings, but group values. That is, the rituals people perform
in Britain reflect the values British society in general holds important. For
example, when the age of majority was reduced from twenty one to
eighteen, the eighteenth birthday became much more important and
often people celebrate this instead of the twenty-first today. Why are
degree ceremonies held but rarely GCSE or A-level ceremonies? Because
a degree is supposed to be of more value than one of these other
qualifications. Why do people make a big splash at weddings but make
divorces as quiet as possible? What does it tell us about British attitudes
that Good Friday is no longer strictly observed as a real holiday, but that
New Year's day is? According to the anthropologists, rituals express the
deepest fundamental values of society, not the individual convictions of
the people in society. In tribal and traditional societies, individual
conviction and social values usually go hand in hand. In ours they often
differ. English Roman Catholics celebrate Guy Fawkes Day despite its
Protestant message, and atheists feel compelled to celebrate Christmas
because society says it must. A study of the rituals of British society is
therefore a key to its deepest and most fundamental values. So too, a
study of the numerous OT ritual texts ought to unlock the fundamentals of
biblical theology.

But by and large they have been neglected for more than a century.
Books on OT religion and theology devote very little space to discussing the
meaning of the sacrifices and other rights described in the Pentateuch,
while commentaries on Leviticus tend to be the Cinderella of their series.
Biblical scholarship has, like much popular thinking, been influenced by
the romantic notion that spontaneity is authenticity, that formality and
ritual represents shame or hypocrisy. This attitude of mind has deterred
people from studying the ritual law, which is hard enough to penetrate
even without the discouragement of being told it is unimportant.
Anthropologists have rightly told us the error of our ways: ritual is indeed
of central importance in the OT. However that does not solve the difficulty
of interpretation: it simply makes the task more important.

II. THE INTERPRETATION OF SACRIFICIAL RITUAL

How should sacrificial ritual be interpreted? Some non-sacrificial rituals
are quite easy to follow because they often include the words that

accompany the rights, such as in the case of a wife's suspected adultery (Nu. 5:11–31) or a failure of the duties of a brother-in-law (Dt. 25:5–10). But with the sacrifices, the rites of ordination, and even the day of atonement ceremonies the problems of interpretation are often baffling. The rites are usually carefully described, but we are left with few clues as to what was said during them or why they should be performed in a particular way. Four different types of animal sacrifice are mentioned, yet on first inspection there seem but trivial differences in procedure and the reason for using one type of animal rather than another is opaque.

The reason for this obscurity is not far to seek. Evidently the meaning of these rites was so obvious that it was unnecessary to spell it out in words. We know why people give flowers at weddings, or funerals, or to the Queen when she goes on tour. It does not need explaining. Similarly, it is not necessary to explain why there are fireworks and bonfires on November 5th, unless there are foreigners present or children who do not know the story of Guy Fawkes. So too in ancient Israel. It was understood by everyone what a burnt offering symbolized, why the priest could eat of the flesh of the sin offering and guilt offering but not of the burnt offering. It was plain to the worshippers of ancient Israel why sometimes the sacrificial blood was poured out at the foot of the altar, why at others it was smeared on the horns of the altar, and at others sprinkled before the veil of the Holy of Holies. But these points mystify us. We are tempted to guess wildly just to find a point in it all. The only way to arrive at a definitive interpretation of these acts would be to resurrect an ancient Israelite priest and ask him. But unfortunately we cannot. Instead we must make do with hypothesis built on careful and thorough exegesis. We must compare each sacrifice very carefully with the other sacrifices to discover, if we can, what is special to each one and on what occasions one sacrifice is used rather than another. The occasional phrase of explanation 'to make atonement', 'as a soothing aroma', must be carefully noted and every possible interpretation explored.

There are a few works, ancient and modern, that proceed in this way and I believe some insights are emerging.[2] For example, it is clear that the opposition between life and death is fundamental to the whole ritual law. God is the source of life, so that everything brought near to God, whether sacrificial animal or priest must be physically unblemished. Death is the great evil, and everything suggesting it, from corpses to bloody discharge to skin disease, makes people unclean and therefore unfit to worship God.[3] Another theme is the election of Israel: that the Lord has made an exclusive covenant with Israel explains the choice of animals for sacrifice and why some animals are unclean and therefore not to be eaten by Israelites.[4] Thirdly, in sacrifice it appears that the worshipper identifies himself with the animal he offers.[5] What he does to the animal, he does symbolically to himself. The death of the animal portrays the death of himself. In the animal's immolation on the altar his own surrender to God is portrayed.

Finally, it must be recognized that in sacrifice, the same point is often made in a variety of ways. With most animal sacrifices it was customary to offer a cereal offering of wheat and also to pour out a libation of wine. In the symbolic system of Israel, clean animals offered in sacrifice represented the Israelite worshipper, and so did wheat and wine. Thus burning of part of the wheat and pouring out the wine, like the slaughter of the animal and pouring out its blood, portrays the worshipper dying for his sin and giving himself entirely to God. Meat, bread, and wine made a banquet in ancient Israel, so that the whole procedures represented a wonderful meal in honour of God the creator, who supplied man with all his physical and spiritual needs.

It may then be objected that the burnt offering and its traditional accompaniments, the cereal offering and the drink offering, each symbolized much the same thing, thereby rendering the latter two redundant. However, repetition is characteristic of symbolism[6] and indeed of much great art. Saying the same thing in a variety of ways reinforces and enhances communication. Remarks made only once are generally unimportant and soon forgotten. Elegant repetition and variation characterize great music, drama, literature and liturgy. The message of the burnt offering ritual, dramatically setting out the effect of sin and the need for total consecration to God's service, is powerful enough on its own. Intensified by the accompanying of cereal offering and libation, it becomes overwhelming.

These broad principles of sacrifice have been stated simply in order to allow those unfamiliar with the topic to have an overview, but it must be underlined that arriving at a secure interpretation is fraught with difficulty. It involves both close observation of the rites themselves using methods by anthropologists to interpret the ritual of contemporary primitive societies and careful exegesis of those few passages which explain the significance of sacrifice.

In *Purity and Danger* (1966), Mary Douglas analysed the whole ritual system enshrined in the laws of Leviticus in a way that for the first time showed them to be a coherent and meaningful whole, not a 'hotch-potch' of unrelated ceremonies, laws and regulations. She insisted that it is necessary to understand the whole ritual system and not just parts of it, or more precisely to understand the parts of it in the light of the whole. This may be illustrated by her approach to the food laws. Earlier commentators picked on certain elements in the food laws as suggestive of a particular interpretation. For instance sheep were clean because they reminded man of his divine shepherd, while serpents were unclean because they recalled the agent of the fall. But multitudes of animals in the list found no easy explanation of this type, for example camels, eagles, grasshoppers, etc. Douglas drew attention to that feature in Leviticus 11 and Deuteronomy 14 that the biblical writers seem to concentrate on, namely the means of locomotion of the animals, how many feet and what type of feet they have. From surveying the lists as a whole she deduced that the animal world mirrors the human world. Just as there are three principle divisions among men, Gentiles, Jews and priests, so there are three classes of animals: unclean, that cannot be eaten; clean, i.e. edible; and sacrificial beasts. Her theory of correspondence between the human and the animal kingdoms is confirmed by other texts scattered through the Pentateuch.[7]

These insights are corroborated in the earliest commentaries on these laws. For example, the second century BC Letter of Aristeas sees the behaviour of clean animals as models of human conduct.[8] Acts 10 links the preaching of Peter to the Gentiles with eating unclean animals. In other words, as soon as men of all nations could belong to the people of God, those food laws which had symbolized Israel's election and served to separate her from the nations became irrelevant too.[9]

This parallelism between the human and animal worlds clarifies one of the most discussed issues in the interpretation of sacrifice: what is the relation between the worshipper and the sacrificial victim? What is symbolized by the imposition of the worshipper's hands on the animal's head?

According to some OT theologians the laying on of hands has little significance. It is simply a statement that the animal belongs to the worshipper and it expresses the hope that the benefits of the sacrifice should accrue to him.[10] However this is such an obvious point that it hardly seems to be worth making. It also fails to do justice to the Hebrew term used of the laying on of hands; *sāmak* does not just mean 'place' the hand but 'press' (Is. 59:16; Ezk. 24:2; 30:6; Am. 5:19). The very action of pressing down on the animal's head suggests an attempt to establish an identity between worshipper and victim.

Another possibility is that the imposition of hands conveys the worshipper's sins to the animal, which then dies in the worshipper's place. This is certainly the most probable interpretation of Lv. 16:21, where in the day of atonement ceremony the high priest lays *both* his hands on the scapegoat's head, confesses 'over him all the iniquities of the people of Israel . . . all their sins; and he shall put them upon the head of the goat, and send him away into the wilderness.' But as Péter has pointed out,[11] here two hands are used instead of the one hand used elsewhere in sacrifice, so that it is not obvious that the two gestures are the same or that both have the same significance in sacrifice. Furthermore, as Kiuchi has argued,[12] it seems likely that in the sin offering at least, it is the priest not the animal who bears the worshipper's sins. And finally the idea that the animal actually carries sin itself would make it difficult to use in atoning for sin or cleansing the sinner and sanctuary. The innocence of the sacrificial victim is presupposed in these rites.

So the most probable explanation of the imposition of the hand in sacrifice is that thereby the victim is identified with the offerer.[13] This has been recognized by Edmund Leach[14] who states, 'the plain implication is that, in some metaphysical sense, the victim is a vicarious substitution for the donor himself.' This interpretation is strengthened by the comment in some Hittite texts that the animal is a substitute for the worshipper.[15] It is confirmed further by Gn. 22:13 which states that Abraham offered up the lamb 'as a burnt offering *instead of his son*'. Now while this could be taken simply as a statement of fact, it seems more probable that Genesis 22, like many stories in Genesis, is also paradigmatic and elucidates the OT understanding of sacrifice in general.[16] It shows an animal suffering vicariously in a man's place.

Now this substitutionary concept of sacrifice fits in very well with the symbolic interpretation of clean and unclean animals advocated above, which sees parallels between the animal world and the human situation. The Israelite, a member of the clean nation, chooses a clean animal to sacrifice on his behalf. The imposition of hands makes the equation even more explicit. But a sacrifice is not merely a suitable animal being offered for the group of people symbolically identified with it. The individual Israelite must choose it himself and then place his hands on its head in a dramatic declaration that he is this animal, that it is taking his place in the ritual.

A second characteristic of all the sacrifices is that at least part of each offering is burnt on the altar and makes a 'pleasing odour' (RSV) to the LORD (e.g. Lv. 1:9; 2:2; 3:5; 4:31). In what way do sacrifices please God? The adjective translated 'pleasing' (*nîḥōaḥ*) by RSV comes from the root 'rest' and would therefore be better translated 'soothing', 'pacifying', 'quietening'.[17] The word suggests divine uneasiness which is quieted by sacrifice.

This understanding of the phrase 'pleasing odour' as 'soothing aroma' is confirmed by its very first use in the OT in Gn. 8:21, a passage of great significance for the OT view of sacrifice. When Noah left the ark he offered burnt offerings, 'then the LORD smelled the soothing aroma, and the LORD said to himself "I shall not curse the land again any further because of man, for the ideas of man's mind are evil from his youth." '. This verse echoes and contrasts with Gn. 6:5 where God's motives for sending the flood are explained. 'The LORD saw that the evil of man was great in the earth and every idea of the plans of his mind was nothing but evil all the time.' Why did God view man's inveterate sinfulness as a reason for sending the flood in 6:5 but as a ground for mercy in 8:21?

The comment that 'the LORD said to himself' comes immediately after the 'the LORD smelled the soothing aroma'. The obvious implication of the sequence of verbs 'the LORD smelled . . . said' is that God's thoughts about mankind were prompted by his appreciation of the sacrifice. This was a common view among older commentators. Indeed, Gunkel, Skinner and von Rad[18] hold that the sacrifice was essentially propitiatory: 'He offered . . . to quiet the remains of his wrath'.[19] 'Noah's first act is to offer a sacrifice, not of thanksgiving but as v.21 shows of propitiation: its effect is to move the Deity to gracious thoughts towards the new humanity.'[20] However, Cassuto[21] sees no need for further atonement after all the suffering and death in the flood: the sacrifices were simply an expression of thanks for deliverance and trust in God for the future. Westermann concurs.[22] They object that God's attitude to Noah has already been seen to be gracious from the moment 'he remembered Noah' (8:1). It can hardly be said that the offering of the sacrifice changed God's attitude to Noah.

However, this is not really what Gn. 8:21 is asserting. From the very start 'Noah found favour in the eyes of the LORD' (Gn. 6:8). It is God's attitude to the rest of mankind that is turned around: Gn. 8:21 stands in particular contrast to Gn. 6:5 'The LORD saw that the evil of man was great in the earth and every idea . . . of his mind was nothing but evil all the time'. Now, for the very same reason, the LORD declares that he will not curse the ground further. And the only hint that the narrative gives for this change of heart is 'God's smelling of the soothing aroma'. Skinner states: 'that the pleasing odour is not the motive but merely the occasion of his gracious purpose (Knobel) may be sound theology, but it hardly expresses the idea of the passage'.[23] Ultimately, of course, the acceptance of every sacrifice depends on God's antecedent gracious purpose, whereby he appointed the sacrificial system as a means of atonement for reconciliation between God and man. A fundamental principle of the Levitical law is 'I have given (the blood) for you upon the altar to make an atonement for your souls' (Lv. 17:11). This is not to deny sacrifice's importance; rather it is to assert its real efficaciousness, because God has declared it so and promised to respond to it.

Looked at in this light, we can view Noah's offering of sacrifice as a prototype of the work of later priests, who made atonement for Israel, or of Job, who offered burnt offerings for his sons and for his 'friends' (Jb. 1:5; 42:8). Here, however, Noah's sacrifice is effective for all mankind.

The third important key to understanding sacrifice is the verb 'make atonement' (*kipper*), which like 'soothing aroma' is used in connection with most of the animal sacrifices (e.g. Lv. 1:4; 4:20; 5:16). Like many terms associated with sacrifices it is extremely difficult to pinpoint its exact meaning, even its etymology is a matter for dispute. Is Hebrew *kipper* related to Arabic *kafara* 'to cover'? If it is, making atonement could be seen as in some way 'covering' sin and thereby making it invisible to God. Or should it be associated with Akkadian *kuppuru* 'to wipe'? In this case atonement may be viewed as a wiping away of sin or its associated pollution, so that God can continue to dwell with man. Or is it linked with the Hebrew noun *kōper* 'ransom price', a sum of money paid in Hebrew law instead of exacting the death penalty? The animal would then be viewed as in some sense a payment, whereby the sinner, instead of paying with his own life for his sins, paid instead with the animal's life. Though the third alternative has probably more to commend it than the others, it is usage of a word that determines its meaning, not its historic etymology.

The careful study of *kipper*, 'make atonement', by Kiuchi[24] has led to the following conclusion. 'Make atonement' is a broad idea[25] involving several subsidiary ones. The offering of sacrifice makes atonement and this involves a variety of consequences. Altars and priests are 'sanctified'

(Ex. 29:33, 36, 37) i.e. made fit to officiate in worship. 'Lepers' and others are cleansed (Lv. 12:7, 8; 14:20). Sinners are forgiven (Lv. 4:20) and guilt is carried (Lv. 10:17). Sin and uncleanness lead a person from the realm of life into the realm of death. Sacrifice stops this process, indeed reverses it. It gives life to those doomed to die.

One of the most important statements about sacrifice is Lv. 17:11 'for the life of the flesh is in the blood; and I have given it for you upon the altar to make atonement for your souls; for it is the blood that makes atonement by reason of the life.' Yet the very brevity of this statement makes it obscure. Though Milgrom[26] has argued that only peace offerings are being discussed here, it seems more likely to see it as commenting on the role of blood in every animal sacrifice. Blood in every animal sacrifice makes atonement. How? The last phrase says 'by reason of the life'. This long-winded RSV translation of four Hebrew consonants covers a complicated exegetical problem. What does the preposition *be*, 'by reason of', mean, and whose is the life, the animal's or the worshipper's? All the various proposals have their problems, but fewest are posed by taking 'life' to refer to the animal's life, and *be* to mean 'through'. It is thus the animal's life united to its blood that makes the atonement for human lives (RSV, 'souls') on the altar. 'The above interpretation of v.11 supports the view that the principle of substitution is at work on the altar: animal life takes the place of human life.'[27]

All the animal sacrifices have a common procedural core, i.e. gestures that occur in every sacrifice, laying on of the hand, killing the animal, catching the blood and using it, burning at least part of the flesh on the altar. It therefore seems likely that every sacrifice has a common core of symbolic meaning. This is what we tried to elucidate above. The animal is a substitute for the worshipper. Its death makes atonement for the worshipper. Its immolation on the altar quietens God's anger at human sin. But to say that every animal sacrifice has a common core of ritual meaning is not to say that in other respects the sacrifices are not very different and have a diversity of symbolic meaning. This may be illustrated by looking at three different sacrifices, the burnt offering, the sin offering and the peace offering.

III.   THE SIGNIFICANCE OF PARTICULAR SACRIFICES

The burnt offering is the offering[28] in which the whole animal (except its skin) is burnt on the altar. The burnt offering was a regular offering in the temple offered every morning and evening. It was also offered on great occasions such as the making of the Sinai covenant (Ex. 24:3–8) or the entry into the promised land (Dt. 27:6). Individuals might offer burnt offerings in thanksgiving for deliverance or when a vow was fulfilled (Nu. 6:14; 15:3; Ps. 50; 60:13–15). In the burnt offering the whole animal was burnt, i.e. given to God. If the animal represents the worshipper, then the particular idea expressed by the burnt offering is total consecration by the worshipper to God. It made visible his desire to love God with all his heart, soul and might. It expressed entire allegiance to the LORD and his service. This element of the commitment and self-surrender to God is most evident in Ge. 22 and 1 Ki. 18:38–39.

In the sin offering[29] or more precisely the purification offering, the most distinctive feature is the use made of the sacrificial blood. In the other sacrifices the victim's blood is simply given to God by being poured over the sides of the altar. In the purification offering however it is handled much more discretely. Sometimes it is used to smear on the horns of the altar of sacrifice, sometimes it is taken into the tabernacle itself and smeared on the incense altar or sprinkled on the curtain, and once a year the high priest takes the blood into the Holy of Holies and sprinkles it on the ark of the covenant, the throne of God. In this case it seems that the blood is viewed as a kind of spiritual disinfectant purifying the sanctuary of the pollution associated with sin and uncleanness. Unatoned sin cannot be tolerated by God and he must either punish it or leave the sanctuary. By purifying the sanctuary and the offerer or those he represents, the sin offering makes possible the continued dwelling of the holy God with sinful man.

The peace[30] or fellowship offering was most likely to be offered spontaneously and was the most joyful offering. It was offered at the ordination of the priests (Lv. 8:22–29) and over a hundred thousand peace offerings were presented at the dedication of the temple (1 Ki. 8:63). Individuals might offer them when they made vows, or their prayers or vows were answered, or even when they wished to enjoy a meat meal with their friends (Lv. 17:5). The Passover lamb was a kind of peace offering.

In the peace offering only a few choice portions were burned on the altar, the rest was shared by the priest and worshipper. In all the other sacrifices the worshipper received nothing back, but in the peace offering most of the flesh was shared out by the worshipper with his family and friends, thus making the sacrificial meal a joyful barbecue.

But if the animal in some sense represents the worshipper, how can the worshipper eat some of the sacrificial victim? Does not the practice of the peace offering undermine the interpretation of the laying on of hands given earlier? At first sight it is paradoxical, but it is not unintelligible. In the peace offering God is the host. When the animal is slain, its blood poured over the altar, and the flesh partly burnt, the worshipper is giving himself to God. Then having received the gift from the worshipper God shares it with him. What was acted out in this sacrifice was the believer's daily experience: God had given him life and health initially, and every day in grace renewed these gifts. In every sacrifice the worshipper gave himself back to God in penitence and commitment, and in return received back a renewal of physical and spiritual life. Usually however there was no immediately visible sign of this renewal of life, but in the peace offering there was. The shared luxury of a meat meal was a tangible, indeed edible, token of God's continuing mercy and grace. It was this that made peace offerings usually such joyous occasions.

This glance at three sacrifices has attempted to show that while they all have a common core meaning, each has distinctive meaning of its own. They all presuppose that the animal victim is a substitute for the worshipper, makes atonement for him, and thereby restores him to favour with God. But whereas the burnt offering focuses on the total consecration of the worshipper to God, the sin offering focuses on the purification from sin, and the peace offering on God's continued blessing of the worshipper.

IV. THEOLOGY OF THE SACRIFICIAL SYSTEM

What then are the theological principles expressed through the sacrificial system, or in the words of Monica Wilson, 'the group values' revealed in sacrifice? It is generally agreed that the most important concept in Israel's self-understanding, at least as the OT writers see it, is the covenant, most obviously the Sinai covenant. In this covenant the LORD declared his choice of Israel to be his special people segregated from and hopefully holier than the nations of the world (Ex. 19:4–6). Israel for her part was obliged to obey the laws set out in the Ten Commandments and the rest of the Pentateuch. She was promised great blessings if she obeyed and threatened with dire punishment if she transgressed.

It is these covenant principles that are expressed visually in sacrifice. First, God's choice of Israel is recalled every time an animal, or wheat, or wine, was picked to be offered. Second, God's demand to be holy, to keep the commandments and so on was recalled in every sacrifice. It was not simply that the right species had to be picked, it had to be a perfect blemish-free specimen of that species. The total consecration to the service of God required of every Israelite was most clearly portrayed in the burnt offering when the entire beast was immolated in the fire. But Israel both corporately and individually often fell short of this ideal, and under the covenant sin was never ignored, indeed it provoked God's anger. Leviticus 26 and Deuteronomy 28 contain lengthy descriptions of the terrible judgements that Israel's sin may provoke including famine, disease, death and loss of the land of promise. God the giver of life may take it away from his people if they fail to live by his commandments. This message is underlined in every sacrifice, in that the animal representing the Israelite is condemned to death. Its shed blood declares that the wages of sin is death. The centrality of sin within the OT consciousness is emphasized by the fact that all these sacrifices have an atoning aspect at their core, that all of them create a 'soothing aroma' (Lv. 1:9, 13; 3:5, 16; 4:31) that appeases divine wrath. But the very institution of sacrifice signals the irrepressible hope built into the covenant, that however much

Israel sins, restoration and new life are possible if she repents (Lv. 26:40–45; Dt. 30:1–10): the animal dies so that the Israelite may live. Life in its fullness is God's ultimate plan for Israel, indeed as Gn. 8:21 (cf. Gn. 12:3) says, for the whole world, and every sacrifice declares the gospel of hope, that the God who so hates sin that he contemplates destroying all mankind has through sacrifice provided a way of salvation. And these great truths were reaffirmed, not just by individuals when they needed to offer sacrifice for themselves or their families, but by the priests who day by day offered the full range of sacrifices on behalf of the whole nation (Nu. 28–29). In this way Israel through her spiritual leaders symbolically reconsecrated herself to the LORD's service, praised him for his mercy, and was assured of the forgiveness of her sins.

NOTES

1. M. Wilson, *American Anthropologist* 56 (1954) 241, quoted by V.W. Turner, *The Ritual Process* (London: Routledge & Kegan Paul, 1969) 6.

2. For the surge of recent publications in this area, see bibliography.

3. For discussion see E. Feldman, *Biblical and Post-Biblical Defilement: Law as Theology* (New York: Ktav, 1977); P.P. Jenson, *Graded Holiness* (JSOTS 106) (Sheffield: SAP, 1992) 56–88.

4. E. Firmage, 'The Biblical Dietary Laws and the Concept of Holiness', in J.A. Emerton (ed.) *Studies in the Pentateuch* (VTSup 41) (Leiden: Brill, 1990) 177–208; W.J. Houston, *Purity and Monotheism: Clean and unclean animals in biblical law* (JSOTS 140) (Sheffield, SAP, 1993); J.E. Hartley, *The Book of Leviticus* (WBC) (Waco: Word, 1992) 140–47.

5. Cf. E.R. Leach, *Culture and Communication* (Cambridge: Cambridge University Press, 1976) 89.

6. E.g. J.B. Pritchard (ed.), *ANET* (Princeton: Princeton University Press, 1955²) 349–356.

7. Douglas developed her ideas further in *Natural Symbols* (New York: Barrie & Rockcliffe, 1970), and in *Implicit Meanings* (London: Routledge & Kegan Paul, 1975). J. Soler ('The Dietary Prohibitions of the Hebrews', *New York Review of Books* 26.10 (14 June 1979) 24–30, C.M. Carmichael ('Some Sayings in Genesis 49', *JBL* 88 (1969) 435–444, and idem, *The Laws of Deuteronomy* (Cornell: Cornell University Press, 1974) 160–162, came to essentially similar conclusions by different routes. E. Firmage, 'Biblical Dietary Laws', and W.J. Houston, *Purity and Monotheism*, thoroughly discuss the issue. Recently M. Douglas has put forward a different symbolic interpretation of the food laws, 'The Forbidden Animals in Leviticus', *JSOT* 59 (1993) 3–23. Her new suggestion, equating the unclean animals with oppressed people in Israel, is an attractive one, but explains the data less satisfactorily than her earlier proposals.

8. Letter of Aristeas, lines 144ff., in J.H. Charlesworth, *The Old Testament Pseudepigrapha* II (New York: Doubleday, 1985) 22–24.

9. G.J. Wenham, 'The Theology of Unclean Food', *Ev Q* 53 (1981) 6–15.

10. E.g. R. de Vaux, *Studies in OT Sacrifice* (Cardiff: University of Wales, 1964) 28; R. Rendtorff, *Leviticus* (Neukirchen: Neukirchener Verlag) 43–47; J. Milgrom, *Leviticus 1–16* (AB) (New York: Doubleday, 1991) 151–152; B.A. Levine, *Leviticus* (Philadelphia: Jewish Publication Society, 1989) 6; R. Knierim, *Text and Concept in Leviticus 1:1–19* (Tübingen: Mohr, 1992) 35–40.

11. R. Péter, 'L'imposition des mains dans l'Ancien Testament', *VT* 27 (1977) 48–55.

12. N. Kiuchi, *The Purification Offering in the Priestly Literature* (JSOTS 36) (Sheffield: JSOT Press, 1987) 87–109.
13. So B. Janowski, *Sühne als Heilsgeschehen* (Neukirchen: Neukirchener Verlag, 1982) 220–221; R. Péter-Contesse, *Lévitique 1–16* (Geneva: Labor et Fides, 1993) 42.
14. Leach, *Culture* 89.
15. Pritchard, *ANET* 350–351, 355.
16. Cf. G.J. Wenham, 'The Akedah: a Paradigm of Sacrifice,' in J. Milgrom FS (forthcoming).
17. Rendtorff, *Leviticus* 68; cf. Hartley, *Leviticus* 22–23; R.P. Knierim, *Text and Concept* 67–76.
18. G. von Rad, *Genesis* (London: SCM, 1972²) 121–122.
19. H. Gunkel, *Genesis* (Göttingen: Vandenhoeck & Ruprecht, 1910³) 65.
20. J. Skinner, *Genesis* (ICC) (Edinburgh: T. & T. Clark, 1930²) 157.
21. U. Cassuto, *A Commentary on the Book of Genesis*, II (Jerusalem: Magnes, 1964) 117.
22. C. Westermann, *Genesis 1–11* (Minneapolis, Augsburg, 1984) 453, describes it as a 'celebration of the act of salvation.'
23. Skinner, *Genesis* 157–158.
24. Kiuchi, *Purification Offering* 87–109.
25. Linguistically *kipper* is a supernym while 'cleanse, sanctify' etc. are hypernyms, cf. dwelling (supernym), house, bungalow (hypernyms).
26. J. Milgrom, *JBL* 90 (1971) 149–156.
27. Kiuchi, *Purification Offering* 107.
28. For discussion of the burnt offering, see commentaries on Leviticus 1; also R. Knierim, *Text and Concept*.
29. On the sin offering, see commentaries on Leviticus 4; also J. Milgrom, *Studies in Cultic Teminology and Theology* (Leiden: Brill, 1983); Kiuchi, *Purification Offering*.
30. On the peace offering, see commentaries on Leviticus 3; also R. Schmid, *Das Bundesopfer in Israel* (Munich: Kösel Verlag, 1964).

FOR FURTHER READING

A. General Works

G.A. Anderson and S.M. Olyan (eds.) *Priesthood and Cult in Ancient Israel* (Sheffield: SAP, 1991).
B. Janowski, *Sühne als Heilsgeschehen*, (Neukirchen: Neukirchener Verlag, 1982).
C.F. Keil, *Manual of Biblical Archaeology*, (Edinburgh: T & T Clark, 1887).
N. Kiuchi, *The Purification Offering in the Priestly Literature* (JSOTS 36) (Sheffield: JSOT Press, 1987).
J.H. Kurtz, *Sacrificial Worship of the Old Testament* (Edinburgh: T & T Clark, 1863 (reprinted Klock & Klock, 1980)).
R.P. Knierim, *Text and Concept in Leviticus 1:1–9* (Tübingen: Mohr, 1992).
J.Milgrom, *Studies in Cultic Terminology and Theology* (Leiden: Brill, 1983).
A. Schenker, *Studien zu Opfer und Kult im Alten Testament* (Tübingen: Mohr, 1992).
R. de Vaux, *Studies in Old Testament Sacrifice* (Cardiff: University of Wales, 1964).

B. Works dealing with related issues

M. Douglas, *Purity and Danger* (London: Routledge & Kegan Paul, 1966).
F.H. Gorman, *The Ideology of Ritual* (JSOTS 91) (Sheffield: SAP, 1990).

W.J. Houston, *Purity and Monotheism: Clean and Unclean Animals in Biblical Law* (JSOTS 140) (Sheffield: SAP, 1993).
P.P. Jenson, *Graded Holiness* (JSOTS 106) (Sheffield: SAP, 1992).
E.R. Leach, *Culture and Communication* (Cambridge: Cambridge University Press, 1976).

C. Commentaries

T.R. Ashley, *The Book of Numbers* (WEC) (Grand Rapids: Eerdmans, 1993).
J.E. Hartley, *Leviticus* (WBC) (Waco: Word, 1992).
R. Péter-Contesse, *Lévitique 1–16* (Geneva: Labor et Fides, 1993).
B.A. Levine, *Leviticus* (Philadelphia: Jewish Publication Society, 1989).
J. Milgrom, *Leviticus 1–16* (AB) (New York: Doubleday, 1991).
J. Milgrom, *Numbers* (Philadelphia: Jewish Publication Society, 1990).
R. Rendtorff, *Leviticus* (Neukirchen: Neukirchener Verlag, 1985).
G.J. Wenham, *The Book of Leviticus* (NICOT) (Grand Rapids: Eerdmans, 1979).
G.J. Wenham, *Numbers* (TOTC) (Leicester: IVP, 1981).

6

Sacrifice in the Ancient Near East

MARTIN J. SELMAN

I. INTRODUCTION

Anyone who attempts to understand sacrificial concepts and practices in the ancient Near East outside Israel has to begin by facing several major challenges arising from the nature of the enterprise.

(i) The subject is extremely varied. Even though evidence for any aspect of ancient Near Eastern civilization is inevitably distributed unevenly, the problem is particularly acute in the case of sacrifice. An initial difficulty is the unusually varied assortment of text types, ranging from passing references in mythical literature to the highly technical language of ritual texts. Further, the available evidence does not always display an inner consistency, especially when one tries to harmonize the archaeological record with literary materials. Since the scope of this survey is far too limited to investigate all these issues, some practical limitation has to be imposed. We will confine ourselves therefore to an investigation of Mesopotamia and Ugarit, since these areas are of greater relevance than, for example, Egypt in any comparison with the OT.

(ii) There is little agreement about whether to adopt a descriptive or comparative approach. Direct comparisons between the Bible and its contemporary world are always of course intrinsically attractive, but it is important to recognize that apparently similar practices occurring in different places may in fact be of widely divergent significance. Unfortunately, the real nature of these underlying differences has not always received proper recognition, especially by those who have approached the subject from the standpoints of Christian theology or comparative religion.[1] Any adequate comparison, however, must take account of the distinctive features in sacrificial practice and terminology as well as external similarities. The approach adopted in this study will therefore be firstly to describe and interpret the various kinds of sacrifice in the light of their own context, and only then to make comments of a comparative nature. In order not to minimize these differences, categories borrowed from traditional Christian theology or from traditional approaches to Israelite sacrifice will generally be avoided.

(iii) A particular problem exists with interpreting ancient sacrificial texts. Ancient scribes were in fact much more concerned with giving detailed practical instructions to those carrying out the rituals than with explaining the inner meaning of such rituals to people who did not share their cultural presuppositions. This problem is not a new one of course, and will be familiar to all who have struggled to understand the sacrificial texts of the OT. The result is, however, that far more can be said about what was done in sacrifice than about what the rituals meant to those who performed and watched them. It also demands great caution from those who are trying to interpret rituals they may not yet fully understand.

(iv) Finally, because an up-to-date overall survey of this subject is still not yet available, 'some fundamental questions therefore are still unresolved' (H. Ringgren).[2] This is particularly unfortunate in the case of the key areas of Babylonia and Assyria. One major reason for this continuing lack is that sacrifice in its narrower sense played a comparatively minor role within the Mesopotamian religion as a whole. Ritual was a much more important concept, and it may well be that the difficulty of disentangling that which may rightly be called sacrifice from the larger issues of religious ritual and ceremonial has led to scholars' reluctance to address the subject in a comprehensive manner.

II. SACRIFICE IN MESOPOTAMIA

1. Definition

Any investigation of sacrifice in Mesopotamia has to face the question of what is actually meant by the term 'sacrifice'. As a starting point, it is essential to distinguish between offerings given to temples generally and sacrifices made specifically to the gods, even though no such formal distinction is made in Sumerian or Akkadian literature. Under the heading of offerings are to be included the vast range of goods which were brought, indeed often required, for the upkeep of ancient temples. The temple, especially in third millennium Sumer, was a large estate, comparable in size to that of the state, and to some extent independent of it.[3] Although from the Old Babylonian period onward in the early part of the second millennium BC, the influence of the temple gradually declined as the authority of the king increased, the amounts of offerings given to the temple remained substantial. These offerings included a wide variety of agricultural gifts, including large herds of cattle, sheep, and goats, mainly designed for the support of the temple administration and economy. Their purpose was not dissimilar to that of the tithes and offerings given for the upkeep of the Jerusalem Temple and its staff.[4]

Sacrifice on the other hand is a term to be reserved for that which was presented to a deity. This does not mean that the concept of sacrifice in Mesopotamia was necessarily the same as that which is known from the OT. In Israel, for example, sacrifices were usually offered to God upon an altar, whereas in Mesopotamia sacrifice was often presented without the use of an altar. Also, sacrifice in Mesopotamia was usually performed by priests using the wide range of offerings already presented to the temples, whereas in Israel laymen had opportunity to sacrifice directly to God by bringing the victim to the altar and killing it there.

2. Care and Feeding of the Gods

The main concern in Mesopotamian sacrificial practice was undoubtedly the care, and especially the feeding, of divine images. This view of sacrifice was fundamentally influenced by the idea that deities were represented by man-made images, and led to a much greater concern with the image's own mundane needs than with the person and requirements of the deity as such. As a result, sacrifice in Mesopotamia was a rather more down to earth affair in comparison with the concepts of sacrifice repeatedly advocated by the OT writers.

The text most usually offered as an example of the care and feeding of the gods is actually a late one, dating from the Seleucid period at Uruk (biblical Erech), but it is quite clear that Babylonian religion even in those Hellenistic times showed very little change from practices and beliefs of much earlier days.[5] According to this text the gods were given four meals a day, differentiated in size rather than by the variety of their menu. Two were in the morning and two in the afternoon or evening. Interestingly, the term used for these was *naptanu*, which in fact was also a word for an ordinary meal.[6] This seems to indicate that the worshippers did not distinguish between a meal offered as a sacrifice to a deity and one which they ate themselves. The two activities seem to have been regarded as essentially one and the same, without any awareness that the difficulty of persuading a statue to consume regular meals might lead to a consideration of the different natures of divine and human beings and of their differing needs for food.

On the basis of several texts, the following procedure for one of these meals can be reconstructed. A table was first placed before the image, and then a bowl of water was provided for washing. After this, food and drink, especially beer, were served, during which time musicians played appropriate music. When the meal was completed, the shrine was fumigated, apparently to remove the smell of food. Finally the table was cleared and water was offered in a bowl for the image to wash its fingers. It is not known how the god was actually thought to eat the food, though a curtain was drawn in front of the table while the deity was actually eating and while he washed his or her fingers. Apparently the deity was thought to eat just by looking at the food! The menu could be very varied. It might include oxen, sheep ('good sheep, sheep fit for the temple, fattened sheep'), lamb, poultry (geese, ducks, doves), incense, soup, bread, flour, sesame, wines, beer and fruit.

A good example of the daily routine is provided in a text from Babylonia of the Seleucid period:

(i) 'During the night *umun sermal-ankia* (an incantation) is recited for Anu and an *elum umma* (a hymn) for the gods as the *dīk bīti* (awakening of the temple) in Ubshuukinaki.

(ii) At dawn the gate is opened. The night vigil is ended.

(iii) Water for the hands is brought and oil is taken.

(iv) The main morning meal comes, the singers sing and the main (meal) is removed.

(v) The second meal (= the second course?) comes. The second meal is removed.

(vi) The main afternoon (*lilātu* = last part of the day) meal comes, the singers sing (and the main afternoon meal is removed).

(vii) (The second afternoon meal comes). The second afternoon meal is removed.

(viii) 'The gate is locked.'[7]

An important variant on this practice was an Assyrian ritual called *tākultu*. Evidence for the *tākultu* is known from texts of the Neo-Assyrian period, but its origin reaches back to Middle Assyrian times in the latter centuries of the second millennium BC. In this ritual, the king offered sacrifices to the chief deity of a temple or a group of temples, and then pronounced a blessing for the town, the land, and the king of the city of Ashur. As a result of the *tākultu* meal, all the gods were then asked to pour out an abundant blessing on the king of Ashur. It seems that the real purpose of this ritual meal, therefore, was to ensure prosperity in the land and the welfare of the king.[8]

Another very important aspect of the feeding of the gods was the food and drink offerings regularly provided for the spirits of the dead. Much Mesopotamian religion was animistic in character, and particularly as far as ordinary people were concerned, religion was probably more about placating the spirits and demons rather than the major gods who had temples and images of their own. When a person died, it was believed that his spirit entered the underworld, the place where 'dust is their food and clay their sustenance'.[9] It was therefore necessary to provide the spirits of the deceased with a more satisfying diet, for if this responsibility was neglected, the spirits might return to earth hungry and thirsty:

The gods which seize (upon man)
Have come forth from the grave;
The evil wind-gusts
Have come forth from the grave;
To demand the payment of rites and the pouring of libations

They have come forth from the grave.[10]

Such wandering spirits were greatly feared, and a great responsibility rested on later generations to exercise proper care by making regular offerings to their ancestors. These issues could affect national life as well as individual families. For example, Ammisaduqa, a king of the first dynasty of Babylon, made offerings to various spirits of the dead who had no-one to provide for them in an attempt to ensure the security of his kingdom.[11] In contrast, the seventh century BC Assyrian monarch Ashurbanipal carried out vengeance even on the ancestors of his Elamite enemies: 'The graves of their former and later kings, who had not feared Ashur and Ishtar, my sovereigns, and who had harrassed the kings of my fathers, I ravaged, destroyed, and exposed to the sun. Their bones I took to Assyria; upon their spirits I imposed restlessness and cut them off from food offerings and libations of water.'[12]

Sacrificial food was not the only item provided for the images of Mesopotamian deities. Clothing and other materials were also offered in order to dress the image, while further gifts and sacrifices were made on special occasions such as regular festivals for the repair or building of a temple. A particularly interesting event was the installation of a new divine statue. This was the moment when the lifeless creation of the craftsmen needed to be endowed with the strength and power of deity, and for this there was a special ritual, often called *mīs pī*, 'the washing of the mouth'. In one account of this ceremony, the phrase 'washing of the mouth' occurs at each stage of the ritual, and fourteen times in all. The rituals began in the temple workshop, from where the statue was brought at night by a torchlight procession to the river side where further sacrifices of such things as a ram, beer, and flour were offered to a variety of deities, planets, and stars. Work on the statue was finally completed at the river side with the insertion of its eyes, which were opened at dawn by a priest with the aid of a tamarisk twig. The trappings of royalty such as a processional throne and an appropriate divine headdress were then given to the deity, before the statue was led back to the temple to be installed in its shrine.[13]

3. Rituals and Incantations

Although sacrifices offered as food to divine images were important in maintaining both human and divine societies, in the wider context of Mesopotamian religion the practice was comparatively minor. The main religious preoccupation of the texts was not sacrifice but ritual. Not that these two categories should be kept separate from one another, for many rituals included some form of sacrifice, though the latter was not necessarily offered to a deity. Rituals however were performed on a great variety of occasions and were accessible to a much wider range of people than those who witnessed the artificial ceremonies of the feeding of the gods. Though some rituals specifically included the king and high officials of temple and state, many others involved just a priest and a single anonymous suppliant.

Rituals were often collected into groups of texts, many of them in series. Two of these series were known as Shurpu and Maqlu, words which both really mean 'burning'. The series were written down on clay tablets, sometimes as many as nine altogether. Closely associated with the rituals were various incantations, prayers, and omens. So close was the connection in fact that the series of ritual texts were often more preoccupied with the incantations than with the rituals themselves, with details of the latter being confined to either the first or the last tablet in the series. In the Shurpu series, for instance, the ritual tablet is only the first out of a total of nine. In practice, however, Mesopotamian thought did not divide a ritual and its incantations, for words and actions were regarded as different aspects of one activity.

Rituals were prescribed for a wide variety of circumstances. Many were concerned with the removal of some kind of trouble, such as sickness or evil spirits, while others were carried out as a means of obtaining purity or fertility. Three of the better known types are briefly described here, in order to give some indication of how the thought patterns and practices of ritual pervaded Mesopotamian culture. The first example concerns the two series mentioned above, Shurpu and Maqlu. The Shurpu texts listed various evils which might happen to a person and from which the rituals might deliver him. For example, a person may have committed an offence, whether moral or cultic in character. He might have 'eaten what is taboo to his god(dess)', or 'pointed his finger behind the back of his fellow'. The god Ea, a god of magic who was also one of the three highest authorities in the Mesopotamian pantheon, might then instruct another god of magic, Marduk, also the chief god of Babylon, to purify the sufferer through the rituals of sympathetic magic. Actions involving objects symbolizing the afflicting evils or sins such as the peeling of an onion or the plucking of goats' hair were carried out, and were often followed by burning. The rituals were also always accompanied by appropriate incantations. In fact, the Shurpu texts contain more details of the prayers and incantations addressed to the gods than of the actual rituals. In the Maqlu series, the rituals and incantations were directed against various forms of black magic, and in these the burning rituals were rather more significant. Wax or wooden figurines of the sorcerer, or more often the sorceress, were burnt, with incantations addressed to the effigy or to the fire-god. The act of burning an object to which the evil was thought to have been transferred symbolized both destruction of the cause of trouble and liberation for the sufferer.[14]

Another set of rituals concerned the *bīt rimki* or 'wash house'. This was a place where preparations were made for various sacral duties and for purification. The purification rituals included various forms of ritual bathing for such diverse people as priests, a penitent king, a corpse during

funeral rituals, and even divine images. The images received ritual
washings in daily, monthly and annual cultic cycles. The purpose was to
transfer or remove evil influences, though one had to be careful not to use
unclean water, since this could bring further bad influences.[15]

A third type of ritual was the so-called *namburbi* ritual.[16] These had a
very specific purpose, namely, to ward off portended evil or to undo its
effects (the term *namburbi* meant '(Ritual for) the undoing of it', ie., of the
portended evil). They had close associations with omens, since they were
intended to negate the inevitable outcome already predicted by an omen.
According to Oppenheim, they were 'the answer of the theologians to the
diviner'.[17] Divination of all kinds, of course, occupied a central role in
ancient Near Eastern religion. The ultimate aim of the *namburbi* rituals
was to 'sanctify' (*qudduśu*) the threatened person. This was achieved by
the use of purification techniques applied both to the site where the ritual
took place and to the sufferer. For example, a reed hut might be marked
off as a suitable place for purification, where the threatened person
washed himself and put on clean clothes. Offerings usually comprising
simple food and drink offerings were frequently made to various deities,
though slaughtered animals would occasionally be included. Although
such offerings were intended to make the gods feel at home, the rituals
were essentially apotropaic in character. They might involve the
destruction of a portentous object such as the drowning of an animal, the
setting up of an obstruction such as smearing a door with a mixture
including bats' blood and crushed spider, or the substitution of another
image as a means of transferring evil from the person who was expected to
suffer. Although as in previous examples, the rituals were accompanied
with prayers, in this case the rituals seem to have been of greater
importance.

The rituals as a whole were based on an underlying thought structure
which demonstrated itself in three distinct modes:

(a) *Sympathetic or symbolic magic*

An example may be taken from one of the Shurpu rituals, as in the
following phrase, 'by the conjuration of Ea, let the curse be peeled off like
this onion, let it be wrenched apart like this date, let it be entwined like
this wick'. The action performed in such cases, accompanied by an
appropriate incantation, was thought to symbolize the removal of evil.
The use of both audible and visible means was a double security doubtless
intended to convince both priest and worshipper as well the troublesome
spirit.

(b) *Substitution or transfer*

This pattern might be employed when a person was ill or under the curse
of death. An animal might be dressed as a human being and laid near the
afflicted person, or a wax image of the sufferer might be laid in a family

grave together with clay images of those spirits that were thought to be causing the affliction. In this way, the disease or evil spirit was encouraged to attack the ritual object, so transferring its attentions from the sufferer. It is to be noted in passing that this approach dealt with cause as well as effect!

(c) *Direct exorcism*

This method depended on how the troublesome spirit was identified, and was based on the idea that the spirit needed another place to which it could be sent. If the spirit's identity was unknown, a long list of possible types of spirit was mentioned, concluding with the phrase 'whatever its name'. When on the other hand, a particular spirit was in mind, its name might be inscribed on the image of the spirit, and the image was then broken and buried.

4. Conclusions concerning sacrifice in Mesopotamia

(i) The nature of sacrifice in Mesopotamia was determined by contemporary concepts of divinity. Because the gods were thought to possess human as well as divine qualities, sacrifice had a much more domestic flavour than it does in the OT. The primary reason for this was probably more to do with the sacrifices made to unseen spirits rather than to the gods in their temples, since the former seem to have been much more accessible to ordinary people. Those spirits who were near at hand, indeed, often far too close for comfort, could apparently be approached with the kind of gifts that belonged to ordinary human life. The fact that even the great gods apparently accepted the same food and drink offerings only confirmed that sacrifice, although carried out according to strict rules, remained in essence an activity closely associated with the regular pattern of human existence. This conclusion is not affected by the sense of threat that many felt from the spirit world. Indeed, it is quite striking that it was thought that the threat of evil could be averted by actions as routine and familiar as providing the hospitality of a meal.

(ii) The emphasis on the feeding of gods and spirits reveals the interdependence of the human and divine worlds. Deities and spirits were felt to have human needs and depended on human beings to meet them, while conversely humanity relied on well-fed gods as a necessary basis for power and blessing. In fact, in the view of Oppenheim, a process of transubstantiation was thought to take place by which the physical offerings were converted into divine power and strength.[18] What should be stressed here, however, is that the ultimate purpose of the feeding of the gods had more to do with the need for king, land, and people to be blessed rather than that the gods were pleased. To that extent, Mesopotamian sacrifice was anthropocentric rather than theocentric, and was obviously susceptible to being manipulated for human purposes.

(iii) It is consistent with the previous paragraph that the correct performance of ritual enjoyed a higher priority than concern for the interests of the gods. For instance, the two chief gods of magic, Ea and Marduk, probably received more attention than other deities, not so much because of their own intrinsic worth as for what they might do for those who brought them sacrifices and offerings. This led to a more mechanical approach to sacrifice than that advocated in the OT, and meant that in Mesopotamia the magician was as important as the priest. In fact there was no great distinction between the two, or between them and the diviner.

(iv) The purposes of the sacrificial practices of Mesopotamia seem much more limited in comparison with Israelite practice in the OT. The idea that sacrifice might establish or restore a sense of communion between the deity and the worshipper is not found in Mesopotamian texts, while the absence of any concept of the importance attached to blood rituals in Israelite sacrifice is quite striking. To satisfy the gods' hunger and thirst and the worshippers' need for blessing were quite sufficient motives for the offering of sacrifice.

III.   SACRIFICE IN SYRIA/PALESTINE

1. Sources

Our main sources for sacrificial practice in Syria/Palestine outside the OT, which itself can hardly be said to be silent on the subject of Canaanite sacrifices, are the fourteenth and thirteenth century BC texts from Ugarit in northern Syria. These texts are of two types, poetic myths and epics, and the so-called 'practical' texts. Although the religious stories in the myths and epics refer several times to various kinds of sacrifices,[19] it is probably unwise to use them as a basis for reconstructing the cultic practices of Ugarit during the period in which our texts were written. It seems more likely that they relate to practices and ideals associated with earlier periods. Unfortunately this awareness has not always been shared by biblical scholars,[20] but the temptation to assume that the myths and epics can tell us about what went on in ordinary Ugaritic temples must be resisted.

Although the number of extant 'practical' texts is much smaller than the literary compositions, it is to them that we must turn as our main source for the actual practice of sacrifice. The texts themselves are quite varied, including lists of offerings, pantheons, and a few steles, but it seems quite clear that the cultus at Ugarit shared many of the same cultural presuppositions as those found elsewhere in the ancient Near East. For example, a regular pattern of cultic offerings and rituals was based on the calendar, with special weekly and monthly ceremonies supplementing the main annual feasts. According to one important text (KTU 1.112), three types of gifts were made in these regular offerings, namely, animals, vegetable products, including bread/grain and wine, and minerals. A tendency for gifts to be made in groups of threes and sevens is also noticeable. As in Mesopotamia, the king and the royal family played a key role in actually presenting many of the offerings to the gods.[21]

Two cautionary notes must be sounded, however. The first is that the available evidence does not allow us to assume that there was a single pattern of religious practices throughout Syria. Each city seems to have had its own traditions and emphases, and although considerable similarities did exist between practices at various sites such as Emar, Ras Ibn Hani, and Alalah, it would be unwise to assume that we can do much more than derive samples of sacrificial practice in ancient Syria. Secondly, the extent and significance of Ugarit's sacrificial cultus should not be overestimated. The numbers of animals involved are much smaller than those described in the OT, with no more than thirty-eight being used on any one occasion. While the view has been expressed that 'the most important religious action at Ugarit was, of course, sacrifice', this is a somewhat misleading statement, since it is based mainly on the frequency with which sacrifice was offered in the official cultus.[22] In the light of our overall knowledge, it is more accurate to conclude that, 'the sacrificial cult remains a modest one'.[23]

Three issues of special interest emerge concerning the practice of sacrifice in Ugarit, namely, the sacrificial terms used in the texts, the meaning of the *šlmm* sacrifice, and the special issue of human sacrifice. An examination of these issues is not only essential for a correct understanding of what took place at Ugarit, but will also clearly illustrate that sacrifice in Syria was in several ways closer to that in ancient Israel than to that in Mesopotamia.

2. Terminology

Three of the most frequently used terms at Ugarit have a clear affinity with important Hebrew sacrificial terms:

(a) *dbḥ*. The Ugaritic form of this widely known Semitic root is usually a noun (cf. Heb. *zebaḥ*, 'a sacrifice, sacrificial meal, slaughter'), though it can occur as a verb (cf. Heb. *zābaḥ*, 'to sacrifice'). Its use is very similar to that of its Hebrew equivalents, in that it can refer either to a sacrificial meal or to sacrifice with blood.

(b) *šlmm*. This is the commonest term for sacrifice in the practical texts. It is clearly cognate with the Hebrew (*zebaḥ*) *šelāmîm* ('peace/ fellowship/communion offerings'), though it is not certain whether the final *–m* in the Ugaritic form is a plural suffix or an enclitic. In Ugarit, *šlmm* is usually employed for animal sacrifice, and is often found in combination with the verb, *lḥm*, 'to eat'. It also frequently occurs in

combination with the term *šrp* ('burnt offering'?) in the phrase *šrp w*
('and') *šlmm*.

(c) *šrp*. This noun appears to be a term for a particular type of
sacrificial offering, and is frequently association with *šlmm*. Since it is also
usually mentioned in the context of 'fire', (*'išt*), it is most likely to be a
'holocaust' or a 'burnt offering' (the root *šrp* is well-known in the Semitic
languages, appearing in Hebrew mainly as a verb meaning 'to burn', cf.
śerāp̄îm, 'burning ones'). Although therefore the cognate Hebrew words
do not have a sacrificial meaning, *šrp* does seem to be closely related to a
type of sacrifice well known in the OT, that is, the 'burnt offering' or 'whole
offering' (Heb. *'ôlâ, kālîl*).

3. The Significance of *šlmm*

Despite the obvious attractiveness of interpreting *šlmm* in the same way as
the Hebrew (*zebaḥ*) *šelāmîm*, the relationship between the two expressions
is by no means straightforward. The basic problem is that in spite of the
comparative frequency with which *šlmm* occurs as a sacrificial term, its
precise meaning remains unclear. The issue is complicated by at least four
factors: (a) the variety of meanings of words formed from the root *šlm* in
Semitic languages; (b) the existence of a deity Salim in Ugarit; (c) the
unlikelihood of the singular form of the word (*šlm*) having a sacrificial
meaning; and (d) the lack of any explanation of *šlmm* in the ritual texts
themselves.

Closer comparison of the Hebrew and the Ugaritic terms in fact shows
that to claim they are more or less identical in meaning is unwarranted.
For example, in complete contrast with what is known of Israel, the
citizens of Ugarit sometimes offered *šlmm* sacrifices in connection with the
cult of the dead and the ancestor cult. Further, the Levitical association
between a *šelāmîm* offering and a blood ritual, and the fact that Israelite
priests shared part of the animal offered in a *šelāmîm* sacrifice have no
parallel in Ugarit. Another difficulty is that in contrast to Hebrew usage,
in Ugaritic the terms *šlmm* and *dbḥ* are not associated with each other.

On the other hand, *šlmm* and *šelāmîm* are not totally distinct. Both the
Ugaritic and Israelite sacrifices were eaten by the worshippers. They also
seem to share common features with practices elsewhere in the ancient
Near East, especially other parts of the Northwest Semitic area and
Greece. The typical Greek *thysia*, for example, was a sacrifice in which
part of an animal was burnt on an altar and part was eaten as a cultic meal,
while Punic inscriptions contain references to a *ṣewa'at* sacrifice where
part was given to the priest and the rest to the offerer.

In fact, many scholars believe there is a direct relationship between
Israelite communion sacrifices and these wider practices. The nature of
the relationship may be explained in two alternative ways. While some
believe that the Greek and Northwest Semitic customs shared a common
origin (Rost, de Vaux), others have argued that the Israelites inherited the

practice of a partially burned animal sacrifice from the Canaanites either via the Greeks and Minoans (Schmid) or the Myceneans (Gill).[24] Despite the differences between the Ugaritic *šlmm* and Hebrew *šelāmîm* therefore, it does seem that there was a 'basic resemblance' between the Ugaritic and Israelite practices.[25] This similarity is in marked contrast with Mesopotamian practice, where neither the burning of parts of an animal sacrifice nor the idea of a communion sacrifice seems to have been known. Although it has been claimed that the Akkadian term *šulmānu* ('greeting; (official) gift')[26] provides a link between Mesopotamia and the sacrifices of peoples to the west, the proposed association remains unsupported.[27] The Akkadian term is not a sacrificial word, and has no clear connection with the practice of sacrifice.

When one turns to the practices associated with burnt offerings, the evidence seems to confirm the picture described above concerning the *šlmm* and *šelāmîm*. The burnt offering, for example, was known in various parts of the Northwest Semitic area, including not only the Ugaritic *šrp* and the Israelite *'ôlâ* and *kālîl*, but also Punic *kalil* and Neo-Punic *'lt*. Both these latter terms are philologically as well as semantically equivalent to the Hebrew ones, while *'ôlâ* and *'lt* are also cognate with the Greek *holokautōma*. When therefore the Ugaritic scribes combined the terms for two of their major sacrifices in the phrase *šrp wšlmm*, they were demonstrating that these important elements of their sacrifcial system were part of a wider pattern evident in Greece, Israel, and other parts of Syria. Mesopotamia on the other hand, did not participate in either of these types of sacrifice.[28]

4. Human Sacrifice

A special problem is raised by references in the OT to sacrifices offered to the god Molek.[29] Each of the passages concerned mentions 'passing a child through the fire to Molek', and it is widely agreed that these passages, along with a number of others in the OT,[30] are concerned with the practice of child sacrifice in Israel. Some evidence exists to suggest that similar practices were known occasionally in Syria/Palestine, though they were probably most frequent among the Phoenicians.[31] They were employed mainly in times of crisis and as part of foundation rituals, as is demonstrated both by the OT (e.g. 1 Ki. 16:34; 2 Ki. 3:27) and by Punic and classical sources.[32]

A more difficult issue is the interpretation of the term Molek. For a while, many scholars accepted that the Deuteronomists actually created the divine name 'Molek/Molok', on the basis of a term *molk* found in Punic inscriptions.[33] This latter word was thought to be a technical term for sacrifice which was then adapted by the OT writers by adding vowels from the Hebrew word *bōšet*, 'shame' (cf. the change of Mephibaal to Mephibosheth) to make it into the name of a god. However, this view has recently been effectively abandoned on the basis of wide-ranging surveys of the available evidence.[34] While *molk* was a general term for sacrificial offering, it was confined to the Punic inscriptions, and must be distinguished from the name of a Syro-Palestinian deity known as Malik, later Milku/i or Molek. This god was worshipped as an underworld deity in Mari, Ugarit, Israel, and was also known in Ebla. He was closely associated with a cult of the dead, which included offerings made to deified ancestors variously known as shades (*rᵉpā'îm, rpum*) and as *malikū, mlkm*. His cult was probably associated more with popular rather than official religion, and was conducted irregularly in Israel until the time of Josiah. It included child sacrifice, though for what precise purpose remains unclear.

The only clear evidence for child sacrifice in fact comes from the OT and from classical and Punic texts sources concerning the Canaanite world. It is not mentioned in Ebla or Mari, its existence is doubtful in Ugarit, and if it was known in Mesopotamia it was still rare there. One can only conclude that child sacrifice was not a major element in the sacrificial cult of the ancient Near East.

IV. SIGNIFICANCE FOR THE OT

(i) Several aspects of Israelite sacrifice are found in a variety of contexts outside the OT. They fall into two groups, according to whether or not they were acceptable to the writers of the OT. The first is certain basic features of two of the major types of sacrifice, the burnt offerings and communion sacrifices, which the Israelites clearly shared with their neighbours. In contrast to this, the second group includes a number of practices regularly condemned in the OT, such as food offered to gods,[35] sacrifices offered in connection with exorcism and magic,[36] and child sacrifice. The existence of these two quite different patterns makes it clear that the OT was able to distinguish between those aspects of sacrifice which Israel could adopt as part of their common ancient Near Eastern culture and those that were harmful to Israel's faith. The mere fact of an overlap in some areas does not seem to have caused any difficulty, which is all the more surprising given the vehemence with which foreign religious practices were often denounced in the OT.

(ii) Israel's links were much stronger with Syria/Palestine, and to some extent with Greece, than with Mesopotamia. This conclusion applies particularly to practices associated with the burnt offering and the communion or fellowship offering, but also includes elements of sacrificial terminology which was common to Hebrew and Canaanite. It is important to recognize, however, that the common features are at best treated neutrally in the OT, and that even where sacrificial practices were outwardly similar, the values associated with them are treated very differently in the OT. It is certainly not possible to go as far as one recent author who has suggested that an Israelite worshipper of Yahweh might say of Canaanite sacrifice, 'it was the "other gods" who were "pagan", not the sacrifices'.[37] Our investigation of *šlmm* and *šelāmîm*, for example, has revealed how wide the variations can be between sacrificial practices that seem superficially comparable. Sacrifice is a complicated phenomenon whose meaning depends on an interweaving of cultural, anthropological, and linguistic elements as well as religious ones. Verbal and formal similarities alone are insufficient grounds for concluding that Israelite sacrifices were basically the same as their Ugaritic or Canaanite counterparts. Even within Syria and Palestine, individual sacrifices seem to have developed in different ways even in the various cultural centres, quite apart from the theological influences that tended to make Israel distinct from its neighbours.

(iii) Despite the existence of similarities between Israel and the rest of Syria/Palestine, there remain two major aspects of Israelite sacrifice for which no obvious parallel exists. The first is the various atonement sacrifices of the OT. Though some analogies have been proposed, they do not have the same significance as they do in the OT. Further, the nearest parallels are more concerned with the removal of evil than with meeting the personal moral standards of a supreme deity.[38] The second case concerns the Passover for which, despite all scholarly endeavour to explain its origins, no real equivalent exists outside the OT. The attempts of scholars to derive the main Passover ritual from apotropaic blood rituals in Israel's nomadic period, and Unleavened bread from Canaanite agricultural practices, remain uncertainly founded on internal literary analysis of OT texts.

(iv) Several general features also tend to set OT sacrifice apart from the practices of its neighbours. The monolatrous outlook of most of the OT writers, for example (probably to be distinguished from the views of the majority of ancient Israelites), resulted in a greater concern with Yahweh's character and demands expressed through sacrifice than the rather vaguer requirements of the pantheon and spirit world thought to exist throughout much of the ancient Near East. A second difference is the lack of any overt theological system concerning sacrifice outside the OT. Ugaritic sacrifice, according to de Tarragon,[39] was concrete rather than speculative, and Ugaritic religion was more naturalistic than theological. The similar lack of any comprehensive view of Mesopotamian sacrifice has already been noted. Thirdly, it is of considerable significance that an emphasis on sacrificial atonement was generally lacking outside ancient Israel. This difference of outlook probably derives from different understandings of the purpose of sacrifice. Whereas in Israel, it had to do with maintaining a right covenant relationship with Yahweh, elsewhere (and often in Israel too!) it tended to serve the needs of the worshippers themselves (cf. the outlook of the Persian kings in Ezr. 6:10; 7:23). Finally, nothing outside the OT remotely corresponds to the covenantal context of Israelite sacrifice, either in theory or in practice. In other words, it is precisely some of the most important and fundamental

features of Israelite sacrifice that are the most distinctive in the setting of
their contemporary culture.

NOTES

1. E.g. J.G. Frazer, *The Golden Bough* (London: Macmillan, 1907–1915[3]). See also the
comments of G. Ashby, *Sacrifice: its nature and purpose* (London: SCM, 1988) 1–25;
A.R.W. Green, *The role of human sacrifice in the ancient Near East* (ASORDS 1) (Missoula:
Scholars, 1975) 3–17, especially the comment on p. 16, 'The basic problem in dealing with
the subject was one of method'.

2. *TDOT*, vol. 4, 16.

3. See e.g. A. Falkenstein, *The Sumerian temple city* (MANE 1) (Malibu: Undena, 1974)
(original French version, 1954).

4. For a description of a system of offerings given to a temple at Drehem, near Nippur,
see B. Lafont, *RA* 77 (1983) 97–117. In this case, no distinction was made between gifts
made for the support of the temple and its staff and those which would be given directly to
the deities.

5. G.J.P. McEwan, *Priest and Temple in Hellenistic Babylonia* (Wiesbaden: Steiner,
1981). For the text, see for example, J.B. Pritchard (ed.), *ANET* 343–345.

6. The word *nindabū*, 'food, provisions', was also used in both cultic and secular
contexts. Cf. *CAD*, N, 236–238, 319–323.

7. Translation from G.J.P. McEwan, *Priest and Temple in Hellenistic Babylonia*
(Wiesbaden: Steiner, 1981) 170. Text in F. Thureau-Dangin, *Rituels accadiens* (Paris:
Leroux, 1921) 92f., 10–14.

8. For further details, see R. Frankena, *Tākultu, de sacrale maaltijd in het Assyrische
ritueel* (Leiden: Brill, 1954) (see also *Bibliotheca Orientalis* 18 (1961) 199–207).

9. *CT* XV, P1.45, 1.8.

10. See W.G. Thompson, *The devils and evil spirits of Babylonia* (London: Luzac, 1904) Vol.
ii, Tab. Y.

11. See W.G. Lambert, *JCS* 22 (1968) pp.1ff.

12. H.C. Rawlinson, *Inscriptions from Western Asia* (London: 1891) Vol. 5, 61, 48ff.

13. For details, see S. Smith, 'The Babylonian ritual for the conservation and induction
of a divine statue', *JRAS* (1925) 37–60.

14. For further details on these series, see E. Reiner, *Šurpu, a collection of Sumerian and
Akkadian incantations* (AfO Beiheft 11) (Graz: 1958); G. Meier, *Die assyrische
Beschwörungssammlung Maqlû* (AfO Beiheft 2) (Berlin: 1937).

15. See further, J. Laessøe, *Studies on the Asyrian ritual and series bīt rimki*,
(Copenhagen: 1955).

16. Some 140 of these texts have been collected and studied in various articles by R.
Caplice. See R. Caplice, *The Akkadian Namburbi texts: an introduction* (SANE 1/1)
(Malibu: Undena, 1974).

17. A.L. Oppenheim, *Ancient Mesopotamia* (Chicago: Chicago University Press, 1964)
226.

18. Oppenheim, *Ancient Mesopotamia* 191.

19. E.g. CTA 14 (Keret) ii:62-79; iii:130-1; iii:156–iv:171 (J.C.L. Gibson, *Canaanite
myths and legends* (Edinburgh: T. & T. Clark, 1978) 83–84, 86–87; CTA 19 (Aqhat) iv:
184–6, 191–2 (Gibson, op. cit., 120).

20. Eg. J. Gray, *The Biblical doctrine of the reign of God* (Edinburgh: T. & T. Clark,
1979).

21. For a helpful proposal concerning the kind of method that should be adopted in
describing the sacrificial literature at Ugarit, see G. del Olmo Lete, 'The cultic literature of
Ugarit: hermeneutical issues and their application to KTU 1.112', in K. Hecker and W.

Sommerfeld (ed.), *Keilschriftliche Literaturen* (Berliner Beiträge zum Vorderen Orient) (Berlin: Reiner, 1986) 155–164.

22. A. Caquot and M. Sznycer, *Ugaritic religion* (Leiden: Brill, 1980).

23. J.M. de Tarragon, *Le culte à Ugarit d'après les textes de la pratique en cunéiformes alphabétiques* (Paris: Gabalda, 1980) 39.

24. R. de Vaux, *Ancient Israel* (London: Darton Longman & Todd, 1965²) 440–441; L. Rost, 'Erwägungen zum israelistischen Brandopfer', in *Von Ugarit nach Qumran* (FS O. Eissfeldt) (Berlin: 1958) 177–183; R. Schmid, *DasBundesopfer in Israel. Wesen, Ursprung und Bedeutung des AT Schelamim* (Munich: Kösel, 1964); D. Gill, 'Thysia and šelāmîm: Questions to R. Schmid's Das Bundesopfer in Israel', *Bib* 47 (1966) 255–262.

25. J.C. de Moor, 'The peace-offering in Ugarit and Israel', in *Schrift en Uitleg* (FS W.H. Gispen) (1970) 112–117; B. Janowski, 'Erwägungen zur Vorgeschichte des israelitischen Šelāmîm-Opfer', *UF* 12 (1980) 231–259.

26. G. von Soden, *AHW* 1268.

27. Contrast the views of B.A. Levine, *In the presence of the Lord* (SJLA 5) (Leiden: Brill, 1974) 18–20 and G.A. Anderson, *Sacrifices and offerings in ancient Israel* (HSM 41) (Atlanta: Scholars, 1987) 44–49.

28. For a similar conclusion, see G.A. Anderson, op.cit., 3–4, 27–55.

29. Lv. 18:21; 20:2–5; 2 Ki. 23:10; Je. 32:35.

30. E.g., 2 Ki. 16:3; 17:31; 21:6; Je. 7:31; Dt. 12:31.

31. S. Brown argues that Phoenician child sacrifice is unique in its positive acceptance of child-killing in a ritual context (*Late Carthaginian child sacrifice and sacrificial monuments in their Mediterranean context* (JSOT/ASOR Monograph Series 3) (Sheffield: SAP, 1991).

32. See e.g., R. de Vaux, *Ancient Israel* (London: Darton, Longman & Todd, 1965²) 445–446; J. Day, *Molech: a god of human sacrifice in the Old Testament* (Cambridge: Cambridge University Press, 1989) 86–91.

33. O. Eissfeldt, *Molk als Opferbegriff im Punischen und Hebraïschen und das Ende des Gottes Moloch* (Halle: Niemeyer, 1935).

34. G.C. Heider, *The cult of Molek: a reassessment* (JSOTS 43) (Sheffield: JSOT Press, 1985); J. Day, *Molech: a god of human sacrifice in the Old Testament* (Cambridge: Cambridge University Press, 1989).

35. Cf. Ps. 50:7–15, and the phrase 'bread/food of God' in Lv. 21:6,17,21,22; cf. 3:11,16; Nu. 28:2; Ezk. 44:7). This phrase has not yet been satisfactorily explained, though it seems to be a general term covering all Israelite sacrifices.

36. Cf. e.g. Lv. 19:26; 2 Ki. 23:24.

37. G. Ashby, *Sacrifice: its nature and purpose* (London: SCM, 1988) 28.

38. A. Caquot has suggested the existence of an equivalent to Yom Kippur at Ugarit (CTA 32), but the comparison is extremely hypothetical. The text has no parallel in Ugaritic ritual, and it is quite unclear whether the event was a regular or unique occurrence. Cf. A. Caquot and M. Sznycer, *Ugaritic religion* (Leiden: Brill, 1980) 17–18; A. van Selms, *UF* 3 (1971) 235–248; J.M. de Tarragon, *Le culte à Ugarit* (Paris: Gabalda, 1980) 92–98.

39. de Tarragon, *Le culte à Ugarit* 74.

FOR FURTHER READING

General

A.R.W. Green, *The role of human sacrifice in the ancient Near East* (ASORDS 1) (Missoula: Scholars, 1975).

J. Quaegebeur (ed.), *Ritual and sacrifice in the ancient Near East* (Orientalia Lovaniensia Analecta 55) (Leuven: Peeters, 1994).

W. von Soden, *The ancient Orient* (Grand Rapids: Eerdmans, 1994) (ET of German original, 1985) 188–202.

Mesopotamia

R. Caplice, *The Akkadian namburbi texts: an introduction* (SANE 1/1) (Malibu: Undena, 1974).

J. Laessøe, *Studies on the Assyrian ritual and series bit rimki* (Copenhagen: Munksgaard, 1955).

G.J.P. McEwan, *Priest and temple in Hellenistic Babylonia* (Wiesbaden: Steiner, 1981).

A.L. Oppenheim, *Ancient Mesopotamia* (Chicago: Chicago University Press, 1964) 183–198.

E. Reiner, *Šurpu: A collection of Sumerian and Akkadian incantations* (AfO Beiheft 11) (Graz: 1958).

A. Sachs, 'Akkadian rituals', in J.B. Pritchard (ed.), *ANET* 331–345.

F. Thureau-Dangin, *Rituels accadiens* (Paris: Leroux, 1921)

Syria/Palestine

A. Caquot and M. Sznycer, *Ugaritic religion* (Leiden: Brill, 1980).

J. Day, *Molech: a god of human sacrifice in the Old Testament* (Cambridge: Cambridge University Press, 1989).

G.C. Heider, *The cult of Molek: a reassessment* (JSOTS 43) (Sheffield: JSOT Press, 1989).

B. Janowski, 'Erwägungen zur Vorgeschichte des israelitischen Šelamim-Opfer', *UF* 12 (1980) 231–259.

J.C. de Moor, 'The peace-offering in Ugarit and Israel', in *Schrift en Uitleg* (FS W.H. Gispen) (1970) 112–117.

H. Ringgren, *Israelite religion* (London: SPCK, 1969) 158–169.

J.M. de Tarragon, *Le culte à Ugarit d'après les textes de la pratique en cunéiformes alphabétiques* (Paris: Gabalda, 1980).

7

Sacrifice in the World of the New Testament

ROGER T. BECKWITH

This chapter is a counterpart to M.J. Selman's chapter 'Sacrifice in the Ancient Near East'. Just as that chapter provides a contemporary context for OT teaching on sacrifice, in this chapter something similar is attempted for NT teaching on sacrifice. The contemporary context here is not Babylonian and Canaanite but Greco-Roman and Jewish, for Christianity was originally a Jewish faith, first preached and practised among Jews, but among Jews who lived in a world where Greek culture and Roman power reigned supreme.

The traditional religion of the Greeks and Romans was a form of polytheism, in which some of the gods worshipped were benevolent and others malevolent, and in which even those who were benevolent shared the vices as well as the virtues of their worshippers. The gods were worshipped by sacrifice, and, as in Judaism, both animal and vegetable offerings were made, though the detailed ceremonial differed from Judaism considerably, and free use was made of images as the representatives of the gods. The purpose of sacrifice also had various similarities to Judaism. Thank-offerings, propitiatory offerings and sacred meals were practised, and very frequently sacrifices were offered in fulfilment of vows, which had been made to secure some benefit. Sacrifice was mainly concerned with securing earthly benefits and averting earthly disasters, and whole offerings were made for the latter purpose to the gods and spirits of the underworld. Two marked differences from Jewish sacrifice were that human sacrifice was not excluded, and that in the ecstatic cult of Dionysus (Bacchus), the worshippers were believed to eat their deity in his animal representative.

Not surprisingly, traditional Greco-Roman religion had come under criticism from philosophers and poets, on both rational and moral grounds. By NT times, a more spiritual notion of the supreme God was becoming common among Greeks and Romans, and virtue was becoming recognized as the supreme good. The value of sacrifice had become a matter of dispute, though still generally practised and even insisted upon.[1]

An interesting application of sacrificial ideas in Greek and Roman literature is the subject of Martin Hengel's book *The Atonement*.[2] He draws attention to the frequent theme of the dying hero, giving his life for his people or his friends. He sees this idea reflected in Jn. 15:13 and Rom. 5:7, and considers, plausibly enough, that it came into Judaism from Greek sources in the intertestamental period. Occasionally, those Greek heroes who die for their people are said to die for the nation's laws, and he compares this with the Maccabean heroes, who gained an everlasting name by dying, not just for their people, but for their God and his laws (1 Macc. 2:50–51,64; 6:44; 2 Macc. 13:14). There is also an exhortation to be willing to die for God's truth in Ecclesiasticus (Sir. 4:28); and in Daniel, which Hengel dates in the same period, Shadrach, Meshach and Abednego are commended for yielding their bodies, that they might not serve nor worship any god, except their own God (Dn. 3:28). The parallel with Greek ideas is in the last two passages rather remote, and even the Maccabees were much more markedly religious in their aims than their Greek counterparts; but Hengel is probably right in arguing that the emphasis of the Maccabean literature on the personal heroism of the Maccabees is rather more Greek than Hebrew in origin.

Though the examples of Samson and Jonathan, dying for their people and praised for it, can be quoted from the OT, the OT is remarkably restrained in giving glory to men, and constantly emphasizes that all glory rightly belongs to God. Nor is this truth absent from the Maccabean literature, which leaves one in no doubt that the source of the heroism of the Maccabees was their faith in the Lord.

As Hengel goes on to say, in Greek and Roman literature the hero dying for his people is often spoken of in sacrificial terms and is said to atone for them. At these points religious language is certainly used, and it is sacrificial in character. The danger that threatens the nation is traced to the anger of the gods, perhaps provoked by a human crime, and the hero who averted that danger at the cost of his own life is considered to have appeased their anger. Hengel intermingles these instances with examples of the horrible practice of human sacrifice, presumably because no clear distinction is drawn in his sources; but only if the human sacrifice was voluntary can the parallel with the other examples be considered close.

In the Fourth Book of Maccabees, which is a moralizing work of the first century AD, strongly influenced by Greek philosophical thought, the story of certain martyrs of the Maccabean period is retold. They did not die in battle (like many of those discussed hitherto) but were cruelly executed for their faith. Their deaths are spoken of in sacrificial terms, as an atonement for the nation. The dying words of one of the martyrs are:

Be merciful to thy people, and be satisfied with the punishment of me on their account. Let my blood be a purification for them, and take my life in recompense for theirs (4 Macc. 6:28–29).

Elsewhere the writer comments:

They became a recompense for the sin of the nation, and the Divine Providence saved Israel, previously afflicted, through the blood of those pious ones and the propitiation of their death (4 Macc. 17:22).

Hengel does not quote these passages, and it seems doubtful whether they go back to the same source as the material he mentions. Since they are cases of unjust execution, they rather recall the Suffering Servant of Isaiah 53, who, despite his innocence, is unjustly oppressed, judged and cut off, and whose grave is made with the wicked (vv.7–9), and who is similarly spoken of as a sacrifice for the sin of the nation (v.10, cf. v.8). One is also forcibly reminded of the execution of Jesus Christ, the most innocent of all sufferers, whose death was being sacrificially interpreted by himself and his disciples at about the same period when 4 Maccabees was written.

To pass on now from the Greco-Roman to the more purely Jewish context, the first thing to note is that the literal sacrifices of the Pentateuchal Law were still being offered in the NT period, and continued to be offered until the destruction of the Temple by the Romans in AD 70. The most accessible comprehensive account of first-century practice is still that given by A. Edersheim in his book *The Temple: its Ministry and Services as they were at the time of Jesus Christ* (1874), based upon the rabbinical literature, though in detail it of course needs to be compared with later studies of the OT sacrifices. Edersheim accepts, probably rightly, the statements of Josephus and the rabbinical literature about the general implementation of Pharisaic teaching even in the Temple. Though the Pharisees, Sadducees and Essenes differed in their interpretation of the Mosaic Law on many points, and though the Sadducees held the high priesthood from about 110 BC onwards, yet such was the influence of the Pharisees with the people that in practice the Pharisaic interpretation was followed.[3] The Sadducean and Essene interpretations are known to us from literary records,[4] but how far they were ever practised is uncertain. The Sadducean and Essene interpretations are both probably attempts to reform traditional Pharisaic practice from Scripture, and consequently have a good deal in common. They tend to opt for the more obvious or literal meaning, as in the famous case of Lv. 23:11,15, where they take 'sabbath' to mean the weekly sabbath, and not the rest-day of the festival, as the Pharisees understood it. The devotion of the Pharisees to tradition meant that certain additional customs not mentioned in the OT, such as the water-pouring at the feast of Tabernacles, were also practised in the Temple.

In the Pharisaic conception of salvation, the place of the ritual of the Temple, and especially of the great sin offering of the Day of Atonement, was important but not basic. Pharisaism was a religion of action rather than reflection, in which the first requirement was to obey God's Law, one part of his Law (but only one) being the law of sacrifice. By obedience to any part of the Law one could achieve merit. The Pharisees did not have a clear conception of the gravity of human sin, but (unlike the Sadducees) they did believe in an individual future judgement after this life, and as the basis for this judgement they adopted the notion so common in human religions that God will weigh our good deeds against our bad and see which preponderate. However, they held that many of our evil deeds could be paid for in advance by suffering or death, or atoned for by penitence and the sin offering of the Day of Atonement. In this way a person's prospects in the judgement to come could be made much more promising.[5] The NT idea that God demands absolute obedience, and that anything less than this warrants condemnation (an idea held not only by Paul, with his emphasis on faith, but also by James, with his emphasis on good works), is absent from standard Pharisaic thinking.

In the Intertestamental literature, the spiritualization of sacrificial ideas which we find in the Psalms and Prophets continues. Examples are Sir. 35:1–3; Test. Lev. 3:6; IQS 8, 9; Philo, *Som.* 2:183. The instances from the Dead Sea Scrolls are particularly interesting, because the Qumran community had separated itself from the Temple until better times arrived, and was thus actually substituting spiritual sacrifice for literal, to a degree which even the Jews of the Dispersion, who could visit the Temple only occasionally, did not equal. When the Temple was destroyed in AD 70, rabbinic Judaism followed a similar course, as the prayers of the later Jewish liturgy indicate. Christianity had probably done so rather earlier in the same century (certainly Gentile Christianity), though Christianity of course saw its great and only sacrifice of *atonement* not in any spiritual sacrifices offered by Christians but in the death of Jesus Christ.

Around the beginning of the Christian era, there was much discussion of Abraham's unfulfilled sacrifice of Isaac – unfulfilled, because God rejects human sacrifice, yet acceptable to God, because Abraham was willing to surrender his dearest possession, his only son. An NT example of this discussion is Heb. 11:17–19, but it is also discussed in 4 Maccabees, the *Biblical Antiquities* of pseudo-Philo, the Aramaic Targums and the rabbinical literature. In these places it is often stated that Isaac was himself willing to be sacrificed, and that the sacrifice was not only acceptable to God, though unfulfilled, but atoned for Isaac's descendants. G. Vermes has argued that the Akedah (or binding) of Isaac, as it is usually called, provided a model for NT writers in their interpretations of Jesus' death,[6] but as the earliest examples of this tradition of thinking are the least explicit, it is difficult to know which came first. All that the evidence of Hebrews entitles us to say is that the first Christians attached importance to the willingness of the offerer of a sacrifice both in the unfulfilled sacrifice offered by Abraham and in the fulfilled sacrifice offered by Christ.

There was also at this period much discussion of the Suffering Servant of Isaiah 53. In later Judaism, as in modern biblical study, this mysterious figure has sometimes been identified with Israel and sometimes with the prophetic author, but as the prophecy itself expressly distinguishes him from both (from Israel in v.9, and from the prophet in vv.4–6), these interpretations have never given much satisfaction. It is important therefore to note that in the earlier Jewish tradition, as represented by the Targum on the Prophets, the halakic midrash Siphre and the Babylonian Talmud, he is often identified with the Messiah.[7] The NT claim that Jesus was both the Messiah and the Suffering Servant was therefore consistent, in this respect, with contemporary Jewish interpretation. It was only after Judaism had rejected Jesus as its Messiah, and after the decline of any form of Jewish messianic expectation following the failure of the second Jewish revolt of AD 135, that the messianic interpretation of Isaiah 53 fell into disrepute, just as the messianic interpretation of Daniel 9 did at the same period.

The sacrifice of Jesus utterly surpassed the anticipations of either Greco-Roman or Jewish religion. As Hengel points out, it did not just expiate a particular crime or avert a particular earthly calamity, like the deaths of Greco-Roman heroes, but it expiated all the sins of mankind and averted eternal judgment, and this before the tribunal of the true God and as an act of his divine grace. Even so, the pre-existing beliefs of the Greeks and Romans at least explain why the Christian message was meaningful to them and found converts among them. Paradoxically, it was perhaps because Jewish religion had less to learn that it was so unwilling to learn what it needed to. A messiah who was divine as well as human, who by his own sinlessness shamed the sinfulness of men, and challenged them to accept atonement as a totally undeserved gift from God, proved a stumbling-block. Yet it could hardly be denied that his sacrifice credibly fulfilled the shadows and prophecies of the OT, and in a way which contemporary Judaism could understand, even though the shadows and prophecies were transcended by the fulfilment.[8]

NOTES

1. A useful modern summary of sacrifice in Greco-Roman religion is found in F.M. Young, *The Use of Sacrificial Ideas in Greek Christian Writers* (Cambridge (Mass.): Philadelphia Patristic Foundation, 1979), chap.1. A fuller account is given by W. Burkert, *Greek Religion: Archaic and Classical* (ET, Oxford: Blackwell, 1985).

2. ET, London: SCM, 1981.

3. There is a discussion of this question in R.T. Beckwith, *The Old Testament Canon of the New Testament Church* (London: SPCK, 1985) 32–34.

4. In the case of the Sadducean interpretation, we are dependent on the accounts given in the rabbinical literature, but in the case of the Essene interpretation we have the evidence

of writings probably emanating from the Essenes themselves or their precursors, viz. 1 Enoch, the Book of Jubilees, the Aramaic Testament of Levi and the Qumran Temple Scroll.

5. It will be evident from this that the writer cannot accept the revolutionary account of Pharisaism given by E.P. Sanders in his *Paul and Palestinian Judaism* (London: SCM, 1977) as true to the ancient sources. On rabbinical ideas of atonement, see J. Jeremias, *The Eucharistic Words of Jesus* (ET, London: SCM 1966) 229–231, and Büchler and Strack-Billerbeck there quoted.

6. *Scripture and Tradition in Judaism* (Studia Post-Biblica 4) (Leiden: Brill, 1961) chap.8. For a different view, see P.R. Davies and B.D. Chilton, 'The Aqedah: a Revised Tradition History', *CBQ* 40 (1978) 514–546.

7. See A. Neubauer, S.R. Driver and E.B. Pusey, *The 53rd Chapter of Isaiah according to the Jewish Interpreters* (Oxford: 1876–77; reprinted New York: Ktav, 1969).

8. The writer would like to acknowledge great help in the composition of this chapter from material prepared by P.M. Head.

FOR FURTHER READING

W. Burkert, *Greek Religion: Archaic and Classical* (Oxford: Blackwell, 1985).
A. Edersheim, *The Temple: its Ministry and Services as they were at the time of Jesus Christ* (London: Religious Tract Society, 1874).
M. Haran, *Temples and Temple-Service in Ancient Israel* (Oxford: Clarendon Press, 1978).
M. Hengel, *The Atonement* (London: SCM, 1981).

8

The Self-Offering and Death of Christ as a Sacrifice in the Gospels and the Acts of the Apostles

PETER M. HEAD

The aim of this essay is to investigate and discuss the ways in which the four canonical evangelists present and interpret the passion and death of Jesus of Nazareth. Of particular interest is whether and/or how the ideas and terminologies of 'sacrifice' were used by the evangelists to express the significance of Jesus' death.[1] Nevertheless we shall not limit our attention only to those passages which can be shown to treat Jesus' death as 'sacrificial'. Rather we shall discuss any such 'sacrificial' terminology within the broader context of the theological intentions of each evangelist. Our overall intention is concerned with providing for, and contributing to, a biblical theology of Jesus' passion and death. So, for example, we shall be interested in the shaping of the whole gospel narratives; the interpretative teachings of Jesus; and the redactional (or editorial) interests that appear in the passion narratives proper. After discussing the gospels individually (Mark, Matthew, Luke & Acts, John), our conclusion will focus on the common elements in their presentations.

I. THE GOSPEL ACCORDING TO MARK

Even the casual reader of Mark's gospel is impressed by the action-packed style of the narrative; the breathless succession of events races before us from the abrupt beginning to the enigmatic ending of the gospel. The reader is faced repeatedly with the question, 'Who is this man?'. Introduced simply in the opening verse as 'Jesus Christ', the question of his identity is constantly posed in the first half of the book: 'What new teaching is this?' (1:27); 'Who can forgive sins but God alone?' (2:7); 'Who then is this, that even wind and sea obey him?' (4:41); 'Where did this man get all this? What is the wisdom given to him?' (6:2); 'Do you not yet perceive and understand?' (8:17,21); 'Do you see anything?' (8:23). This comes to a focus at 8:27 when Jesus asks the disiples: 'Who do men say that I am?' . . . 'But who do you say that I am?'

The ultimate answer to this question is found on the lips of a Gentile soldier as he sees Jesus die upon the cross: 'Truly this man was the Son of God!' (15:39). Here is the climax to Mark's presentation—not simply that Jesus can be recognized only as 'Son of God' at the point of his death, but that his death in some unique way expresses his divine sonship.[2] The importance of Jesus' death for Mark is not really the subject of any dispute. There are early indications of his fate (2:20; 3:6); and the theme of conflict which is prominent in Mark (particularly in 2:1–3:6 and 11:27–12:40) provides the human backdrop for the events of the passion.

Many scholars regard the passage which follows Jesus' question to Peter as the key to Mark's interpretation of Jesus' death. Following Peter's answer: 'You are the Christ', and the command to secrecy, Jesus begins a new type of teaching concerning the suffering of the Son of Man (8:31–32). This saying is the first of three passion predictions (8:31; 9:31; 10:33) which focus the attention of the reader on the death and resurrection of Jesus. They appear within and provide the structural framework for the whole passage from 8:27–10:45.[3] The structure of this passage can be seen outlined in the table below:

Place	Prediction	Misunderstanding	Teaching
Caesarea 8:27	8:31	8:32–33	8:34–37
Galilee 9:30	9:31	9:33–34	9:35–37
Judea 10:1	10:33–34	10:35–41	10:42–45

There is little doubt that Mark presents here a deliberate structure.[4] Throughout the section there is a continuing emphasis on Jesus' journey to Jerusalem. Concerning the passion predictions themselves three things attract attention. First, the third prediction (10:33–34) corresponds particularly closely with the course of events chronicled in Mark (delivered to the Jews, 14:53; sentenced, 14:64; sent to the Roman authorities, 15:1,10; mocked, spat upon, scourged, 14:65; 15:15-20; killed, 15:20–39,44; and raised from the dead, 16:1–8). Secondly, the consistent use of 'Son of Man' in these sentences. Thirdly, the important term *dei* ('it is necessary') is used in 8:31. It is necessary for the Son of Man to suffer because it is thus written (9:12; 14:21). While no OT passages are mentioned by Mark in this connection, the theological rationale—fulfilment of the promises made under the old covenant—is clear, and in fact is even more prominent in Matthew and Luke.[5]

Mark 10:35–45 is the climax of this section. Third in the series of misunderstandings-followed-by-teaching, it takes up the question of discipleship in some detail, particularly in relation to Jesus' death. In answering the question raised by two disciples, Jesus refers to his impending suffering in terms of a cup which must be drunk and a baptism. 'Baptism' suggests the sense of being overwhelmed by some disaster or catastrophe.[6] Similarly, 'cup' is a widely used symbol in the OT, where it is used to indicate someone's destiny or fate, in both good and bad senses (e.g. Pss. 11:6; 16:5; 23:5). The most prominent aspect of the background is in the use of 'cup' to describe a visitation of God's wrath. The *locus classicus* is Is. 51:17–22 where the people of Jerusalem are described as those 'who have drunk at the hand of the LORD the cup of his wrath, who have drunk to the dregs the bowl of staggering.'[7] This usage continued to be used down to the first century and is found in several Jewish sources contemporary with the NT.[8] Thus the suffering to which Jesus looks forward is not merely pointless innocent suffering, but the terrible spectre of alienation from God and suffering under his wrath (cf. Mk. 15:34).[9]

A further misunderstanding on the part of the other disciples provokes further teaching: instead of seeking positions of authority (like the Gentile rulers), the disciples must be servants and slaves. Indeed, according to v.45, the mission of the Son of Man involved exactly the kind of service which the disciples are to exhibit. The final phrase of this verse: 'and to give his life as a ransom for many' refers to the ultimate culmination of the Son of Man's service as his death (as in 8:31; 9:31; 10:33–34) which he here interprets for us as a 'ransom for many' (*lytron anti pollōn*). For Mark, this verse supplies the foundation upon which the imitation of Christ must be based. As Best says:

> Verse 45b offers a suitable ending to the long section on discipleship which commenced at 8.27, for it brings the death of Christ back into the centre of the picture; the discussion began from the first prediction of that death (8.31). Moreover in providing an interpretation of the death it opens up the way for the final journey to Jerusalem and the passion itself.[10]

The phrase *lytron anti pollōn* is obviously a crucial one from our point of view. *lytron* generally refers to 'money paid as a ransom' and is customarily used with respect to the release of prisoners of war and/or slaves and to release from a bond.[11] Although the ransom price (in the LXX) denotes a substitutionary payment,[12] it is never (unlike the verb) linked specifically with a sacrifice.[13] The substitutionary nature of this phrase is clearly illustrated in the parallel in Josephus (*Ant.* 14.107). Josephus reports the visit of Crassus (governor of Roman Syria from 54 BC) to the Temple in Jerusalem. He began to collect a lot of money and intended to strip all the gold from the sanctuary. Eleazar the priest saw this and gave him a bar of gold as a ransom for all the rest (*tēn dokon autō tēn chrysēn lytron anti pantōn edōken*). Crassus gave Eleazar an assurance that he would not steal anything else, but would take the gift, obviously functioning as a substitute (the fact that Crassus reneged and violated his oath by stealing the gold anyway does not change the meaning of the phrase here).

This passage speaks clearly of Jesus' supreme self-sacrifice, although it is less clear that an allusion to any specific OT sacrifice is being made. The parallels between this passage and Isaiah 53 have been often discussed, and no consensus has yet been reached among scholars.[14] Barrett argued that 'the influence of Isa. 53 upon Mark 10:45 is by no means so clear and unambiguous as is often supposed'.[15] If there is a reference to Isaiah 53 here then it could be argued that, since in Isaiah the Servant is given / gives his own life as an offering for sin (Heb. *'āšām*), therefore 'the Messianic Servant offers himself as an *'šm* in compensation for the sins of the people, interposing for them as their substitute'.[16] If Jesus identifies himself with the Servant, he therefore claims that his death shall be the atoning sacrifice or guilt offering referred to in Is. 53:10. But the allusion is far from certain, the text speaks of ransom (from slavery?) rather than forgiveness (of sins), and it seems unwise to base too much on what is not actually clear in Mark's text. Nevertheless, although at one level this text is theologically restrained, it offers an important pointer to Mark's understanding of Jesus death as a substitutionary ransom for many. It is difficult to conceive how such an idea can be entirely divorced from an association with sacrificial categories.

A clear allusion to sacrificial categories does occur in Mark's narrative of the last supper (Mk. 14:22-25). The institutional words of Jesus, particularly v. 24, 'This is my blood of the covenant, which is poured out for many', clearly echo Ex. 24:8, where Moses formalized the terms of the covenant by taking the blood from burnt offerings and peace offerings, and threw half of it against the altar, and half of it over the people, saying, 'Behold the blood of the covenant which the LORD has made with you in accordance with all these words.' The death of Jesus is obviously regarded here as a similar covenant-inaugurating-sacrifice (note again that it is not connected explicitly with sin or expiation). The vicarious nature of the sacrifice is presented—'poured out for many'—in words which are again reminiscent of Is. 53:12: 'he poured out his soul to death'. The benefit accrues to 'many' (cf. 10:45), probably understood here as the inclusive 'many' of the covenant community.[17]

Also relevant to our discussion is the fact that the meal is a passover supper.[18] Jesus appropriates the content of the paschal lamb imagery, in order to speak of the redemptive power of God in making his covenant operative, through his sacrificial death:

> his death is the vicarious death of the suffering servant, which atones for the sins of the 'many', . . . which ushers in the beginning of the final salvation and which effects the new covenant with God.[19]

Mark's passion narrative contains no obviously sacrificial interpretation of Jesus' death.[20] The main theme would appear to be the kingship of Jesus.[21] This kingship is, however, portrayed rather ironically: Jesus is mocked as 'King of the Jews' (Mk. 15:9, 12, 26–32),[22] only to be manifested as 'Son of God' (i.e. Messianic King) at his death (15:39).

II. THE GOSPEL ACCORDING TO MATTHEW

Matthew begins his gospel (Mt. 1:1) with the decisive affirmation that Jesus is both Jewish Messiah ('Son of David') and Gentile hope ('son of Abraham', i.e. fulfiller of God's promises to Abraham that he would bless all nations through Abraham's seed). He further introduces Jesus to the reader in chapters 1 and 2, describing who he is (Jesus, Emmanuel etc., chap.1), and where he came from (chap.2).[23] While many of the themes and terms from chapters 1 and 2 come together again at the conclusion of the gospel (Mt. 28:16–20),[24] at least one (the interpretation of the name of Jesus in 1:21) is grounded for Matthew in the death of Jesus:

> you shall call his name Jesus, for he will save his people from their sins.[25]

Here Matthew anticipates Jesus' teaching in 26:28 (see below). Through his death, 'his people' (that is the *ekklēsia*, both Jews and Gentiles) will receive salvation from sin (a fundamental aspect of the blessings of messianic salvation[26]). Matthew does not here provide any answer to the question *how* Jesus would save his people from their sins, and indeed, throughout the gospel Matthew points to the availability of salvation (including forgiveness) during the earthly ministry of Jesus (e.g. 8:16–17; 9:8; 12:17–21).[27] Nevertheless, it seems clear that Matthew is anticipating the atonement obtained by Jesus' death.

Matthew's gospel is structured, in part at least, along more topical lines than Mark. He tends to bring together logical groups of sayings and then miracle stories.[28] He also holds all teaching about Jesus' death until after the disclosure of Jesus' Messiahship in 16:16, which lends support to the view that 16:21–22 is the most important structural division in the whole gospel.[29] While the whole section 16:21–28:20 can therefore be said to deal with 'the Suffering, Death, and Resurrection of Jesus',[30] the passion predictions in Matthew are presented in a much less structured manner than in Mark (see 16:21–22; 17:22–23; 20:18–19; 26:2). The result of this is that the ransom saying (20:28) is not as climactically placed in Matthew as in Mark. The ordering of the events of the passion and the wording of both the ransom saying and the words of institution generally follow Mark exactly. One characteristic note, which we have already mentioned, is the addition of the phrase 'for the forgiveness of sins' to the words of institution: 'for this is my blood of the covenant, which is poured out for many for the forgiveness of sins' (26:28). Here Matthew reveals the locus of forgiveness, the means by which forgiveness is made available—the self offering and death of Jesus.[31]

Matthew's passion narrative emphasizes several themes when compared with that of Mark.[32] None of these relates directly to a sacrificial understanding of the death of Jesus, but several are of importance. In particular, the OT background of the passion is spelled out more clearly (e.g. the general statement of 26:54; also quotations in 27:9–10 from Je. 32:7 and Zc. 11:12, and in 27:43,50 from Ps. 22).[33] In connection with this it should also be noted that Jesus is presented more explicitly as Messiah (26:68; 27:17,22), and that the eschatological significance of Jesus' death is spelled out more fully (particularly in 27:51–53, but also 26:52–54; 27:3–10, 19).[34] Thus Matthew appears to regard the death of Jesus as the climax of the fulfilment theme which has been prominent throughout the gospel. This also coheres with the christological interest in Matthew's passion: it is Jesus the Messiah who is also Son of God and appears in control of events, who gives himself 'a ransom for many'.[35]

Thus Matthew stands in the tradition of Mark. He sees the death of Jesus as the sacrifice of the new covenant, and understands it along the lines of ransom and substitution (without spelling these out in any way). Matthew also emphasizes the fulfilment of scripture and the eschatological significance of Jesus' death: it is the source and ground of the blessings of the Messianic Age (including, prominently, forgiveness of sins).

III. THE GOSPEL ACCORDING TO LUKE AND THE ACTS OF THE APOSTLES

Of all the gospels, Luke's alone has a sequel. In Acts, Luke begins by referring back to the gospel: 'In the first book, O Theophilus, I have dealt with all that Jesus began to do and teach . . .' (Acts 1.1). The historical perspective involved in this two-volume story of Jesus' ministry has led many scholars to suggest that Luke dispenses with both apocalyptic and atonement in connection with his presentation of the death of Jesus. Käsemann suggested that in Luke: 'a *theologia gloriae* is now in process of replacing the *theologia crucis*.'[36] By this he means that 'the Cross of Jesus is no longer a scandal but only a misunderstanding on the part of the Jews which the intervention of God at Easter palpably and manifestly corrects.'[37] P.G. Voss summarized his discussion of Luke's theology of the death of Jesus by stating that 'in Luke the death of Jesus has neither the character of a sacrifice nor is it understood as an atoning work.'[38]

There is no reason, of course, why every writer in the NT should emphasize the atoning significance of Jesus' death, or indeed utilize sacrificial terminology to do so. It seems likely, however, that this view over-emphasizes the differences between Luke and the other gospels. It is clear that the sermons in Acts often mention the death of Jesus (Acts 2:23–24, 36; 3:13–15, 18; 4:10; 5:30; 7:52; 10:39; 13:28–29; 20:28),[39] although the focus tends to be on his resurrection as God's sign of victory over death (2:24–28, 31–32; 3:13–15, 26; 4:10; 5:30, etc.). Forgiveness of sins is another prominent element in the apostolic preaching, available to those who repent and believe (2:38; 5:31; 10:43; 13:38; 26:18; cf. Lk. 24:47). The blessings of salvation (whether 'forgiveness of sins', healing, or receipt of the Holy Spirit) are never predicated exclusively upon the death of Christ, but are rather seen as products of the whole complex of his death-resurrection-ascension (so clearly in 13:38–39: '. . . through this man . . . by him . . .').[40] In addition, Luke reports that the early preachers commonly referred to Jesus as God's 'Servant' (Gk. *pais*; 3:13, 26; 4:25, 27, 30). While this term could mean 'child', it seems likely that the servant passages of Isaiah were in the background (cf. the quotation of Is 53:7–8 in Acts 8:32–33). Jesus is identified (in his suffering and humiliation) with the servant of Isaiah.[41] In addition, Luke also records Paul's statement to the Ephesian elders in 20:28 (RSV): 'Take heed to yourselves and to all the flock, in which the Holy Spirit has made you overseers, to care for the church of God which he obtained with the blood of his own Son.' Whatever is made of this verse (and the difficulties are both textual and grammatical), it should certainly be regarded as an echo of Pauline teaching on the death of Christ: whereby the church was constituted through an act of redemption.[42]

In his gospel Luke has Jesus' death in focus long before the narrative of the passion itself. When Moses and Elijah appear at the transfiguration they speak of the 'departure which he [Jesus] was to accomplish at Jerusalem' (Lk. 9:31). It is possible that Luke uses the term *exodos* here in order to make a parallel between Jesus' death and the exodus from Egypt (i.e. God's act of redemption which inaugurated the Mosaic covenant). From this moment the narrative begins to focus on the approach to Jerusalem and to Jesus' death (cf. the passion predictions in 9:22, 44).[43] In particular Lk. 9:51 sets the scene for the interpretation of the long travel section (Lk. 9:52–19:27): 'When the days drew near for him to be received up, he set his face to go to Jerusalem.' The RSV here preserves the ambiguity of the word *analēmpsis*, which could refer either to Jesus' death or to his ascension.[44] Luke himself, of course, could be aware of this ambiguity, and have in mind the death-resurrection-ascension of Jesus understood (as in the sermons in Acts) as a unity. It is this long section which contains not only regular notices of the advance to Jerusalem (e.g. Lk. 13:22, 33; 17:11; 18:31, 35; 19:1, 11), but also two more predictions of Jesus' passion (17:25; 18:31–34).[45]

Luke 22 contains what can be described as Jesus' farewell address to his disciples.[46] As such the whole passage assumes a great importance in assessing Luke's understanding of the death of Jesus. We shall discuss here three passages: 22:19, 20 concerning the bread and the cup, 22:24–27 (and Luke's omission of Mk. 10:45), and the issue of the fulfilment of Is. 53:12 in 22:37.[47]

Luke clearly presents the last supper (22:14–22) as a passover meal (vv.7, 15), and describes traditional passover rituals (including two separate cups, vv.17, 20). The interpretation of the bread and wine (in 19b, 20) is as follows:

This is my body which is given for you.
This cup which is poured out for you is the new covenant in my blood.

This whole passage is omitted in some manuscripts (Codex Bezae, the Old Latin and the early Syriac versions), and thus by some English translations (notably REB). As a consequence, differences of opinion concerning the authenticity of this text have resulted in different views of Luke's theology.[48] In this case, however, the omission is limited to only one branch of Western texts, and the vast majority of manuscripts (both early and of diverse provenance, including p[75] and the major uncials) include the long version, and thus recent commentators have regarded its overwhelming attestation as 'the decisive argument in favour of the Long Text'.[49]

Essentially we have two parallel statements, the first concerning the body of Jesus, which is given *hyper hymōn* ('for you'); and the second concerning his blood, poured out *hyper hymōn* ('for you'), which is (seals?) the new covenant. The term 'new covenant' is an obvious allusion to Je. 31:31 (LXX 38:31), brought into being here by means of Jesus' blood (i.e. death). There is almost certainly another allusion to Ex. 24:8: 'Behold the blood of the covenant', especially if we recall the passover setting. Both parts of the saying include reference to the vicarious nature of Jesus' death, and both verbs, 'given' and 'poured out', in this context bear a sacrificial connotation.[50] The last phrase, 'poured out for you', is reminiscent of Is. 53:12 ('he poured out his soul to death'). In view of the more general parallel in which pouring out of one's blood simply means death (e.g. Gn. 9:6; Is. 59:7; Ezk. 18:10; Lk. 11:50) it is impossible to be sure whether Luke intends an allusion to Isaiah here, but if we note Luke's quotation from Is. 53:12 below (22:37), this could be regarded as an anticipation of that passage.

The conclusion to be drawn from this discussion is that Luke does present Jesus' death as a sacrifice. There are allusions to the covenant sacrifice, the sacrifice of the passover, and a generally vicarious sacrificial death, all within this one double phrase. In the context of the last supper Jesus proclaims a new passover meal. His body is in place of 'the bread of affliction' (Dt. 16:3) and his poured out blood is in place of the passover sacrifice, marking out, as it were, those who are the Lord's (cf. Ex. 12:13). At the same time, Jesus' death is regarded as the means by which the new covenant is inaugurated. This coheres with other Lukan passages where it was through Jesus' death (and resurrection-ascension), that forgiveness of sins was made available (characteristic of the new covenant of Je. 31:34, and emphasized in Acts), and the church of God was constituted as his people (Acts 20:28 cf. Je. 31:33–34).

If Luke regarded Jesus' death in this way, it is fair to ask why he does not reproduce the ransom saying in Mk. 10:45 (par. Mt. 20:28), particularly since Lk. 22:24–27 seems to parallel the passages in Matthew and Mark apart from the closing saying. The likely solution to this question is that Luke is not following Mark (or Matthew) at this point, but is recalling an independent tradition.[51] Of the sixty-seven words in Luke's account, only fifteen are paralleled in Mark, and out of that fifteen ten are relatively insignificant (pronouns, particles, articles). Indeed the descriptions of the Gentile leaders and their activity are different, as are the terms of the parallel instruction (Mark uses the contrasts great/servant and first/slave; while Luke has greatest/youngest and leader/servant). This passage should be placed in the same category as Lk. 5:1–11 and 13:6–9. At all three places Luke appears to have access to traditions which overlap with Mark, but prefers to include the independent tradition. This somewhat defuses the argument that Luke objected to the sacrificial interpretation of Jesus' death, but it does suggest (assuming of course that Luke knew Mark) that Luke was not interested in emphasizing this particular understanding of Jesus' death (the evidence of Acts and the passion narrative proper bear this out).

The next passage of interest is 22:37. Here Jesus has taken the initiative and asked the disciples about their provisions for the mission (cf. Luke 10). They lacked nothing then, but now, in the light of the approaching passion, he warns them to be prepared and makes the (probably ironic) comment about the swords. Verse 37 quotes from Is. 53:12 and can be taken in two ways: on the simplest level it could mean that the approaching passion involves the servant (i.e. Jesus) being increasingly opposed by transgressors. On the other hand, in view of the emphatic introductory and concluding formulae, 'that which is written about Jesus' (22:37b) would be his death (cf. Luke's insistence on the necessity of Jesus' death because it is written: 18:31; 24:26–27, 46). The quotation then interprets that death vicariously: Jesus the servant is reckoned with the sinners. Thus the next phrase in Is. 53:12: 'he bore the sin of many' could also be in view. In light of what we said about Luke's use of Isaiah 53 in Acts, and his understanding of Jesus' death in the preceding verses of chap. 22, this seems to be the more likely view.[52]

We have little space for an examination of Luke's passion narrative.[53] Many scholars have noted that Luke presents Jesus as a martyr figure, emphasizing Jesus' innocence, his firm resolve and final confidence (23:28, 34, 43, 46).[54] It is foolish, however, to oppose a martyrological presentation to an atoning one, since in 4 Maccabees that is exactly the point: the death of the martyr atones for sin (eg. 4 Macc. 1:10–11; 6:28–29; 17:20–22).

Thus it may fairly be concluded that, while Luke does not emphasize the significance of Jesus' death as a sacrifice, it is a category with which he is familiar. Further, in reporting the institutional saying and the preaching of the early apostles including Paul, Luke identifies Jesus' death as the new covenant sacrifice. As such, it is the means by which forgiveness of sin is provided and the means by which God's new covenant people are constituted (in fulfilment of Je. 31:31–34).

IV.   THE GOSPEL ACCORDING TO JOHN

It is a truism to say that John's gospel is more christologically explicit than the three synoptic gospels: 'In the beginning was the Word and the Word

was with God and the Word was God. . . . And the Word became flesh
and dwelt among us, full of grace and truth; we have beheld his glory,
glory as of the only Son from the Father' (Jn. 1:1,14). The prologue sets
the scene and provides the theological framework for the rest of the
gospel. Many scholars regard the confession of Thomas: 'My Lord and
My God' as the climax (20:28). According to this view, John's purpose is
fulfilled when his readers also believe as Thomas does (cf. 20:31).[55]

There is a tendency among some scholars to regard John's christological presentation, especially the emphasis on Jesus as revealer of the
Father, as existing in somewhat uneasy tension with the teaching about
the passion and death of Jesus. Käsemann for example was tempted to
regard the passion narrative 'as being a mere postscript' to the gospel.[56]
Bultmann argued that the atonement language contained within the
gospel was not part of John's own position but was church tradition,
which stands as 'a foreign element in his work'.[57] It is important therefore
to realise that it is precisely the crucified Jesus, now raised but bearing the
marks of crucifixion, whom Thomas confesses to be 'Lord and God'
(20:26–28). In addition, there are other important indications that mark
the crucifixion as the climax of the gospel.

The first of these is the 'witness' theme, which is very prominent
throughout the gospel (and also in 1 John). It is specifically related to the
death of Christ: 'He who saw it has borne witness—his testimony is true,
and he knows that he tells the truth—that you also may believe' (19:35).[58]
Secondly, throughout the gospel the narrator has referred to 'the hour'
which was to come (2:4; 7:30; 8:20; 12:23, 27; 13:1; 16:32; 17:1, cf. also
possibly 4:21, 23). This theme clearly links the early sections of the gospel
with the passion, since the 'hour' refers to the time when:

a) Jesus would be arrested and hands laid on him (7:30; 8:20; cf. 18:12);
b) he would be glorified like the seed which died (12:23–24; cf. 19:30);
c) the Passover feast was to be held (13:1; cf. 19:14, 31); and
d) the disciples would scatter (16:32; cf. 18:27).

The 'hour' is spoken of as a glorifying (12:23; 17:1), and in a similar
way Jesus had already spoken of his death as a 'lifting up' (3:14; 8:28;
12:32–34).[59] Thirdly, the *hyper* ('for, on behalf of') sayings throughout
the gospel (6:51; 10:11,15; 11:50–52; 15:13; 18:14) function not only to
interpret, but also to alert the reader to expect the laying down of Jesus'
life. These factors suggest that while John's gospel is written from a
christologically informed perspective, this perspective should not be
opposed to the significance of Jesus' death for John; rather, in
Schnackenburg's words, John's 'Christology is completely oriented
towards soteriology'[60] and this soteriology is oriented towards the death
of Jesus.

A prominent characteristic of Johannine Christology is the manner in
which Jesus takes over and fulfils Jewish holy places. So, for example, the
Jerusalem temple is displaced by 'the temple of his body' (2:21 and cf.

8:59), as are other holy places (Bethel, 1:51; Jacob's well, 4:6–15; Mount Gerizim, 4:20–21; and perhaps Bethzatha, 5:1–9; and the Pool of Siloam, 9:1-11).[61] The result is that, 'In the Fourth Gospel the person of Jesus becomes 'the place' which replaces all holy places.'[62] It is Jesus himself who becomes the *locus* of true worship, as of revelation and salvation.

A complementary characteristic is that Jesus takes over, fulfils and displaces Jewish festivals. Jesus breaks the sabbath regulations, and justifies his actions on the basis of his unity with the Father (5:17–27). Further, he himself is 'the bread of life' (6:35,48), displacing the manna from heaven and passover bread (chap.6), as the true source of God's wisdom and word (cf. Sir. 15:3; 24:19–23).[63] He is source of living water (7:37–39), and 'the light of the world' (8:12, cf. 9:5), replacing and displacing the ceremonies of the festival of tabernacles (7:2, 10, 14, 37; 8:20, 59).[64] And at the Feast of Dedication (10:22–39), he declares that he himself is the one whom the Father consecrated and sent into the world (10:36).[65]

This Johannine characteristic could explain both the prominence and ambiguity of John the Baptist's announcement: 'Behold the Lamb of God who takes away the sin of the world' (1:29, repeated in v.36 as simply 'behold the Lamb of God'). It has never been clear to commentators exactly which 'lamb' is here referred to, and this (among other things) has led several scholars to regard the saying as of marginal interest to John.[66] This hardly follows, especially since John the Baptist is given great prominence in this gospel as a true and decisive witness to Christ.[67] If John the Baptist is 'the ideal witness to Christ',[68] then his first statement regarding Christ's identity and role must be allowed some prominence. Secondly, this is the first clear christological pronouncement after the prologue, and thus not to be regarded as unimportant (since to some extent 1:19–51 functions as an introduction to the rest of the gospel, just as 1:1–18 functions as an interpretative prologue).[69]

The abruptness of these sayings means that we have little interpretative help in the context. In addition the word for 'lamb' (*amnos*) is a relatively uncommon word in the NT.[70] Barrett writes, 'It is certain that this phrase has an OT background, less certain what that background is.'[71] Dodd's suggestion that the lamb referred to is the apocalyptic, conquering lamb (mentioned in Test.Jos. 19:8; Eth. Enoch 90:38; Rev. 7:17; 17:14 etc.), does not adequately take account of the fact that the phrase, 'who takes away the sin of the world', places this saying in the realm of a sacrificial offering which provides forgiveness of sin (cf. 1 Jn. 3:5).[72] Since lambs are relatively common in the OT, and sacrificial lambs not much less so, most of the alternatives have been proposed at some time.[73] One possibility is the lamb mentioned in Isaiah 53. Acts 8:32 indicates the possibility that *amnos* could be used in the translation of Is. 53:7, and in the only other place where *amnos* is used in the NT (1 Pet. 1:19), Isaiah 53 is very prominent.[74] In addition, Isaianic ideas are present in this speech of John the Baptist (Jn. 1:32 echoes Is. 11:2; 42:1, cf. also Jn. 12:38), and we find the combination of *airō* ('to bear, take away') and sins in the Aquila version of Is. 53:12. Another contender is the passover lamb. This seems to be supported by John's presentation of the death of Jesus (cf. 19:14, 31, 36), and the fact that *amnos* was often used to refer to a young lamb (e.g. as a one year old, and as a sheep which does not yet have horns[75]), corresponding to the instruction of Ex. 12:5 which requires that the passover lamb be one year old.[76]

With so many possibilities it is not surprising that most commentators take an 'all the above' approach. As Morris suggests, 'a lamb taking away sin, even if it is distinguished as God's Lamb, is too indefinite a description for us to pin-point the reference'.[77] It seems likely that John has deliberately used an ambiguous term, in order to maintain that Jesus' death fulfils and displaces all the OT sacrifices, by dealing finally with sin.[78]

John's understanding of the death of Jesus is filled out in several other places. Caiaphas' statement (Jn. 11:50 repeated in 18:14) that 'it is expedient for you that one man should die for the people, and that the whole nation should not perish' is accepted and interpreted by John as a death 'for the nation'. This language, while not necessarily sacrificial, indicates that for John, Jesus' death not only had salvific value, but was actually and clearly substitutional: either the people perish or one man does instead of the people.[79]

The *hyper* ('for, on behalf of') passages in John are as follows: 'the bread which I shall give for the life of the world is my flesh' (6:51); 'The good shepherd lays down his life for the sheep' (10:11); 'I lay down my life for the sheep' (10:15: cf. also vv.17,18); and 'Greater love has no man than this, that a man lay down his life for his friends'(15:13). All of these look to the death of Jesus as a voluntary act of self-sacrifice on behalf of (for the benefit of) his people.

It is well known that John's gospel appears to differ from the synoptics in giving the day that Jesus died as the day of the Passover (15th Nisan).[80] Reference to the Passover appears early in the passion account (13:1), and later passages (e.g. 18:28, 39; 19:14, 31, 42) apparently emphasize that the crucifixion took place on the day of the preparation of the Passover. As Smalley points out: 'if Jesus is represented as dying on the day of the preparation of the passover, then his death coincides with the slaughter of the sacrificial passover lambs; and this is theologically suitable in a Gospel which uniquely designates Jesus "the Lamb of God".'[81] This very point is emphasized at 19:36: 'these things took place that the scripture might be fulfilled, "Not a bone of him shall be broken".' Here 'these things' refer to all that the previous verse had in mind, viz., the death of Jesus as the ground of faith. The quotation comes from Ex. 12:46, and there refers to the eating of the passover lamb.[82]

John, then, presents Jesus' death as a passover sacrifice, the means by which sins are forgiven, and as subsitutionary in intent. John's presentation, although very different from the synoptics at certain levels, coheres with theirs in various ways. Particularly important is the combination of various OT themes which are focused in the death of Jesus as the new passover, with the result that Jesus' ministry is regarded as a new exodus. This approach has the advantage (over, for example, that of Forestell) of showing that John's gospel stands in the same theological position as the first epistle: Jesus' blood [i.e. death] cleanses from sin (1 Jn. 1:7), by means of his sacrifice of atonement (*hilasmos*: 1 Jn. 2:2; 4:10). Like the 'Lamb', *hilasmos* is used of various sacrifices in the LXX,[83] and here is said also to provide the means by which sins are forgiven.

V. CONCLUSION

It is apparent that the four gospels are to a large extent united in their view of the importance and necessity of the death of Christ. In the light of contemporary views about the scandal of crucifixion this is no mean thing.[84] The *importance* of the death of Jesus is seen in the amount of space given to it by the evangelists, as well as their presentation of Jesus' ministry as one which climaxes in the cross. The *necessity* of the cross is expressed in many places, and is obviously based on the scriptures: 'the Son of Man goes as it is written of him'.

Although we have seen a multi-faceted presentation of Jesus' death in the four gospels, including but by no means limited to language which alludes to various types of sacrifices, the fundamental aspect of the gospel presentation of the death of Jesus, understood as sacrifice, should probably be regarded as that of covenant inauguration.[85] This is spelled out clearly, albeit in different ways, in all three synoptic gospels, and is implied in John's use of the Passover motif. In addition, Matthew's fulfilment schema and John's displacement schema serve to emphasize the same point: in Jesus, and particularly in his death, the Old is fulfilled and replaced by the New. Jesus' death is the sacrifice of the New Covenant (cf. Ex. 24:8). The blessings of salvation under the new covenant flow from the atonement wrought upon the cross, and the evangelists (as the other NT writers) use a varied cluster of other themes to expand on the theme: the suffering servant, the passover, the sin offering.

The nature of the atonement is never clearly spelled out in the gospels, though it certainly appears to contain a strong substitutionary component; interestingly, only in Matthew and John is the death of Jesus related clearly and explicitly to the forgiveness (or in sacrificial terminology, expiation) of sin(s). Nevertheless, it will be readily seen how this presentation coheres with the Pauline presentation of the death of Jesus, and even more so with the Pauline eschatology of fulfilment.

The gospels then rightly introduce the 'New Testament', representing the inauguration of the New Covenant in the death of Christ, and providing the key which links the OT prophets and the NT apostles: Christ's death being the means by which the New both fulfils and displaces the Old.

NOTES

1. For our purposes we shall concentrate on allusions to particular sacrifices within the OT and contemporary Judaism. On the wide range of terminology and the difficulty of defining 'sacrifice' adequately see, in addition to the earlier essays in this book, S.W. Sykes, 'Sacrifice in the New Testament and Christian Theology' in *Sacrifice* (eds. M.F.C. Bourdillon & M. Fortes; London: Academic Press, 1980) 62–63; D.R. Jones, 'Sacrifice and Holiness` in *Sacrifice and Redemption: Durham Essays in Theology* (ed. S.W. Sykes) (Cambridge: Cambridge University Press, 1991) 9–11.

2. E.S. Johnson, 'Is Mark 15.39 the Key to Mark's Christology?' *JSNT* 31 (1987) 3–22.

3. W.L. Lane, *The Gospel According to Mark* (Grand Rapids: Eerdmans, 1974, 1979) 292.

4. See most recently R.E. Watts, *The Influence of the Isaianic New Exodus on the Gospel of Mark* (Ph.D. thesis, University of Cambridge, 1990) 95–122. Cf. E. Best, *Following Jesus: Discipleship in the Gospel of Mark* (JSNTS 4) (Sheffield: JSOT Press, 1981).

5. See the parallels to Mk. 8:31 in Mt. 16:21; Lk. 9:22, as well as Mt. 26:31, 54, 56; Lk. 13:33; 17:25; 18:31–32; 22:22; 24:7,26–27,44ff. For a detailed examination of the passion predictions of Jesus see H.F. Bayer, *Jesus' Predictions of Vindication and Resurrection* (WUNT II.20) (Tübingen: J.C.B. Mohr [P. Siebeck], 1986).

6. Diod. Sic. 1.73.6: 'swamped with taxes'; Plut. *Galba*, 21.3: 'immersed in debts'; Josephus, *War* IV.137: 'overwhelmed the city'; see also MM 102.

7. This meaning dominates in the prophetic books (Je. 25:25, 27–29; 49:12; 51:7; La. 4:21; Ezk. 23:31ff; Hab. 2:15–16; Zc. 12:2; cf. Ps. 75:8), and is also characteristic of the Apocalypse (Rev. 14:10; 16:19; 18:6). See further L. Goppelt, *TDNT* VI 149–153.

8. 1 QpHab xi.10–15 for the commentary on Hab. 2:15–16: 'the cup of the wrath of God shall confuse him . . .'; Pss.Sol. 8:14–15; Mart.Isa. 5:13.

9. The same note of Jesus' suffering under divine judgement is also present in 14:27, where Jesus quotes from Zc. 13:7: 'I will smite the shepherd . . .'; cf. E. Best, *The Temptation and the Passion* (SNTSMS 2) (Cambridge: Cambridge University Press, 1990²) 157–158.

10 Best, *Following* 127.

11. F. Büchsel, *TDNT* IV 340.

12. So L. Morris, *The Apostolic Preaching of the Cross* (London: Tyndale, 1955) 29.

13. Ex. 21:30(bis); 30:12; Lv. 19:20; 25:24, 26, 51; 27:31; Nu. 3:12, 46, 48, 49, 51; 18:15; 35:31,32; Pr. 6:35; 13:18; Is. 45:13.

14. For positive assessments see J. Jeremias, *New Testament Theology* (London: SCM, 1971) 292–293; R.T. France, 'The Servant of the Lord in the Teaching of Jesus' *Tyn. B.* 19 (1968) 26–52. The evidence does not allow firm conclusions: *diakonein* is said to correspond to the Servant motif in Isaiah 53, but in fact is not used in the LXX, and in any case the Isaianic Servant serves the Lord, Jesus here serves the 'many'; though *dounai tēn psychēn autou* corresponds to Is. 53:10,12, the Servant gives his life; *lytron* corresponds to the sin offering (*'āšām*) of Is. 53:10, but is never so used in the LXX; *anti pollōn* corresponds to the substitutionary ministry of the Servant exercised on behalf of the 'many' (cf. Is. 53:11–12). See also P. Stuhlmacher, 'Vicariously Giving His Life for Many, Mark 10:45 (Matt. 20:28)' in *Reconciliation, Law, & Righteousness: Essays in Biblical Theology* (Philadelphia: Fortress, 1986) 16–29.

15. C.K. Barrett, 'The Background of Mark 10:45', *New Testament Essays* (FS T.W. Manson; ed. A.J.B. Higgins) (Manchester: Manchester University Press, 1959) 1–2. Cf.

also M.D. Hooker, *Jesus and the Servant: The Influence of the Servant Concept of Deutero–Isaiah in the New Testament* (London: SPCK, 1959) 74–79.

16. *BDB* 80.

17. See Jeremias, *TDNT* VI 536–545. Lane writes, 'The "many" are the redeemed community who have experienced the remission of their sins in and through Jesus' sacrifice and so are enabled to participate in the salvation provided under the new covenant' (*Mark*, 507).

18. On the passover viewed as a sacrifice, see Ex. 12:27; 34:25; Nu. 9:7,13; Josephus, *Ant.* 2.312; 3.248; *War* 6.423; *Exod.Rab.* 15.35a,b; Philo, *Vit. Mos.* II.224.

19. J. Jeremias, *The Eucharistic Words of Jesus* (London: SCM, 1966, 1973) 231.

20. Study of the Markan passion narrative has tended to focus on the question of pre-Markan sources; see J.B. Green, *The Death of Jesus* (WUNT 2.33) (Tübingen: J.C.B. Mohr, 1988) 9–14.

21. Suggested by H. Conzelmann, 'History and Theology in the Passion Narratives of the Synoptic Gospels', *Int* 24 (1970) 178–197, on p191; and expounded by F.J. Matera, *The Kingship of Jesus: Composition and Theology in Mark 15* (SBLDS 15) (Chico, CA: Scholars, 1982).

22. Note in particular the purple garment (*porphyran*) of Mk. 15:17, which is characteristically understood as a royal garment (Dio Chrys. 4.71; Josephus, *Ant.* 11.256–257; 1 Macc. 10:62; cf. *BAG*, 694).

23. See K. Stendahl, 'Quis et Unde? An Analysis of Mt 1–2', *The Interpretation of Matthew* (ed. G.N. Stanton) (London: SPCK, 1983; original version, 1960) 56-66.

24. For example: the 'Emmanuel, "God with us" ' of 1:23 corresponds to Jesus' final promise in 28:20; the Gentile interests expressed in the genealogy (1:1–17) and the worship of the Magi (2:1–11) correspond to the command for Gentile mission in 28:19, and trinitarian content is present in both (1:18,20; 2:15; cf. 28:19).

25. 'Thus the entire gospel is to be read in the light of its end', W.D. Davies & D.C. Allison, Jr., *A Critical and Exegetical Commentary on the Gospel According to Saint Matthew* (ICC, vol.1) (Edinburgh: T. & T. Clark, 1988) 210.

26. On salvation from sin as part of Jewish hope see Is. 53:4–6, 10–12; Je. 31:34; Ezk. 36:24–31; also Test. Lev. 18.9; Eth. Enoch 10.20–22; Sl. Enoch 64.5; Pss.Sol. 17.28–29, 41; 11QMelch 2.6–8; *Tg. Isa.* 53:4, 6–7; *Tg. Ezk.* 36:25.

27. See further B. Gerhardsson, 'Sacrificial Service and Atonement in the Gospel of Matthew', *Reconciliation and Hope: New Testament Essays on Atonement and Eschatology* (FS L.L. Morris, ed. R. Banks) (Exeter: Paternoster, 1974) 25–35.

28. This is seen most clearly in the five discourses which all end with the formula, *kai egeneto hote etelesen ho Iēsous* (7:28; 11:1; 13:53; 19:1; 26:1).

29. Due to the repetition of the phrase *apo tote ērxato ho Iēsous* (in 4:17; 16:21). For this view, see in particular J.D. Kingsbury, *Matthew: Structure, Christology, Kingdom* (Philadelphia: Fortress, 1975; London: SPCK, 1976).

30. So Kingsbury, *Structure* 21–25.

31. Matthew's distinctive *eis aphesin hamartiōn* may reflect the influence of Je. 31:34 (=LXX 38:34). Others have suggested a possible derivation from Is. 53:10–12 (Hooker, *Servant* 82).

32. For a detailed study which emphasizes a range of Matthean interests (with Christology being the most prominent) see D.P. Senior, *The Passion Narrative according to Matthew. A Redactional Study* (BETL 39) (Leuven: Leuven University Press, 1975).

33. See R.H. Gundry, *The Use of the Old Testament in St. Matthew's Gospel with special reference to the Messianic Hope* (NovTSup XVIII) (Leiden: Brill, 1967) 201–204.

34. See Senior, *Passion* 307–323. Matt 27:51b–53 is usually regarded as deriving from an apocalyptic interpretation of Ezk. 37:1–14 (paralleled in frescoes at Dura Europos).

35. On 'Son of God', see 27:40, where the passers by ironically echo the devil's tests in 4:2,6: 'If you are the Son of God, come down from the cross' (whereas it is precisely

because he is the obedient Son to his Father that he goes as it is written of him; see 26:39, 42; also cf. 27:43). Matthew clearly presents Jesus' death as occurring at the time of his choosing, signalling this at the outset by the juxtaposition of 26:2 and v.5 (cf. further 26:18, 50, 52–54, 61; 27:50).

36. E. Käsemann, 'Ministry and Community in the New Testament', *Essays on New Testament Themes* (trans. W.J. Montague; SBT 41) (London: SCM, 1964) 92.

37. Käsemann, *Essays* 92. Käsemann builds on H. Conzelmann, *The Theology of Luke* (Philadelphia: Fortress, 1982) 200–201.

38. P.G. Voss, *Die Christologie der lukanischen Schriften in Grundzügen* (StudNeot 2) (Paris & Brugge: Desclée de Brouwer, 1965) 130. Others argue that Luke actively suppressed such an understanding, e.g. D.A.S. Ravens, 'St Luke and Atonement', *Exp Tim* 97 (1986) 291–294.

39. For discussion see E. Richard, 'Jesus' Passion and Death in Acts' in *Reimaging the Death of the Lukan Jesus* (ed. D.D. Sylva; BBB 73) (Frankfurt-am-Main: Hain, 1990) 125–152, especially 134–152.

40. On the inseparability of Jesus' death and resurrection, see A. George, 'La Sens de la Mort de Jesus pour Luc', *RB* 80 (1973) 186–217, especially 215.

41. For discussion see D.L. Bock, *Proclamation from Prophecy and Pattern: Lucan Old Testament Christology* (JSNTS 12) (Sheffield: JSOT Press, 1987) 188–190, 226–230.

42. C.F.D. Moule, 'The Christology of Acts', *Studies in Luke–Acts* (eds. L.E. Keck & J.L. Martyn) (London: SPCK, 1968) 171; cf. C.F. Vine, 'The "Blood of God" in Acts 20.28', *CBQ* 9 (1947) 381–408.

43. Earlier indications of conflict and rejection occur in Lk. 2:34–35; 4:16–30, especially v.24; 6:11.

44. *BAG* 57.

45. The passion predictions in Luke (i.e. 9:22,44; 17:25; 18:31–34) emphasise the necessity of Jesus' death, the themes of suffering and rejection, the fulfilment of Scripture, and the resurrection. It is noteworthy that the resurrected Jesus repeats the same themes in 24:25–27, 44–47.

46. See W.S. Kurz, 'Luke 22:14–38 and Greco-Roman and Biblical Farewell Addresses', *JBL* 104 (1985) 251–268.

47. A recent study (although only concerned with 'L' material) is M.L. Soards, *The Passion According to Luke. The Special Material of Luke 22* (JSNTS 14) (Sheffield: JSOT Press, 1987).

48. Theological differences between versions of Luke (not only here at 22:19b,20, but also 22:43–44; 23:34; 24:51–52, etc.) have recently been emphasised by B.D. Ehrman, *The Orthodox Corruption of Scripture: The Effect of Early Christological Controversies on the Text of the New Testament* (Oxford: Oxford University Press, 1993). I have discussed some of the evidence (and defended a more moderate position) in 'Christology and Textual Transmission: Reverential Alterations in the Synoptic Gospels' *NovT* XXXV (1993) 105–129 (although I discuss only Luke 22:43–44 in any detail).

49. Jeremias, *Eucharistic Words* 159. The commentaries by Marshall and Fitzmyer support this, though the remaining problem is to explain why the text was omitted. Jeremias suggested that the text was abbreviated in the interests of secrecy, since being a liturgical text the rest would have been well known. B.M. Metzger suggests that confusion caused by the mention of two cups led to the omission (*A Textual Commentary on the Greek New Testament* (London: UBS, 1975) 174.

50. For *didōmi* used in this way elsewhere, see Mk. 10:45 (par. Mt. 20:28; 1 Tim. 2:6; Gal. 1:4; Tit. 2:14; 1 Macc. 6:44, cf. 2:50 (*BAG* 193). For *ekchynnō*, see Mk. 14:24 (par. Mt. 26:28); Lv. 4:7; 1 Clem. 7.4.

51. See V. Taylor, *The Passion Narative of St Luke: A Critical and Historical Investigation* (SNTSMS 19) (Cambridge: Cambridge University Press, 1972) 61–64; so also Soards, *Passion* 48.

52. See further D.J. Moo, *The Old Testament in the Gospel Passion Narratives* (Sheffield: Almond, 1983) 132–138, and the literature cited there. Other features which also suggest the importance of the Isaianic servant motif include Luke's emphasis on Jesus' innocence (chap.23, cf. Is. 53:11); Jesus' refusal to speak in self-defence (23:9, cf. Is. 53:7); and the mockery which describes him as 'the Chosen One' (23:35, cf. Is. 42:1); cf. also Lk. 2:32; Is. 49:6. Green suggests that this background explains both the emphasis on the necessity of Jesus' death in Luke and the focus on vindication-exaltation as salvific event (both motifs are held together in Is. 53:11). See further J.B. Green, 'The Death of Jesus, God's Servant', *Reimaging the Death of the Lukan Jesus* (ed. D.D. Sylva; BBB 73) (Frankfurt-am-Main: Hain, 1990) 1–28.

53. J.T. Carroll argues that the crucifixion itself functions as the climax to the confrontation between Jesus and Israel, as the focus of the rejection of Jesus by Jewish people (23:22-25; cf. v.51; also Acts 2:22–23, 36; 3:12–13; 4:10; 5:30; 10:39; 13:27–28); 'Luke's Crucifixion Scene', *Reimaging the Death of the Lukan Jesus* (ed. D.D. Sylva; BBB 73) (Frankfurt-am-Main: Hain, 1990) 108–124.

54. For a balanced assessment see B.E. Beck, '*Imitatio Christi* and the Lucan Passion Narrative', *Suffering and Martyrdom in the New Testament* (FS G.M. Styler; ed. W. Horbury & B. McNeil) (Cambridge: Cambridge University Press, 1981) 28–47. D. Schmidt relates the innocence of Jesus to the Righteous One of Is. 53:11; see 'Luke's "Innocent" Jesus: A Scriptural Apologetic', *Political Issues in Luke-Acts* (eds. R.J. Cassidy & P.J. Schasper) (Maryknoll: Orbis, 1983) 111–121.

55. On the evangelistic purpose of John, see D.A. Carson, 'The purpose of the Fourth Gospel:John 20:31 reconsidered', *JBL* 106 (1987) 639–651.

56. E. Käsemann, *The Testament of Jesus* (London: SCM, 1968) 7.

57. R. Bultmann, *Theology of the New Testament* (trans. K. Grobel) (London: SCM, 1983; reprint of 1952–55 edition; 2 vols.) vol. 2, 54. J.T. Forestell largely follows and amplifies Bultmann's position: revelation and not expiation is the essential Johannine soteriology (*The Word of the Cross: Salvation as Revelation in the Fourth Gospel* (AnBib 57) (Rome: Biblical Institute Press, 1974). For a critique, see M.M.B. Turner, 'Atonement and the Death of Jesus in John: Some Questions to Bultmann and Forestell' *EvQ* LXII (1990) 99–122. The most recent statement of the Käsemann-Bultmann-Forestell position is J. Ashton, *Understanding the Fourth Gospel* (Oxford: Clarendon, 1991) 485–501.

58. See especially 5:31–40 for the major statement (and 1 Jn. 5:6–12); cf. also 1:7–8, 15, 19, 32–34; 3:26 [John]; 3:11, 32–33; 8:13–14, 18; 18:37 [Jesus]; 10:25 [works]; 15:26 [Spirit]; 19:35; 21:24 [Beloved disciple]. Cf. A.A. Trites, *The New Testament Concept of Witness* (SNTSMS 31) (Cambridge: Cambridge University Press, 1977) 78–127.

59. G.C. Nicholson, *Death as Departure: The Johannine Descent-Ascent Schema* (SBLDS 63) (Chico, CA: Scholars, 1983) rightly places these sayings in the broader context of the exalted return of Jesus to the Father, a theme prominent in John and worthy of attention. I cannot but think that he exaggerates his thesis in chap.4 where he argues that the 'hour' and the grain of wheat saying (12:24) refer not to Jesus' death but *rather* to his return to the Father (see pp.145-155). His conclusion that the death of Jesus in John functions (and receives its meaning) only as the means of Jesus' return to the Father (see pp.153, 163) is hardly adequate, as we shall see.

60. R. Schnackenburg, *The Gospel According to St John* (London: Burns & Oates, 3 vols., 1968, 1980, 1982) vol.1, 548.

61. See W.D. Davies, *The Gospel and the Land* (Berkeley: University of California, 1974) 288–318.

62. Davies, *Gospel and the Land* 318.

63. On the messianic associations of the manna from heaven see 2 Baruch 29.8; Mek. on Ex. 16:25; Ecclesiastes Rab. on Ec. 1:9, quoted in R.E. Brown, *The Gospel According to John* (AB) (London/New York: Doubleday, 2 vols, 1966, 1970) vol.1, 265.

64. See Sukk. Mishnah 4.9–10; 5.2–3 and C.K. Barrett, *The Gospel According to St John* (London: SPCK, 1978²) 327, 335.

65. See Brown, *John* 411.

66. See, e.g. Forestell, *Word of the Cross* 194.

67. We find him mentioned in the prologue (1:6-8,15), the first section of the gospel (1:19-42) in which he gives a decisive witness to Christ; later in 3:22–4:3 in which he again witnesses to Christ; and in references in 5:31–47 and 10:40–42; both concerning the truth of John's testimony.

68. W. Wink, *John the Baptist in the Gospel Tradition* (SNTSMS 7) (Cambridge: Cambridge University Press, 1968) 105: 'John is made the normative image of the Christian preacher, apostle and missionary, the perfect prototype of the true evangelist, whose one goal is self-effacement before Christ: "He must increase, but I must decrease" (3:30).'

69. See also Turner, 'Atonement', 121.

70. Found only in Jn. 1:29,36; Acts 8:32; 1 Pet. 1:19.

71. Barrett, *John* 176.

72. C.H. Dodd, *The Interpretation of the Fourth Gospel* (Cambridge: Cambridge University Press, 1953) 233ff. Several recent commentators (e.g. Barrett, Brown, and Beasley-Murray) argue that this could have been John the Baptist's understanding.

73. In addition to the two mentioned here, consideration might also be given to the *tamid*, the lamb offered twice a day in the temple (see Ex. 29:38–46), or the sin offering (Lv. 4:32).

74. It is possible that a more precise allusion to the passover lamb is intended by 'without blemish or spot' (1 Pet. 1:19; cf. Ex. 12:5), but this is in fact a requirement of all OT sacrifices (cf. Lv. 1:3; 3:1; 4:3; Nu. 6:14; 19:2 etc.).

75. See the references in *BAG* 46.

76. Against this is the fact that the LXX consistently uses *probaton* for the paschal lamb.

77. Morris, *John* 147.

78. B. Lindars noted that 1:29, 36 bracket the account of Jesus' baptism. This association suggests that the eschatological cleansing of the one who baptizes with the Holy Spirit is effected by Jesus' sacrificial death (cf. 13:8–10 for a similar association). See B. Lindars, 'The Passion in the Fourth Gospel', *God's Christ and His People* (FS N.A. Dahl; ed. J. Jervell & W.A. Meeks) (Oslo: Universitetsforlaget, 1977) 71–86, especially 72–73.

79. See e.g. Morris, *John* 568; Brown, *John* 442–443; D.A. Carson, *The Gospel According to John* (Leicester: IVP, 1991) 422–423.

80. For recent discussions concerning the relationship between John and the synoptics at this point, see R.T. France, 'Chronological Aspects of "Gospel Harmony" ', *VE* 16 (1986), especially 43–54; R.T. Beckwith, 'Cautionary Notes on the Use of Calendars and Astronomy to Determine the Chronology of the Passion', *Chronos, Kairos, Christos* (FS J. Finegan; eds. J. Vardaman and E.M. Yamauchi) (Winona Lake: Eisenbrauns, 1989) 183–205.

81. S.S. Smalley, *John: Evangelist and Interpreter* (Exeter: Paternoster, 1978) 24.

82. The use of the same phrase in Nu. 9:12 shows that it is a standard term for the passover; Ps. 34:20 does not contradict this.

83. In particular see Nu. 5:8: 'the lamb of atonement'; 1 Ch. 28:20: 'the house of atonement'; Ezk. 44:27: 'the sin offering'; Lv. 25:9: 'the day of *hilasmos*'; (also Ps. 129:4; Am. 8:14; Dn. 9:9; Sir. 18:20; 32:3; 2 Macc. 3:33). Philo uses the term six times, in connection with the day of atonement (*Plant.* 61; *Congr.* 89), and other sacrifices (*Rer. Div. Her.* 179).

84. See M. Hengel, *Crucifixion in the Ancient World and the Folly of the Message of the Cross* (London: SCM, 1977).

85. Cf. B. Cooke, 'Synoptic Presentation of the Eucharist as Covenant Sacrifice', *TS* 21 (1960) 1–44.

FOR FURTHER READING

M. Barth, *Was Christ's Death a Sacrifice?* (SJT Occasional Paper 9, 1961).

J.B. Green, *The Death of Jesus: Tradition and Interpretation in the Passion Narrative* (WUNT II.33) (Tübingen: J.C.B. Mohr [Paul Siebeck], 1988).

R.J. Daly, *The Origins of the Christian Doctrine of Sacrifice* (Philadelphia: Fortress, 1978).

M. Hengel, *Crucifixion in the Ancient World and the Folly of the Message of the Cross* (London: SCM, 1977).

M. Hengel, *The Atonement: A Study of the Origins of the Doctrine in the New Testament* (London: SCM, 1981).

J. Jeremias, *The Eucharistic Words of Jesus* (London: SCM, 1966).

F.J. Matera, *Passion Narratives and Gospel Theologies: Interpreting the Synoptics through their Passion Stories* (New York: Paulist, 1986).

L. Morris, *The Cross in the New Testament* (J.A. McElwain Lectures) (Exeter: Paternoster, 1960)

F.M. Young, *Sacrifice and the Death of Christ* (London: SCM, 1975).

9

The Death of Christ as a Sacrifice in the teaching of Paul and Hebrews

ROGER T. BECKWITH

P.M. Head's chapter gives us ample reason to think that in Mark, in Matthew, in Luke and Acts, and in John and 1 John, the death of Jesus is described, sometimes by himself and sometimes by others, sometimes explicitly and sometimes implicitly, as sacrificial. Thus, in the Synoptic Gospels, he speaks at the Last Supper of 'my blood of the covenant' (or 'the new covenant in my blood') 'which is to be shed for many' (or 'for you'), Matthew's version adding 'for the remission of sins'. He is spoken of in John (and also, incidentally, in 1 Pet. 1:19 and Rev. 5:6–10; 13:8) as the slain 'lamb' of God, who by his precious blood 'takes away the sin of the world' – a lamb being an animal used in various sacrifices, in sin offerings, guilt offerings, burnt offerings and peace offerings, as well as the passover sacrifice. In 1 Peter, again, Christ is said to be a sacrifice 'without blemish', that is, without the moral blemish of sin, not the physical blemishes which disqualified OT sacrifices; and we ourselves are said to be 'sprinkled' with his blood (1 Pet. 1:2, 19). Similarly, in 1 John we are said to be 'cleansed' by his blood 'from sin' (1 Jn. 1:7,9), the language of sprinkling and cleansing being drawn from the OT sacrificial ritual, and perhaps from the Covenant sacrifice of Exodus 24, also alluded to at the Last Supper. This is to recall only some of the more explicit passages, from various books of the NT, in which a sacrificial interpretation of Christ's death is given.

Passing on now to the teaching of Paul, we find there similar statements, along with others. Paul too has his institution narrative of the Last Supper in 1 Corinthians 11, where, as in Luke, Jesus speaks of 'the new covenant' in my 'blood' (v.25). Here, no less than in the Synoptists, the language of the *Covenant* sacrifice of Exodus 24 is being used at the Last Supper, and the Last Supper was probably taking place on the occasion of the feast upon the *Passover* sacrifice of Exodus 12, thus suggesting that Jesus is seen as fulfilling both. By his sacrificial death, it is implied, he inaugurates the predicted 'new covenant' of Jeremiah 31, the covenant which writes the Law not upon stones (like the Sinai covenant) but upon the heart; and which brings not judgement for the transgression of that law but forgiveness—'their sins and their iniquities I will remember no more' (Je. 31:31–34; cf. 2 Cor. 3). Yet Jesus also fulfils the Passover sacrifice, with its two features of the blood which delivers from judgement, and the meal which proffers communion with God. The Passover sacrifice also inaugurated deliverance from bondage, and was regularly observed in commemoration of that deliverance; and the new passover meal, to be held in commemoration of Jesus, speaks likewise of deliverance from bondage, though not from the bondage of Egypt, of course, but from the bondage of sin and death. The link with the Passover is made explicit in 1 Cor. 5:6–8, where Paul directly compares Jesus to the sacrificed Passover lamb ('Christ our Passover has been sacrificed for us, therefore let us keep the feast'), and bids us keep the feast not just for the next week but throughout our Christian lives, not with literal unleavened bread but with the 'unleavened bread of sincerity and truth'.

Another connected passage in Paul is 1 Cor. 10:14–22, where it is the Lord's Supper that is compared not just with the Passover meal but with post-sacrificial meals more generally, the peace offering meals of Israel and the comparable meals of the Gentiles; and the significance for Paul in each case is that the meal proffers 'communion' with the deity to whom the sacrifice has been offered, whether the true God or a false god; for one cannot, Paul says, have communion with both. It is important to observe, with most commentators on 1 Corinthians (Grosheide, Héring, Fee, etc.), that Paul is comparing the Lord's Supper not with the offering of Jewish and pagan sacrifices, but with the feast upon those sacrifices which followed. Thus, the Lord's Supper is a feast upon Christ's sacrifice, but the offering of his sacrifice took place elsewhere.[1]

But if the sacrifice of Christ fulfils both the Covenant sacrifice and the Passover sacrifice, Paul does not seem to leave it there. For, by a commonly received interpretation of Rom. 8:3, he also teaches that Christ's sacrifice fulfils the sin offering:

> For what the Law could not do, in that it was weak through the flesh, God, sending his own Son in the likeness of sinful flesh, and as an offering for sin, condemned sin in the flesh; that the ordinance of the Law might be fulfilled in us, who walk not after the flesh but after the Spirit.

The words here translated 'as an offering for sin' are simply *peri hamartias*, 'for sin'; but since this is a normal way of expressing 'as an offering for sin' in the Septuagint (Lv. 5:7,11; 9:2,3; etc.), there is no strong reason for doubting that this very appropriate meaning is what Paul intends, or at least part of what he intends. Commentators on Romans who interpret the words as 'to deal with sin' (e.g. Sanday and Headlam) are not thereby *excluding* a sacrificial implication.

The context here (in Rom. 8:3) of law and judgement reminds us of an important fact. Though sacrifice belongs to the realm of worship, and law and judgement belong to the realm of the lawcourt, the sin offering brings the two together. The God who is worshipped in sacrifice is also the God who gives the Law and judges sin; and the sin offering is that form of worship by which man approaches God in both his characters, as the one whom he worships and the one whom he has sinned against. If, then, there is a penal element in Rom. 8:3, it may well be because there was a penal element in the sin offering; and the combination of ideas which is explicit in the account of the Suffering Servant of Isaiah 53, who, when he undergoes the punishment of Israel's sins, makes himself a 'guilt offering' for them, may go back to the Pentateuchal ritual, as well as forward to the NT.

When we move on to the Epistle to the Hebrews, we find, among other things, the third main class of Jewish sacrifices, burnt offerings (not just sin and peace offerings) also apparently seen as fulfilled in Christ. It is often considered that the spiritualizing of sacrifice in OT thought reaches a high point in the psalm quoted and interpreted in Hebrews 10, Psalm 40, where the psalmist, offering *himself* to do God's will and fulfil his Law from the heart, seems to set aside the external ceremonies of sacrifice and offering, sin offering and burnt offering:

> Sacrifice and offering thou hast no delight in; mine ears hast thou opened; burnt offering and sin offering hast thou not required. Then said I, Lo, I am come; in the roll of the book it is written of me; I delight to do thy will, O my God; yea, thy law is within my heart (vv. 6–8).

Though the psalmist mentions not only the burnt offering but also the sin offering as giving no pleasure to God,[2] yet the idea of consecration to God's will, which he substitutes, is the spiritual idea most closely akin to the burnt offering. In the sin offering, the emphasis was on the atoning application of the blood; in the peace offering, the emphasis was on the communion meal with God that followed; but in the burnt offering (having no meal attached, and not being primarily concerned with atonement) the emphasis was on the total dedication of the gift to God, wholly consumed by fire. In Hebrews 10, the speaker in Psalm 40 is identified with Jesus; and the total dedication of Jesus to his Father's will, even to the point of the cross, is indeed the perfect human expression of the same ideal. Admittedly, Hebrews 10 does not stress the link with the burnt offering, but rather with the sin offering, as vv.4,11–12 indicate. Yet there is another place in the epistle which speaks of Jesus' prayers in sacrificial terms and seems to confirm that the idea of the sacrificial dedication of his whole life to God was present in the writer's mind. This is Heb. 5:7,

> who in the days of his flesh, having offered up (*prospherō*) prayers and supplications with strong crying and tears unto him that was able to save him out of death, and having been heard for his godly fear . . .

It is at these points that the sacrifice of Jesus comes nearest to the spiritual sacrifices of his followers, though it still differs in being unblemished by sin, and above all in making atonement for the sins of others. It is only 'through him', that is, through his atoning sacrifice or holy priesthood, that their spiritual sacrifices can be accepted by God at all. As Heb. 13:15 expresses it, '*through him* let us offer up a sacrifice of praise continually'; and compare 1 Pet. 2:5, 'to be a holy priesthood, to offer up spiritual sacrifices, acceptable to God *through Jesus Christ*'.

In chapter 9 of the Epistle to the Hebrews, as elsewhere in the NT (see above), a parallel is drawn between the sacrifice of Christ and the covenant sacrifice of Exodus 24. Because Christ's death truly atones, the writer says, 'for this cause he is the mediator of a new covenant' (v.15); then, after comparing a covenant with a testament or will, for which the same word *diathēkē* is used in Greek, and which likewise involves death, he continues, 'wherefore even the *first* covenant (i.e. that of Sinai) hath not been dedicated without blood' (v.18).

In the same chapter, he compares Christ's death with two other sacrifices. One is the red heifer of Numbers 19, a sin offering of which the ashes cleansed those defiled by contact with the dead. This is in 9:13,14:

> For if the blood of goats and bulls and the ashes of a heifer sprinkling them that have been defiled sanctify unto the cleanness of the *flesh*, how much more shall the blood of Christ, who through the eternal *Spirit* offered himself without blemish unto God, cleanse your *conscience* from dead *works* (not dead *bodies*) to serve the *living* God?

Here, as in the teaching of our Lord (Mk. 7:1–23) and Paul (2 Cor. 6:14–7:1), we see the ceremonial cleanness and uncleanness of the OT ritual being replaced by *moral* cleanness and uncleanness. Uncleanness and sin are *connected* ideas in the OT, but in the New they are actually identified: the *true* uncleanness is sin, so the atoning sacrifice of Christ, which deals with sin, deals with uncleanness too.

Finally, Hebrews 9 and 10 compare the sacrifice of Jesus with the Day of Atonement offering of Leviticus 16. It does this in vv.1–12 of chap.9, resuming the theme from v.23 to 10:4, and again in 10:19–25. It is in this extended comparison that the writer shows the superiority of Christ's sacrifice in the most telling ways. First, he points out that the permission for the high priest to go into the Holy of Holies only once a year meant that all the rest of the year he was excluded. This is an indication, he says, that the OT sin offerings could not make the worshipper's conscience perfect (i.e. free it from the guilt of sin), and this was because they, and the associated ceremonies, were merely ordinances of the flesh, or outward ordinances, imposed until a time of reformation (9:1–12).

Secondly, he argues that in the nature of things the OT sacrifices could not atone for men's sins, because they were mere animals, and 'it is impossible that the blood of bulls and goats should take away sins' (10:4).

A third indication that the OT sacrifices could not atone, he argues, is to be found in their repetition (10:1-2). If they had atoned at all, they would have atoned completely, and would not have needed to be repeated, as (he has just said) Christ's sacrifice does not need to be. The fact that they were continually repeated shows that they did not atone. They were not in fact *remedies* for sin so much as *reminders* of it: 'in those sacrifices there is a remembrance made of sins year by year' (10:3).

The implication of this teaching evidently is that any grace which the OT sacrifices conveyed came not from themselves but from the sacrifice of Christ which they foreshadowed. The epistle, especially in chap.11, bears ample witness to the grace of God in OT times, and in vv.4 and 28 of the chapter relates it to OT sacrifices; but the chapter ends by saying that the OT saints nevertheless 'received not the promise, God having provided some better thing concerning us, that apart from us they should not be made complete' (vv.39-40). The retrospective efficacy of Christ's sacrifice becomes explicit in 9:15, where his death is said to have taken place 'for the redemption of the transgressions that were under the *first* covenant'; and the same thing is implied in v.26 of that chapter, as also in Rom. 3:25.

The true Holy of Holies, into which Christ entered at *his* day of atonement, was heaven (Heb. 9:23-8). And that is where we too can now boldly draw near, through faith in his blood (10:19-25). Heaven is the scene of his priesthood (8:1-5), of which this epistle, unlike the rest of the NT, says so much. But it was on earth, essentially, that his *sacrifice* took place. The epistle lays great stress on the importance, in Christ's sacrifice, of his death (Heb. 2:9,14; 9:15-17, 22, 25-28; 13:12, 20). All that was costly in the sacrifice—the part of the donor and the victim—took place at the cross; there remained only the priestly part—the presentation of the sacrifice to God by an acceptable mediator—and we are probably to understand that Christ performed this at his ascension, the time when, as man, he entered his Father's presence in the true Holy of Holies. We are told in 8:3 that he 'offered' (*prospherō*) something there, and this probably refers to the sprinkling or 'offering' of the blood in the Holy of Holies by the high priest on the Day of Atonement (Heb. 9:7,21-26; cf. 12:24), a typical action fulfilled by Christ, perhaps by simply 'appearing in the presence of God for us' (9:24). Once he had appeared there, his sacrifice was over. This is clear from the numerous passages in the epistle which speak of his sacrifice as once for all, past and finished—not only passages which speak of his sacrifice in general terms, as 1:3 does, but also passages which speak of it specifically under its priestly aspect (Heb. 7:27; 9:11-12, 25-28; 10:10-14, 18). This needs to be remembered when theories of eucharistic sacrifice are based upon a supposed continuing work of *sacrifice* being performed by Christ in heaven.[3] Christ's continuing priestly work in heaven is like that of the priests in Ps. 99:6 and Joel 2:17—it is not sacrificial but intercessory (Heb. 7:24-5), and is only in that sense propitiatory (2:17). He may be compared with the *Advocate* who is the propitiation for our sins in 1 Jn. 2:2. His intercession, or advocacy, is propitiatory only in a derived sense: it is propitiatory because it is based upon the once for all propitiation which he offered on the cross.[4]

We have seen how often OT categories are reinterpreted in NT teaching on the sacrifice of Christ. Clearly, it is not a ceremonial sacrifice, any more than the spiritual sacrifices of Christians are, and it does not conform to OT ceremonial rules. This has led some to refer to it as a metaphorical sacrifice, but if we do this, we must realize that we are taking the OT sacrifices as the norm, whereas, according to the NT, they were merely shadows of the true sacrifice to come, which fulfilled them. You cannot build a house without a plan, yet what matters is not the plan but the house. The OT sacrifices provide providential categories for the interpretation of Christ's sacrifice, but they are categories which it everywhere transcends. For the blood of animals, we have the blood of Christ (Heb. 10:4; Mk. 14:24). For spotlessness, we have sinlessness (Heb. 9:14; 1 Pet. 1:19). For a sweet smell, we have true acceptableness (Eph. 5:2). For the sprinkling of our bodies with blood, we have forgiveness (Heb. 9:13–14,19–22; 1 Pet.1:2). For symbolical atonement, we have real atonement (Heb. 10:1–10). From a Jewish point of view, this might indeed be metaphor. From a Christian viewpoint, however, it is eschatological fulfilment.

NOTES

1. For further discussion of this issue, see chap.10.
2. God's rejection of the sin offering also may be due to the fact that, though it acknowledges sin, it assumes sin, whereas God's ideal is obedience. The Epistle to the Hebrews adjusts this concept to leave room for the true sin offering of Jesus, which is at the same time the expression of perfect obedience. For further discussion of Psalm 40, see N.B. Courtman's remarks, chap.3.
3. Notably, the theory propounded by S.C. Gayford, *Sacrifice and Priesthood* (London: Methuen, 1924) and F.C.N. Hicks, *The Fulness of Sacrifice* (London: Macmillan, 1930). On the eucharistic issue, see also the chapter by S. Walton (chap.10).
4. There is a judicious and compendious discussion of detailed points of interpretation in the Epistle to the Hebrews in the New London commentary of F.F. Bruce (London: Marshall Morgan & Scott, 1964). The general teaching of Hebrews on the sacrifice and priesthood of Christ has been vigorously discussed at various periods since the Reformation, and most recently in the period between about 1890 and 1930. The most satisfactory statement of what Hebrews teaches is probably that given by H.H. Meeter, *The Heavenly High Priesthood of Christ* (Grand Rapids: Eerdmans, 1916), building upon the writings of G. Vos.

FOR FURTHER READING

F.F. Bruce, *Commentary on the Epistle to the Hebrews* (London: Marshall Morgan & Scott, 1964).
L. Morris, *The Apostolic Preaching of the Cross* (London: Tyndale Press, 1955).
L. Morris, *The Cross in the New Testament* (Exeter: Paternoster, 1965).
J.I. Packer (ed.), *Eucharistic Sacrifice* (London: Church Book Room Press, 1962).

10

Sacrifice and Priesthood in Relation to the Christian Life and Church in the New Testament[1]

STEVE WALTON

Sacrifice in relation to the Christian life and church, and priesthood as an aspect of that broader area, are categories with a long history of controversy attached to them and a short paper cannot attempt to solve all the problems posed by church history and systematic theology in this area. Our discussion will therefore focus on three themes. First, we shall consider the sacrifice of Christ and the sacrifices of the church, and ask what their relationship is. Second, we shall consider the eucharist and Christ's own self-offering sacrifice, evaluating the biblical reasons that have been suggested for seeing the eucharist as sacrificial. Third, we shall consider the relationship of church leadership to Christian priesthoood.

I. THE SACRIFICE OF CHRIST AND THE SACRIFICES OF THE CHURCH

This area focuses into three key questions: What are the implications of the sacrifice of Christ for Christian believers? In what do the sacrifices of the Christian church consist? What is the relation of Christ's priesthood to that of the Christian church?

1. The Sacrifice of Christ and Christian Believers

Sacrificial imagery in relation to the death of Christ, particularly the priesthood of Christ, is considered most fully in Hebrews within the NT, and this is also one place where the implications of Christ's sacrifice and priesthood for believers are discussed. Three specific passages are relevant.

Heb. 7:23–28 draws out one implication of Christ's sacrifice and priesthood, namely that no other expiatory sacrifice or priesthood is necessary for the believer. The writer has been considering the contrast between the levitical priesthood and Christ's priestly office, and here clarifies that no other means of drawing near to God is necessary for the believer, since Christ lives for ever. This implies that he needs no successor as priest, and also implies that his priesthood goes on for ever: 'he holds his priesthood permanently, because he continues for ever. Consequently, he is able for all time to save those who draw near to God through him, since he always lives' (vv.24–25). Similarly, his sacrifice has been offered 'once for all' (v.27) and has been accepted. Therefore it needs no repetition or replacement.

Heb. 10:19–22 develops this point further, by showing that the priestly work of Christ (that is, his sacrificial death, vv.19–20) makes access to God possible for the believer. This is possible because 'by a single offering he has perfected for all time those who are sanctified' (v.14) and therefore 'we have confidence to enter the sanctuary by the blood of Jesus' (v.19). The link with Christ's priesthood is then drawn explicitly (vv.21–22); the work of this 'great priest' implies that believers may 'draw near', which is shorthand for 'draw near to God'.

Drawing those two passages together, we may say that Christ's priesthood and sacrifice form necessary and sufficient conditions for the believer's access to God. They are necessary, since no other priesthood or sacrifice really dealt with sin (cf. Heb. 10:4), and they are sufficient, since his once-and-for-all sacrifice deals completely with sin and he lives for ever (and therefore exercises a permanent priesthood), which means that he is able to offer the benefits of that sacrifice to those who trust in him. The first implication of the sacrifice of Christ for his church is open access to God, with no need for any human mediator.

In considering why the author of Hebrews reasons in this manner, Moule points to the theme of sacrifice and sanctuary in the apologetic of the earliest Christians.[2] He argues that they would have needed to respond to the accusation from Jews and pagans alike that the Christian church had no temple, altar, sacrifices or priesthood—a cogent objection in a world where all those things were considered necessary for communion with the divine. Thus Moule believes that the argument of Hebrews in particular should be understood as a response to a situation in which Christian Jews were under pressure to revert to Judaism, especially so if the letter should be seen against the backdrop of the Jewish revolt of AD 66–70:[3]

At such a time it is not only a fear of persecution and of being called traitors but also the human yearning for the ordered stability of an ancient system, with objective, tangible symbols, that will drive men back from the bold pioneering demanded by the Christian faith to the well-worn paths of the older way. It is to exactly such a temptation that the Epistle speaks . . . this writer boldly claims that . . . if you would be loyal Jews you are committed to go forward in company with the new Israel of the Christian Church, not back to a pre-Christian stage of Judaism; Judaism itself implies Christianity.

2. The Sacrifices of the Church

Heb. 13:15–16 draws the other implication relevant to our discussion, which is that the sacrifice and priesthood of Christ imply that believers can and should offer spiritual sacrifices. These verses come in a context of the sacrifice of Christ again (Heb. 13:10–13), and the writer goes on from that point to argue that Christians should offer various things which he calls sacrifices, namely (here) praise to God in words, and doing good and sharing what you have (presumably with other Christians in the first instance).[4] Gunton aptly observes:[5]

> The Sacrifice [*sc.* the death of Christ] is the basis and enabler of sacrifices: yet what is offered is not Christ, but that which he came to realize, the gift to God in worship and life of the perfected creation.

By contrast with Christ's offering, which was bloody, the sacrifices which believers offer are unbloody: they consist in aspects of Christian living.[6] Instead of the sphere of the sacred being limited to the temple, the whole of life is sacralized, and hence sacrifice can be offered in the lifestyle of the believer. Further, the kind of sacrifice is worthy of note, that it is a 'sacrifice of praise' (v.15), rather than an expiatory sacrifice, again by contrast with the death of Christ. In the NT by far the commonest model of sacrifice used of believers' sacrifices is the thank-offering,[7] since the death of Christ forms the final and complete expiatory sacrifice, as Hebrews argues most powerfully by its use of *hapax* ('once, once for all') of the death of Christ (Heb. 9:26, 28).

Looking more widely in the NT, it is interesting (and probably significant) that sacrificial language about activities in the life of the believer and the Christian church does not speak of activities which usually merit that terminology today, which suggests how far our use of sacrificial language has moved from that of the Bible. The following activities occur in the context of sacrificial or priestly language:[8]

Praise of God is described in these terms in 1 Pet. 2:9 ('a royal priesthood . . . that you may declare the wonderful deeds of him who called you out of darkness into his marvellous light') and Heb. 13:15 ('let us offer up a sacrifice of praise to God, that is, the fruit of lips that acknowledge his name'). Indeed, the context in 1 Peter is of Christians who are 'living stones . . . built into a spiritual house, to be a holy priesthood, to offer spiritual sacrifices' (2:5), accumulating language redolent with the themes of temple, sacrifice and priesthood.[9]

It is no surprise that praise is described in sacrificial language in the NT, since some of the OT sacrifices were principally praise and thanks sacrifices (e.g. the peace offering in Lv. 7:11–18; the use of a song in Ps. 69:30–31). The earliest Christians, who were predominantly Jews, would carry over the models of sacrifice they knew into their new Christian context.

Witness is also described in sacrificial terms, both in 1 Pet. 2:9 (which I take to be a deliberate ambiguity by Peter encompassing both speaking of God in praise in the congregation and speaking of him to outsiders, cf. Ps. 107:22[10]), and also in Rom. 15:16. Paul here describes his ministry of evangelism as 'a priestly minister (*leitourgon*) of Christ Jesus to the Gentiles in the priestly service of the gospel of God, so that the offering of the Gentiles may be acceptable.'[11] Cranfield argues that 'priestly minister' is the wrong translation here, and prefers simply 'minister'. However, the context of sacrificial language is clear,[12] with the clustering of sacrificial language ('priestly service' [*hierourgounta*], 'offering' [*prosphora*], 'acceptable' [*euprosdektos*] and 'sanctified' [*hēgiasmenē*]). Further, *leitourgos* and its word-group are used in the LXX of *priestly* service of God, as opposed to the service offered by the whole people of Israel (e.g. 2 Ch. 11:14; Joel 2:17; Ezk. 45:4).[13] This suggests that is it appropriate, *pace* Cranfield, to translate 'priestly minister' here.[14] Paul therefore sees his work of evangelism amongst the Gentiles in terms which can be described as sacrificial language.

Prayer is also spoken of in the context of sacrificial language in Rev. 5:8; 8:3, where prayer is compared to incense smoke rising to the throne of God, using the language of OT sacrifices (e.g. Ex. 30:1–6). This may also link into the use of sacrificial language in Ps. 51:17 of the broken and contrite heart, where repentance may be seen as a specific form of prayer.

Also worthy of note in this context is the use of the language of 'drawing near' in Hebrews (*proserchomai*, e.g. 4:16; 7:25; 10:22; 11:6; 12:18–24), appropriating terminology used of the (Jewish) priest approaching the altar to offer sacrifice.[15] The recipients of Hebrews were being encouraged by the writer to see that they had genuine access to the presence of God, access which had previously been limited to the priesthood. Therefore they could 'draw near . . . in full assurance of faith' (Heb. 10:22).

Giving is described in these terms also in Phil. 2:17, where Paul speaks of himself as being 'poured out as a libation upon the sacrificial offering of your faith'. What exactly is his point here? The commentators divide over whether the genitive 'of your faith' (*tēs pisteōs hymōn*) should be taken as subjective ('the sacrifice offered by your faith') or as a genitive of apposition ('the sacrifice which consists of your faith'). In the context of Philippians, it seems more likely to be a subjective genitive, since sacrificial language is used of their gift to Paul in 4:18.[16] Further, the carrying of their gift by Epaphroditus is described using the same terminology (Phil. 2:25). Thus giving is the subject in 2:17, as it is in 2:25 and 4:18.[17]

Heb. 13:16 uses similar language of giving, since it describes sharing what you have as a sacrifice (*thysia*), along with doing good. Tillard describes this as, 'it is a matter of something other than ritual cult: it concerns *a cult which is Christian living itself*.'[18]

Laying down one's life for the gospel is also a sacrificial activity—Phil. 2:17 sees Paul writing in sacrificial terms of the possibility of his own death: 'but even if I am poured out upon the sacrifice and offering of your faith' (*alla ei kai spendomai epi tē thysia kai leitourgia tēs pisteōs hymōn*). He seems to be alluding to the drink offering which was poured out along with the burnt offering (Nu. 15:3–10), as a minor offering alongside the major atoning offering. It is reading too much into the text to see Paul suggesting that his own death, whilst it may be seen in sacrificial terms, is but a minor accompaniment to the major atoning sacrifice of the death of Christ, for here his death is an accompaniment to the sacrifice *of the Philippians' faith*, i.e. their giving to Paul. Similar sacrificial language in connection with the death of a Christian is used in 2 Tim. 4:6 and perhaps Rev. 6:9, where the souls of the martyrs are under the altar.

The consecration of the life to God's will is the use of sacrificial language which underlies all these other uses. Instead of part of life being the sphere of the sacred, the whole of life becomes sacred for the believer. Hence in Rom. 12:1 the offering of the bodies of Christians is described both as 'a living sacrifice' and as 'spiritual worship'. The sphere of worship for the Christian is not primarily the congregation, but the world in which Christ is to be served. Marshall has argued that the worship vocabulary of the NT is used of this service of God in the whole of life and not of (as we would say) congregational worship.[19] This reinforces the point here, which is the same as that noted earlier from Tillard, that the cult in the NT is *Christian living itself*, and not any smaller segment of the Christian life. This is how 1 Pet. 2:5,9 should be understood, where holiness of life marks the priestly people of the church, a holiness that is not merely an 'in church' thing.

In summary, sacrificial language and terminology is used by the NT of a variety of activities, and this points to the central affirmation of the NT, that because of the sacrifice of Christ the whole of life becomes sacralized for the believer. Hence sacrificial language can be used of all kinds of activities.[20]

This is brought into effect by the Spirit. In an interesting allusion to sacrifice in speaking of 'We . . . who have the *firstfruits* of the Spirit' (Rom. 8:23), Paul points to the Spirit as the one who enables Christians to appropriate the access to God achieved by the death of Christ (vv.26–27) and therefore to offer the sacrifices of Christian living (vv.9–17).[21]

The other point worthy of note is that the kind of sacrifice envisaged is never an atoning sacrifice, but always a sacrifice of praise and thanksgiving. Cranmer's later distinction holds true for the NT period:[22]

One kind of sacrifice there is which is called a propitiatory or merciful sacrifice, that is to say, such a sacrifice as pacifieth God's wrath and indignation, and obtaineth mercy and forgiveness for all our sins . . .

And although in the OT there were certain sacrifices called by that name, yet in very deed there is but one such sacrifice whereby our sins be pardoned . . . which is the death of the Son of God our Lord Jesus Christ; nor ever was any other sacrifice propitiatory at any time, nor never shall be.

This is the honour of this our priest wherein he admitted neither partner nor successor . . .

Another kind of sacrifice there is, which doth not reconcile us to God, but is made of them that be reconciled by Christ . . . to show ourselves thankful to him; and therefore they be called sacrifices of laud, praise and thanksgiving.

The first kind of sacrifice Christ offered to God for us; the second kind we ourselves offer to God by Christ.

Whilst certain of the functions of the OT priesthood are carried over into the NT material on the priesthood of the church, one function not given a specifically *priestly* label in the NT is teaching, which was, under the old covenant, an important function of the priesthood (e.g. Mal. 2:6–7; Jdg. 18:3–6; 1 Sa. 14:36–42; Dt. 33:8–10). This is significant for our discussion of priesthood and the leaders of the Christian community.

3. The Priesthoods of Christ, the Christian and the Church

This leads naturally to the discussion of the form of priesthood appropriate to the church in the NT. Only two books of the NT use the word 'priest' of Christians or the church, 1 Peter and Revelation. The two books use the image in slightly different ways, and by this give a both/and answer to the question of whether the NT teaches the priesthood of all believers (i.e. a corporate form of priesthood) or the priesthood of *every* believer (i.e. individual priesthood).

1 Pet. 2:5, 9 uses the corporate picture of priesthood for the church, and transfers the titles of Israel to the Christian church. Thus, whilst Israel as a whole was a priesthood (Ex. 19:6; Is. 61:6), the church as a body now takes on that priestly character, and its priesthood is realized by the offering of spiritual sacrifices (v.5). The offering of sacrifice springs from the priestliness of the church:[23] the church is being built into a spiritual house (*eis hierateuma hagion anenegkai pneumatikas thysias*). Further, v.9 spells out the implications of the priestliness of the church (which is again presented in corporate terms: 'a royal priesthood') in terms very similar to Heb. 13:15, using a phrase which may well carry both senses of declaring the deeds of God—in praise and also in evangelism: 'proclaim the mighty deeds'.

Revelation uses the term 'priests' of the church in three places (1:6; 5:10; 20:6), and the very use of it in this form (rather than the corporate form, 'priesthood') implies that John saw every believer individually as a priest. Thus in 1:6 believers are 'priests to God', in 5:10 believers are made 'priests serving our God', and in 20:6 those who share in the first resurrection are described as 'priests of God and of Christ'. Believers are 'priests' here, and there is no exclusion of some believers as priests (and therefore others as not): it is a metaphor used to describe Christians without discrimination.

Revelation does not seem to draw implications from the priestliness of believers as such. In two places it couples the description of believers as 'priests' with the description of them as 'a kingdom' (1:6; 5:10) and in two places draws the implication of reigning (5:10; 20:6), but this seems more appropriate to the image of kingship than of priesthood. Thus believers corporately form a priesthood, and individually may be described as priests.

What, then, of the relationship of Christ's priesthood to that of the believer and the church? The NT authors never draw this relationship out explicitly, but we may suggest two propositions, which go some way towards defining this relationship.

First, because Christ is a priest, believers can offer sacrifice. This is the thrust of Hebrews' discussion of priesthood, especially in 13:10–16. Because Christ has once and for all dealt with sin, believers have access to the presence of God and therefore can approach the throne of grace with confidence (4:14–16; 10:19–25), and this must imply a priestliness of the Christian, for access to God is one central factor to priestliness in the OT.[24]

Second, because of the sacrifice of Christ, believers are constituted as priests, and they exercise that priesthood in offering spiritual sacrifices. This is the thrust of 1 Pet. 2:4–10. It is as people come to Christ, the living stone which people rejected and God valued differently, that they are built into the new temple and become part of the royal and holy priesthood which is to offer spiritual sacrifices through Jesus Christ. Similarly in Rev. 1:5–6, believers are made priests because of Christ's work of freeing them from their sins by his blood, by his priestly sacrificial work. The same thought is present in Rev. 5:9–10. The work of Epaphroditus, as we have noted above, is described in a similar, sacrificial manner by Paul (Phil. 2:25).

Thus the two angles from which the NT authors come at the issue never quite answer our contemporary question in the form we have posed it, but they seem in combination to be saying that the church's priesthood is a *dependent* priesthood, in that it is dependent upon both the sacrifice and priesthood of Christ for its initiation and continuance. It is fundamentally different from the OT form of priesthood, because sin has been once and for all dealt with in the death of Christ, and because Christ the priest of the new covenant lives for ever (Heb. 9:11–15; 7:23–28).

II.   THE EUCHARIST AND CHRIST'S SELF-OFFERING SACRIFICE

This subject is a potential minefield, and we must therefore be clear what we are attempting. We shall look purely at the question of whether there are NT grounds for the view that the eucharist should be seen as in some sense a sacrifice and, if so, what kind of sacrifice.[25] This involves the issue of the use of sacrificial language about the eucharist (which is more obviously present in the Fathers than the NT) and the relation of the Last Supper (assuming it to be a Passover[26]) to our view of the eucharist in this connection.

What biblical reasons are offered for seeing the eucharist as in some sense a sacrifice? On the whole there are three grounds presented by the various authors.

1. Malachi 1:11 and the Eucharist

First, the Fathers saw the eucharist as the fulfilment of Mal. 1:11 ('in every place incense and pure offerings will be brought to my name'), with its prophecy of world-wide sacrifice. This is the passage most frequently quoted in the first three centuries when the Fathers want to find a biblical passage to discuss the eucharist in sacrificial terms.[27]

In response, it needs to be noted that this does not prove all that is sometimes suggested, since the passage in Malachi is discussing the *minhâ* or meal offering, which was not expiatory, and which was unbloody. Thus Justin comments:[28]

> The offering of fine flour, which was ordered to be offered on behalf of those who were being cleansed from leprosy, was a type of the bread of the eucharist. For Jesus Christ our Lord ordered us to do this in remembrance of the suffering which he suffered on behalf of those who are being purged in soul from all iniquity.

It is noteworthy that it is universally true in the early period that this is the understanding of the eucharist adopted by the Fathers when considering it as a sacrifice: they relate it to Mal. 1:11 and draw conclusions about it as a *thanksgiving* sacrifice, not an expiatory sacrifice. And in some cases (e.g. Did. 14:1–2) the offering made in the eucharist is that of the Christian's heart and conscience.[29] Even in some of Justin's writing the verb *prospherō* is used of the offering of the bread and wine to the celebrant and not to God.[30]

The further question, of whether the Fathers were correct to understand the verse in these terms, must be answered with an unambiguous 'No', since the verse (viewed from a Christian perspective) relates rather to the acceptability of the Gentiles through the sacrifice of Christ. Thus Baldwin rightly relates it to Eph. 2:11–22 and similar passages:[31]

> Thus the inadequacies of the sacrificial system, which had so troubled the prophets, were seen by Malachi as about to be transcended, as indeed they were in the sacrifice of Jesus Christ. Through this sacrifice those who were strangers to the covenants of promise would be reconciled to God (Eph. 2:11–22).[32]

2. Sacrifice in the Ancient World and the Eucharist

The second biblical argument put forward for seeing the eucharist as
sacrificial is that of G. D. Kilpatrick in his *The Eucharist in Bible and
Liturgy*.[33] His argument hinges on his view of sacrifice in the ancient
world, which he claims is to do with release of life and power, following a
hint in Oesterley.[34]

Kilpatrick argues that this explanation of sacrifice explains other types
of sacrifice, and notes the importance of blood in this context (e.g. Dt.
22:20–25; Ex. chaps. 12, 29 and 24:5–8), in particular that blood was
reserved for God alone.[35] Then he discusses a number of biblical
examples where life given up in sacrifice seems to release life and power
for other purposes.

He first considers 2 Kings 3,[36] and argues that the sacrifice of the king's
son on the city wall was to release life and power to strengthen the wall.
He therefore translates v.27, 'And there was great wrath upon Israel and
they departed from him and returned to their own land.'

He sees Exodus 12 as providing a similar example,[37] where the blood on
the doorposts at the exodus was to prevent the entry of the destroyer who
(he postulates) in the original version of the story 'did his rounds alone'.
Thus the doorway was reinforced by the blood of sacrifice to prevent his
entry.

A third example he cites is Numbers 22–24,[38] where Balaam asks Balak
to offer sacrifice on seven altars when Balak wants Balaam to curse Israel
(23:1–7). Kilpatrick comments, 'We may infer that they [*sc.* the
sacrifices] are offered to reinforce the curse or the blessing with the life
and strength so released.'[39]

He discusses other examples,[40] notably Korah's rebellion (Nu. 16), and
notes that the offering of incense there led to the power released breaking
loose and destroying those who burned it (vv.35–36). King Uzziah (2 Ch.
26) suffered similarly by being struck with a serious skin disease when he
attempted to burn incense in the temple. Kilpatrick concludes:[41]

> the world was divided into two, the place and conditions in which superhuman
> power could be safely released in sacrifice, and the rest of the world and the
> conditions in which it could not. The former was holy and the latter profane.

When he applies this line of thinking to the eucharist, he comes to
interesting conclusions about its sacrificial nature. In particular, he
argues that to see the Last Supper as a Passover (which he sees Mark as
doing) indicates that it was sacrificial (see especially Mk. 14:12).

On turning to the evidence of 1 Cor. 11:27–34,[42] he throws light on the
puzzling v.30 by arguing that the parallel situations to those who are ill
and those who have died are precisely King Uzziah in 2 Chronicles 26 and
Korah in Numbers 16.[43] This may be a suggestive insight as to the way
Paul's mind works.

He then argues that the phrase *mē diakrinōn to sōma* in v.29 should be understood as meaning 'not *separating* the body', and that 'the body' here means the eucharistic bread. Thus 'not separating the body' means to treat it as profane, rather than holy. He concludes from this line of exegesis that Paul saw the eucharist as a sacrifice.

Turning to Jesus himself, he suggests that the common ground between Mk. 14:24 and 1 Cor. 11:25 is the references to covenant and blood.[44] Since the Sinai covenant sacrifice was made with blood, and Jesus in the Last Supper is setting up his covenant sacrifice for his people, this suggests that Jesus did intend the Last Supper to be viewed as sacrificial.

Having argued that sacrifice involves the release of power, Kilpatrick must go on to show the effect of this release of power in the eucharist. He argues from Mt. 26:28 that one effect is forgiveness, evidenced by the phrase 'for the remission of sins'. He further cites Jn. 6:48–71, and argues that v.54 points to the eucharist as giving eternal life. He traces the thinking of the Fathers on this, notably Ignatius (*Eph.* 20:2), who describes the eucharistic elements as 'medicine of immortality' (*pharmakon athanasias*).[45]

Much could be said in response to Kilpatrick's discussion, but we make only a few observations.

First, Kilpatrick seems to have misunderstood the OT material he discusses, since he fails to distinguish pagan forms of sacrifice from those forms of sacrifice which were integral to the religion of Israel. None of the examples of sacrifice he cites is stated in the text to be approved by God, either explicitly or implicitly, and most are said to meet with God's disapproval. To argue from a view of sacrifice that is found only in pagan or semi-pagan contexts to seeing the eucharist as sacrificial in a similar manner must be questionable, to say the least.

Second, Kilpatrick makes the classic mistake with the accounts of the Last Supper of confusing the thing signified with the sign itself. It is beyond dispute that the bread and wine of the Last Supper speak of the sacrificial death of Christ on the cross. But *the thing signified* (the death of Christ) being sacrificial does not mean that *the sign itself* is sacrificial. The strongest statement that could be made is that of Aulén:[46]

> The eucharist of the Last Supper was not in itself a sacrifice, but it has nevertheless a sacrificial character, because everything is concentrated around that final, self-giving sacrifice which immediately followed.

In other words, the Last Supper is not itself a sacrifice, but points to a sacrifice.

Third, Kilpatrick misunderstands the nature of the Passover. Two lines of approach to this topic show this. The first is to notice that in the Passover the properly sacrificial act was the pouring out of the blood of the victim at the base of the altar, and this was performed by the priest in the temple. The meal in the home was presided over by the father of the house, and was not regarded as sacrificial. Tillard explains well: 'The meal was a participation, in thanksgiving and hope, in the redemptive power of the commemorated event, by the virtue of the eating of the lamb, the bitter herbs and the unleavened bread.'[47] We shall return to this in discussing the question of priesthood and ministry below.

Moreover, as Green notes, the Passover itself in its annual celebration was not regarded as an atoning sacrifice. Rather it was a memorial of the first Passover, which was an atoning sacrifice. Green presses the point home by going on to note that it is with the original redemptive Passover that Jesus compares his death, and thus concludes that 'Like the Passover, the Holy Communion is the memorial of an atoning sacrifice, but is not itself an expiatory offering.'[48] Thus the analogy with the Passover argues against the position Kilpatrick seeks to establish.

Kilpatrick's position appears to have been arrived at on grounds other than biblical ones, and he has then sought to find support for that view in Scripture by eisegesis. The Fathers obviously give this kind of support, since all the impetus towards the eucharist being seen as a sacrifice happens in the Patristic period.

3. Pleading the Sacrifice?

The third set of biblical arguments put forward for seeing the eucharist as in some sense a sacrifice is expressed by Hebert:[49]

> The true celebrant [*sc.* in the eucharist] is Christ the high priest, and the Christian people are assembled as members of his Body to present before God his sacrifice, and to be themselves offered up in sacrifice through their union with him.

Again, Pittenger writes:[50]

> . . . the eucharist as sacrifice is not a substitute for the perfect sacrifice of Calvary, as if there were anything lacking in the utter completeness of that act of Christ's. It is not a substitute for, or a sacrifice in addition to, Calvary; it is, rather, an entrance into and a pleading of 'the merits' of that sacrifice, made possible because the Church is the mystical Body of the Lord and thereby can make that sacrifice its own. The Church is enabled to make its sacrificial action identical with the once-for-all event on Calvary because it is the same Christ who offered himself on Calvary, and who gives himself in his Body the Church . . . The eucharist is a sacrifice because it is that 'offering of Christ once made', herein pleaded and offered to the Father, set between 'our sins and their reward'.

Or again, Moberly writes:[51]

> Through this symbolic enactment . . . she [*sc.* the church] in her Eucharistic worship on earth is identified with his sacrificial self-oblation to the Father; she

is transfigured up into the scene of the unceasing commemoration of his sacrifice in heaven; or the scene of his eternal offering in heaven is translated down to, and presented, and realized in the worship on earth.

The central thought in each of these writers is that the sacrifice of the cross is in some sense continually being offered, or that we in the eucharist 'plead' the sacrifice of the cross, or that Christ himself in heaven is now pleading his sacrifice. Thus the direction of the eucharist ceases to be from God to people, but the eucharist becomes an offering by people to God. This is often linked with use of the word variously translated as 'remembrance' or 'memorial' (*anamnēsis*), especially following the work of Dix.[52]

On *anamnēsis*, Buchanan, Gregg and Jeremias between them have done enough to show that it cannot mean 'memorial' in the sense of a recalling of an event from the past into the present.[53] The 'real presence', if we may use that term, in the Passover celebration is the presence of the participants in the past, rather than the hauling of the past event into the present. Thus the participants were to say, 'This the Eternal did *for me* when *I* went forth from Egypt.'[54]

In arguing for a 'pleading' view, Heb. 7:25 and Rom. 8:34 are the NT passages most commonly used as the basis of the idea that Jesus pleads his sacrifice now before the Father: 'he always lives to make intercession for us' and 'Christ Jesus . . . who indeed intercedes for us'. Sykes explains:[55]

> The fact that, as it appears, Christ *continually* intercedes with his blood in the presence of God on behalf of sinners (Heb. 9:24) provides the essential key to the readiness of the early church to speak of the eucharistic worship of the church as a sacrifice. The memorial of the 'new covenant in my blood' (1 Cor. 11:25) is the rehearsal of the foundation act of the new age, the sacrifice of Christ. If that sacrifice is being eternally pleaded on behalf of sinners by the exalted Christ in the heavens, it is but a short step to say that the prayer of the Christian body at the eucharist joined with that of Christ, its head, is itself the offering of a sacrifice.

But the verb *entygchanō* (translated 'make intercession') has a quite different meaning from the claimed sense of 'pleading', since it means that Christ is *around* in heaven on our behalf, rather than that he is trying to persuade the Father to accept us because of his death. His presence is his plea. Thus Calvin comments on Rom. 8:34:[56]

> For he [*sc.* Christ] is not to be thought to beseech his Father humbly upon his knees, with his hands stretched out; but because he appeareth still with his death and resurrection, *which are instead of an eternal intercession* and have the efficacy of lively prayer, that they may reconcile the Father to us, and make him entreatable, he is worthily said to make intercession for us.

Likewise, Westcott:[57]

The modern conception of Christ pleading in heaven His Passion, 'offering His Blood', on behalf of men, has no foundation in the Epistle [*sc.* to the Hebrews]. His glorified humanity is the eternal pledge of the absolute efficacy of His accomplished work. He pleads, as older writers truly expressed the thought, by His Presence on the Father's throne.

Indeed, as W. Stott has shown,[58] the thinking of Hebrews is incompatible with the idea of our Lord presently offering his blood or himself to God. Heb. 9:24 is clear that there is no altar in heaven. The context of 7:25 is 7:26–28, where the implication of the death of Christ, that he has no further need to offer sacrifices, eliminates the need for any re-presentation of the sacrifice of Calvary. This was perceived in the Fathers by Chrysostom, who wrote on Heb. 13:8, 'Do not think because you have heard Jesus is a priest, that he is always offering sacrifice. He offered sacrifice once and for all and thenceforward he sat down.'[59]

Therefore, any conception of a 're-presentation' or 'offering' or 'pleading' of the sacrifice once offered (and note the use of 'once and for all' in Hebrews in this context!) by Christ has no biblical foundation. This view of the eucharist cannot be said to be biblically defensible.

4. Towards a Biblical Understanding of the Eucharist

What should we say as to a correct biblical understanding of the relation of the eucharist to the sacrifice of the cross? J.R.W. Stott offers five suggestive propositions,[60] which we will close this section of the paper by discussing briefly.

First, we remember Christ's sacrificial death. He said, 'Do this in remembrance of me' (1 Cor. 11:24–25), and whatever else the meaning of *anamnēsis*, it certainly involves straightforward thinking on that past event, recalling it to mind. This is aided by the dramatic actions with the bread and wine, which focus the minds of those present upon the events of the cross.

Second, we partake of its benefits. Thus Paul writes, 'Is not the cup of thanksgiving for which we give thanks a *participation* in the blood of Christ? And is not the bread which we break a *participation* in the body of Christ?' (1 Cor. 10:16). Thus in the Lord's Supper the church of God feeds spiritually on the 'benefits of his passion', and shares together in Christ.

Third, we proclaim his sacrifice: 'For as often as you eat this bread and drink this cup, you proclaim the Lord's death' (1 Cor. 11:26). Therefore the eucharist points back and speaks of the Lord's death. It is sometimes claimed that the verb *katangellō* used here can mean 'proclaim to God', almost 'present as a sacrifice before God', but in every other NT use of the word it refers to proclamation to people, not to God. Its most frequent use is of proclaiming 'the word' or 'the gospel' or 'Christ'.[61] Thus the claim has no biblical foundation.

It is for this reason that evangelicals have classically understood the need for preaching in the context of the eucharist, for the 'proclamation' made by the bread and wine is dumb without explanatory words. Obviously these are partly provided by the repetition of the words of institution, but the analogy with the Passover Haggadah suggests that the proclamation would be by way of explanation of the significance of the events to which the sign points (cf. Ex. 13:7–8).

Fourth, we attribute our unity to Christ's sacrifice. This Stott draws from the fact that in the NT the eucharist is never intended to be celebrated solo, but always in fellowship with other believers (cf. 1 Cor. 11:20, 33). This Paul makes explicit in writing, 'Because there is one loaf, we who are many are one body, for we all partake of the one loaf' (1 Cor. 10:17). Thus the eucharist points the church afresh to its unity, which is solely due to the death of Christ and which breaks down human dividing walls (cf. Eph. 2:11–22), creating a new multi-racial, multi-cultural society.

Fifth, we give thanks for the sacrifice of Christ, and in doing so offer our lives up to his service. Stott here refers to Rom. 12:1, which is not linked to any discussion of the eucharist, and he is at his most questionable here. Whilst it is true that the NT does argue from the sacrifice of Christ to the servant lives of believers in the service of God (e.g. 1 Pet. 2:21), this link is nowhere made in the context of discussing the eucharist.

This is not necessarily to question the appropriateness of a prayer of response after the reception of the eucharistic elements,[62] for in refocusing upon the cross in the eucharist it is surely right to be reminded of the implications of the cross for the Christian life in giving ourselves up to Christ's service. However, we simply observe that this is a connection never made explicitly in the NT witness about the eucharist.

III.   CHRISTIAN LEADERSHIP AND PRIESTHOOD

It has long been noticed that the NT nowhere uses the word 'priest' to describe leaders in the Christian community, and that this term is applied (in a Christian context) only to Christ himself and to the whole church, as we have discussed above.

Why, then, has part of the Christian church persisted in the use of this category to describe its ordained leaders? The principal answer to this comes from the Patristic period, and can be traced through the development of a sacrificial view of the eucharist to the idea that the person who presides at the eucharist must in some sense be priestly. This comes to full flower in Cyprian in the third century.[63] However, the Anglican Reformers were clear that their retention of the term 'priest' was, first, because of its antiquity as a title for elders in the church, and, second, because of the etymological argument that the English word 'priest' is properly derived from *presbyteros* (='elder') and not from *hiereus*

(='sacrificing priest'). Thus Hooker defends the use of the term along precisely these lines.[64]

In closing, we shall briefly examine why the vocabulary of priesthood was absent from the NT discussions of the elder or other leaders. Four important reasons suggest themselves.

First, the continuation of Jewish priestly sacrifices, at least until AD 70, must have been one factor in the emerging Christian movement's refusal to use the vocabulary of priesthood and sacrifice of their ministers. Hodge acutely observes:[65]

> Every appropriate title of honour is lavished upon them. They are called the bishops of souls, pastors, teachers, rulers, governors, the servants or ministers of God; stewards of the divine mysteries; watchmen, heralds, but never priests. As the sacred writers were Jews, to whom nothing was more familiar than the word priest, whose ministers of religion were constantly so denominated, the fact that they never once use the word, or any of its cognates, in reference to ministers of the gospel, whether apostles, presbyters, or evangelists, is little less than miraculous. It is one of those cases where the silence of Scripture speaks volumes.

This reflects the emphasis of Hebrews, that the OT sacrificial system found its fulfilment in the death of Christ. Lightfoot expresses this well:[66]

> All former priesthoods had borne witness to the necessity of a human mediator, and this sentiment had its satisfaction in the Person and Office of the Son of Man. All past sacrifices had proclaimed the need of an atoning death, and had their antitype, their realisation, their annulment, in the cross of Christ.

Further, the first Christians really do seem to have grasped that the whole of life is sacralized by the death of Christ, and therefore the vocabulary of sacrifice is rarely applied in the NT to what Christians do when they meet together. The NT authors' use of this terminology is to do with serving God in the world, as we have seen above in discussing the application of the vocabulary of sacrifice to the Christian life.

Second, because the early Christians saw the death of Christ as the fulfilment of the OT sacrificial system, they saw the Christian assembly (*ekklēsia*) as analogous to the synagogue, rather than the temple. This has been argued with respect to Christian forms of worship, for example, but we should here note its implication for the title applied to the leaders of the congregation. In the synagogue the leader was known as an 'elder' (the Greek word would be *presbyteros*), and this is suggestive for the early Christians' use of *presbyteros* as the commonest term for their leaders in the local setting.

An interesting sidelight on this is the modern Roman Catholic tendency to use 'presbyter' as the term for their ordained ministers, rather than 'priest'. Robert Taft, a Roman Catholic liturgical scholar, observes, 'I was made a priest at my baptism: I was made a presbyter at my ordination.'[67] In this Taft displays a NT understanding which it is difficult to fault.

Third, Tillard's analogy with the Passover (discussed above) has interesting implications for a view of the eucharist, and in particular for presidency at the eucharist. He points out that the meal of the lamb which had been offered in the temple, eaten in the home, was presided over by the father of the family, and that the priestly act was antecedent to the meal—it took place (strictly) at the first Passover in Egypt or (more loosely) in the temple when the priest poured out the victim's blood at the base of the altar.

Tillard goes on to argue that the priestly function in the eucharist had already been performed in the historical event of the cross, and thus when Christians met to celebrate the eucharist, they considered that act to be analogous to the Passover meal in the home, not to the original Passover sacrifice in the day of Moses, nor to the Passover sacrifice at the temple. This meant (Tillard claims) that they were not inclined to use priestly terminology of the one presiding at the eucharistic meal. He also notes that this point is strengthened if the eucharist is to be linked to a 'fraternity' banquet and not to a Passover.[68]

Finally, we observe that in any case the early Christian communities appear not to have been greatly concerned about who presided at the eucharist. If the scholarly consensus about 'the breaking of bread' being the eucharist is correct,[69] we may note that Acts 2:46 implies a multiplicity of eucharists and therefore (unless the apostles rushed from house to house saying eucharistic prayers!) a multiplicity of presidents. It is even questionable whether our modern conception of 'presidency' would have been recognized by the earliest Christians, with the strong emphasis they had on the community 'celebrating' the eucharist (e.g. in 1 Cor. 10–11, where all the verbs for the celebration of the eucharist are plural, with the sole exception of the call to individual self-examination in 11:27–29).

Beckwith claims, in common with much other scholarship, that the NT is silent on the question of who is to officiate at the eucharist.[70] Horvath,[71] reacting to *Baptism, Eucharist and Ministry*'s claim that this is the case,[72] offers three verses in which he believes Paul is presented as presiding at a eucharistic celebration (Acts 20:7–15; 27:35; 1 Cor. 10:16).

The first seems uncontroversial. The second is at least arguable, since it pictures Paul 'breaking bread' after the shipwreck, having urged his companions to eat. Bruce, whom we have noticed sees Acts 2:46 as a clear reference to eucharistic thanksgivings, is ambivalent, suggesting that the breaking of bread here might have had a different significance for the non-Christian sailors than it had for Paul and his Christian companions, who would have treated it as a eucharistic thanksgiving.[73] However, Marshall correctly observes that Paul's actions do not go beyond normal Jewish practice, in blessing God for the food to be eaten.[74]

Horvath's third claimed instance of Paul presiding (1 Cor. 10:16) seems odd, for he claims that Paul, in speaking of 'the bread that *we* break', was describing *himself* presiding, presumably *in absentia*. There seems to be no justification in the text for this; it seems more natural to see the use of 'we' as 'we Christians' than as 'we apostles' or 'we elders'. This is more likely in the light both of the contrast in 1 Corinthains 10 with pagan table fellowship, and also of the emphasis in 1 Corinthians 11 on the Christian community celebrating the eucharist together.

Overall, Horvath's case fails to convince. He can produce only one firm example, which is simply an example of practice in one instance, with no explicit or implicit statement as to whether this practice was normative. Certainly, the events of the rest of the evening were not normative (Acts 20:9–12)! The consensus of scholarship, that the NT makes no pronouncements on who should be the 'president' at eucharistic celebrations (if there was such a person recognizable at all), seems secure.

Thus until the development of the later period, in which presidency at the eucharist did become important, and therefore priestly vocabulary was attached to the one who presided, priestly language was simply irrelevant to the eucharist.

These four points together add up to the thought that the early Christians were wise to avoid the application of priestly terminology to their leaders, because they feared the loss of the centrality of the priestly act of Christ on the cross. Church history suggests that we today might be wise to heed them.

NOTES

1. I acknowledge the kind support and encouragement of the Church Pastoral-Aid Society in the preparation of this paper, the bulk of which was completed whilst I was a member of CPAS staff.
2. C.F.D. Moule, 'Sanctuary and Sacrifice in the Church of the New Testament' in *JTS* 1 (1950) 29–41.
3. Moule, 'Sanctuary', 37.
4. So Moule, 'Sanctuary', 38.
5. C. Gunton, 'The Sacrifice and the Sacrifices: From Metaphor to Transcendental?', in R.J. Feenstra & C. Plantinga (eds.), *Trinity, Incarnation, and Atonement: Philosophical and Theological Essays* (Library of Religious Philosophy, vol. 1) (Notre Dame: University of Notre Dame Press, 1989) 225.
6. So R.J. Daly, SJ, 'The New Testament Concept of Christian Sacrificial Activity' in *BTB* 8 (1978) 99–107.
7. For discussion of the various forms of sacrifice found in the OT, see F.M. Young, 'New Wine in Old Wineskins, XIV: Sacrifice' in *Exp Tim* LXXXVI (1974-75) 305-309; R.P. Shedd, 'Worship in the New Testament Church' in D.A. Carson (ed.), *The Church in the Bible and the World* (Exeter/Grand Rapids: Paternoster/Baker, 1987) 136–137.
8. Cf. R.T. Beckwith, *Priesthood and Sacraments* (Abingdon: Marcham Manor Press, 1964) 16; idem, 'The Relation between Christ's Sacrifice and Priesthood and those of the Church: An Attempt at a Summary Statement', *Churchman* 103 (1989) 232.
9. Daly, 'New Testament Concept', 103–104.

10. D.G. Peterson, *Engaging with God: A Biblical Theology of Worship* (Leicester: Apollos, 1992) 268–269 notes the wider context of 1 Peter, especially 3:15, in support of this point. He also sees the same *double entendre* in *homologountōn* (translated 'confess' in NRSV) in Heb. 13:15, comparing the use in Mt. 10:32; Jn. 9:22; 12:42, where it is is used of 'confessing' to 'outsiders' (ibid. 246, 259, n.41).

11. See C.E.B. Cranfield, *Romans*, vol.II (ICC) (Edinburgh: T. & T. Clark, 1979) 754ff. for a thorough discussion in which he argues that Paul's ministry here is comparable to that of the OT Levite, not the priest, principally from the use of the term *leitourgos* in the LXX and the context of *christou iēsou*. For the contrary view, see Daly, 'New Testament Concept', 102–103.

12. As Cranfield acknowledges, *Romans* II, 755.

13. Peterson, *Engaging with God* 150.

14. In agreement with J.D.G. Dunn, *Romans 9–16* (WBC 38B) (Dallas: Word, 1988) 859–860 ('the cultic language of the following clauses puts this almost beyond dispute'); and J.A. Fitzmyer, *Romans* (AB 33) (New York: Doubleday, 1993) 711–712.

15. See discussion in J.M. Scholer, *Proleptic Priests* (JSNTS 49) (Sheffield: JSOT Press, 1991) chap. 3. Peterson, *Engaging with God* 238–239, refers to LXX usage, which is used of priestly ministry in offering sacrifices, e.g. Lv. 21:17, 21; 22:3.

16. G.B. Caird, *Paul's Letters from Prison* (New Clarendon Bible) (Oxford: Clarendon Press, 1976) 127.

17. Also worth noticing is 2 Cor. 9:12, where giving is also described using *leitourgia*. See Shedd, 'Worship', 147–148.

18. J.M.R. Tillard, *What Priesthood Has the Ministry?* (Grove Ministry & Worship Booklet 13) (Bramcote: Grove Books, 1973, 12) (italics mine).

19. I.H. Marshall, 'How Far Did the Early Christians Worship God?', *Churchman* 99 (1985) 216–229; cf. the discussion of Acts 13:2 in Peterson, *Engaging with God* 150–151.

20. Young, 'New Wine', 307 points out that the early Christians were not the only ones to 'spiritualise' the idea of sacrifice in this way. She cites Ben Sira and the Dead Sea Scrolls, as well as the later rabbis, as treating other things such as good deeds, fasting, prayer, repentance and the study of *torah*, as equivalent to offering animal sacrifices.

21. C. Gunton, 'Christ the Sacrifice: Aspects of the Language and Imagery of the Bible', in L.D. Hurst & N.T. Wright (eds.) *The Glory of Christ in the New Testament: Studies in Christology in Memory of George Bradford Caird* (Oxford: Clarendon Press, 1987) 238, citing H.-G. Link & C. Brown, 'Sacrifice' in *NIDNTT* vol. 3, 417. Cf. Fitzmyer, *Romans* 510, who refers to Lv. 22:12; 23:15–21 for the origins of the idea of 'firstfruits' in Israelite practice.

22. Thomas Cranmer, 'A Defence of the True and Catholic Doctrine of the Sacrament of the Body and Blood of Our Saviour Christ', in H. Jenkyns (ed.) *The Remains of Thomas Cranmer*, vol. II (Oxford: Oxford University Press, 1833) 448–449.

23. J.N.D. Kelly, *The Epistles of Peter and of Jude* (Black's NT Commentaries) (London: A. & C. Black, 1969) 90–91; C.E.B. Cranfield, *The First Epistle of Peter* (London: SCM, 1950) 49–50.

24. Beckwith, *Priesthood*, chap. 2; likewise Scholer, *Proleptic Priests* 207.

25. For discussions of wider reasons for seeing the eucharist as a sacrifice, see J.I. Packer (ed.), *Eucharistic Sacrifice* (London: Church Book Room Press, 1962); J.L. Houlden, 'Sacrifice and the Eucharist' in Archbishops' Commission on Christian Doctrine, *Thinking about the Eucharist* (London: SCM, 1972) 81–98; R. Williams, *Eucharistic Sacrifice: The Roots of a Metaphor* (Grove Liturgical Study 31) (Bramcote: Grove Books, 1982); C. Buchanan (ed.), *Essays on Eucharistic Sacrifice in the Early Church* (Grove Liturgical Study 40) (Bramcote: Grove Books, 1984).

26. See the discussions in J. Jeremias, *The Eucharistic Words of Jesus* (London: SCM, 1966[2]); I.H. Marshall, *Last Supper and Lord's Supper* (Exeter: Paternoster, 1980); G.D. Kilpatrick, *The Eucharist in Bible and Liturgy* (Cambridge: Cambridge University Press, 1983), especially Lecture IV; and the commentaries.

27. See, for example, Did. 14:1; Justin, *Dial.* 41. R.P.C. Hanson discusses these texts and others extremely helpfully in his *Eucharistic Offering in the Early Church* (Grove Liturgical Study 19) (Bramcote: Grove Books, 1979). See also Houlden, 'Sacrifice', 84–86.

28. *Dial.* 41.

29. Hanson, *Eucharistic Offering* 5.

30. *Apol.* I, 67:5, discussed in Hanson, *Eucharistic Offering* 8.

31. *Haggai, Zechariah and Malachi* (TOTC) (London: IVP, 1972) 227–230 (the quotation is from 230). Cf. idem, 'Malachi 1:11 and the Worship of the Nations in the Old Testament', *Tyn. B* 23 (1972) 117–124; J. Swetnam, 'Malachi 1,11: An Interpretation', *CBQ* 31 (1969) 200–209.

32. See also chap. 4, Sect. III, for further discussion of this verse.

33. See n.26 above. See also his 'The Eucharist as Sacrifice and Sacrament in the NT' in J. Gnilka (ed.) *Neues Testament und Kirche* (Freiburg: Herder, 1974) 429–433.

34. W.O.E. Oesterley, *Sacrifices in Ancient Israel* (London: Hodder & Stoughton, 1937) 33–41; cf. also 177–190, cited in Kilpatrick, *Eucharist in Bible* 46.

35. *Eucharist in Bible* 46.

36. *Eucharist in Bible* 47.

37. *Eucharist in Bible* 47.

38. *Eucharist in Bible* 47–48.

39. *Eucharist in Bible* 48.

40. *Eucharist in Bible* 49ff.

41. *Eucharist in Bible* 50.

42. *Eucharist in Bible* 53.

43. *Eucharist in Bible* 53–54.

44. *Eucharist in Bible* 54.

45. *Eucharist in Bible* 54–57.

46. G. Aulén, *Eucharist and Sacrifice* (Philadelphia: Muhlenberg, 1958) 158.

47. Tillard, *What Priesthood* 18.

48. E.M.B. Green, 'Eucharistic Sacrifice in the New Testament and the Early Fathers' in Packer, *Eucharistic Sacrifice*, especially 64ff. (the quotation is from p.64).

49. A.G. Hebert, quoted in *The Lambeth Conference* (1958, Part 2) (London: SPCK, 1958) 85.

50. W.N. Pittenger, *The Christian Sacrifice* (New York: Oxford University Press, 1951) 109–110.

51. R.C. Moberly, *Ministerial Priesthood* (London: John Murray, 1897) 255.

52. Dom G. Dix, *The Shape of the Liturgy* (Westminster: Dacre Press, 1945) 243–247.

53. D.W.A. Gregg 'Hebraic Antecedents to the Eucharistic *anamnēsis* Formula', *Tyn. B* 30 (1979) 165–168; idem, *Anamnesis in the Eucharist* (Grove Liturgical Study 5) (Bramcote: Grove Books, 1976); Jeremias, *Eucharistic Words* 237–255; C.O. Buchanan, *ARCIC and Lima on Baptism and Eucharist* (Grove Worship Booklet 86) (Bramcote: Grove Books, 1983) 13–14. See also the discussion in G.D. Fee, *The First Epistle to the Corinthians* (NICNT) (Grand Rapids: Eerdmans, 1987) 552ff.

54. *Pes.* (Mishnah) 10:6 (italics mine).

55. S.W. Sykes, 'Sacrifice in the New Testament and Christian Theology', in M.F.C. Bourdillon & M. Fortes (eds.), *Sacrifice* (New York: Academic Press, 1980) 77 (italics his).

56. John Calvin, *Romans* (Edinburgh: Calvin Translation Society, 1844) 235 (italics mine).

57. B.F. Westcott, *The Epistle to the Hebrews* (London: Macmillan, 1920²) 232.

58. W. Stott, 'The Conception of "Offering" in the Epistle to the Hebrews', *NTS* 9 (1962–63) 62–67.

59. Homily on Heb. 13:8.

60. J.R.W. Stott, *The Cross of Christ* (Leicester: IVP, 1986) 260–261.

61. See Acts 3:24; 4:2; 13:5,38; 15:36; 16:17; 17:3,13,23; 26:23; Rom. 1:8; 1 Cor. 2:1; 9:14; Phil. 1:17,18; Col. 1:18. This is a complete list of NT uses of *katangellō* as found in *VKGNT*, Band 1, Teil 1, 678.

62. As e.g. in the Church of England's *Alternative Service Book*, Rite A, Holy Communion service, 144–145 (§§52–53), at this point following the pattern of the *Book of Common Prayer* service.

63. Cyprian considered that Christian ministers formed a special priesthood, and argued that the privileges of the levitical priesthood were transferred to this group of Christian ministers, whom he saw as offering the eucharist, of which he spoke in sacrificial terms. See his Epistles 3, 4, 43, 59, 63, with the summary in Hanson, *Eucharistic Offering* 18–19.

64. R. Hooker, *Ecclesiastical Polity* V, 77, 2: 'I rather term the one sort presbyters than priests, because in a matter of so small moment I would not offend the ears to whom the name of priesthood is odious, though without cause . . . seeing then that sacrifice is now no part of the church ministry, how should the name of priesthood be thereto applied? Wherefore whether we call it a priesthood, or presbytership, or a ministry, it skilleth not: although in truth the word presbyter doth seem more fit, and in propriety of speech more agreeable than priest with the drift of the whole gospel of Jesus Christ.'

65. C. Hodge, *Systematic Theology*, vol. II (London: Nelson, 1883) 467.

66. J.B. Lightfoot, *Philippians* (London: Macmillan, 1898[2]) 265.

67. Cited by C.O. Buchanan in *News of Liturgy* 140 (Aug. 1986) 1.

68. Tillard, *What Priesthood* 18–19; so also Beckwith, 'The Relation', 232–233.

69. F.F. Bruce, *The Acts of the Apostles* (London: Tyndale, 1952[2]) 100 (Bruce continues to maintain this position in the 3rd edn. (Leicester: Apollos, 1990) 132). He cites Otto's argument that the emphasis on the act of breaking the bread, a 'circumstance wholly trivial in itself' was 'the significant element of the celebration', in R. Otto, *The Kingdom of God and the Son of Man* (London: Lutterworth, 1943[2]) 315. The following come to similar conclusions: H. Conzelmann, *Acts of the Apostles* (Hermeneia) (Philadelphia: Fortress Press, 1987) 23 (Excursus); I.H. Marshall, *Acts* (TNTC) (Leicester: IVP, 1980) 83–84; C.S.C. Williams, *A Commentary on the Acts of the Apostles* (Black's NT Commentaries) (London: A. & C. Black, 1957) 72; E. Haenchen, *The Acts of the Apostles* (Oxford: Blackwell, 1971) 191–193; Jeremias, *Eucharistic Words* 118–121.

70. Beckwith, 'The Relation', 233.

71. T. Horvath, 'Who Presided at the Eucharist? A Comment on BEM', *JES* 22 (1985) 604–607.

72. *Baptism, Eucharist and Ministry* (Faith and Order Paper 111) (Geneva: World Council of Churches, 1982) Ministry statement, Commentary on §14.

73. F.F. Bruce, *The Book of Acts*, revised edn. (NICNT) (Grand Rapids: Eerdmans, 1988) 492–493.

74. Marshall, *Acts* 413–414. See the discussion of Jewish blessings in Fee, *First Corinthians* 467, n.26. In agreement with Marshall are L.T. Johnson, *The Acts of the Apostles* (Sacra Pagina, vol. 5) (Collegeville: Liturgical Press, 1992) 455; Haenchen, *Acts* 707; Conzelmann, *Acts* 220.

FOR FURTHER READING

R.T. Beckwith, 'The Relation between Christ's Sacrifice and Priesthood and Those of the Church: An Attempt at a Summary Statement', *Churchman* 103 (1989) 231–239.

R.J. Daly, SJ, 'The New Testament Concept of Christian Sacrificial Activity' in *BTB* 8 (1978) 99–107.

E.M.B. Green, 'Eucharistic Sacrifice in the New Testament and the Early Fathers', in J.I. Packer (ed.), *Eucharistic Sacrifice* (London: Church Book Room Press, 1962) 58–83.

D.W.A. Gregg, *Anamnesis in the Eucharist* (Grove Liturgical Study 5) (Bramcote: Grove Books, 1976).

G.D. Kilpatrick, *The Eucharist in Bible and Liturgy* (Cambridge: Cambridge University Press, 1983).

J.B. Lightfoot, 'The Christian Ministry' in his *Philippians* (London: Macmillan, 1898²) 181–269.

I.H. Marshall, *Last Supper and Lord's Supper* (Didsbury Lectures 1980) (Exeter: Paternoster, 1980).

I.H. Marshall, 'How Far Did the Early Christians Worship God?', *Churchman* 99 (1985) 216–229.

D.G. Peterson, *Engaging with God: A Biblical Theology of Worship* (Leicester: Apollos, 1992).

R.P. Shedd, 'Worship in the New Testament Church', in D.A. Carson (ed.), *The Church in the Bible and the World* (Exeter/Grand Rapids: Paternoster/Baker, 1987) 120–153.

J.R.W. Stott, *The Cross of Christ* (Leicester: IVP, 1986).

J.M.R. Tillard, *What Priesthood Has the Ministry?* (Grove Ministry & Worship Booklet 13) (Bramcote: Grove Books, 1973).

11

Sacrifice for Christians Today

MARTIN J. SELMAN

I. SACRIFICE AND WORSHIP

The aim of this chapter is to explore in some small way how the Bible's teaching on sacrifice might be relevant for contemporary Christian worship. This task is clearly different from that attempted in the other essays, but it is no less important. Anyone who wants to worship God according to biblical principles must take account of the whole range of the biblical teaching about sacrifice. Even though Christians no longer need to put their gifts on a physical altar, there is a direct connection between sacrifice as described in the Bible and worship today. That link involves the outward forms of worship as well as its inner meaning, as Paul illustrates in his appeal to Christians to 'offer your bodies as living sacrifices' (Rom. 12:1) and in his testimony that he was 'being poured out like a drink offering' (2 Tim. 4:6).

Many Christians today will actually be familiar, though often unconsciously, with the presence of biblical sacrificial language in hymns and songs in current use. Songs such as 'We bring the sacrifice of praise', 'Lay our lives before you', Charles Wesley's hymn, 'Kindle a flame of sacred love on the mean altar of my heart', and the conclusion to Graham Kendrick's Servant King: 'To bring our lives as a daily offering of worship to the Servant King', all bring the world of biblical sacrifice into contemporary worship.[1]

The relationship between worship and sacrifice, however, goes much deeper than mere literary metaphor, as careful study of the Bible clearly indicates. Even in pre-Christian OT worship, sacrifice was concerned with a great deal more than observing correct ritual. Sacrifice could even be a means by which a person might experience the glory and majesty of God. When Isaiah stood before the altar, for example, he saw the Lord (Is. 6:1–7), and when Solomon dedicated the temple, 'fire came down from heaven and consumed the burnt offering and the sacrifices, and the glory of the LORD filled the temple' (2 Ch. 7:1). It was only when Jesus offered himself on the cross, however, that the potential for encountering God through sacrificial worship was fully realized. The mysterious ripping apart of the temple veil as Jesus breathed his last decisively demonstrated that sacrifice had fully opened the way into God's very presence (Mt. 27:51; Heb. 6:19–20). What is more, by Jesus' death believers received a new opportunity to bring their own offerings into God's presence (Heb. 10:19–22). The clear implication is that far from Jesus bringing about the abolition of sacrificial thought and practice, he actually encouraged its spread and development.

Sacrifice is not merely associated with worship, it lies at its very heart. This understanding has recently been expounded by S.W. Sykes, who argues that the ideas, language, and practices of sacrifice are central to the relationships that people enjoy with God.[2] Since Christians express their relationship with Jesus most fully through worship, which in biblical thought is symbolized externally and internally by sacrifice, sacrificial worship is the proper means for communicating the meaning of that relationship. Or to put it another way, the most profound way to show one's love for God in worship is to lay everything on his altar. Christina Rosetti's famous carol, 'In the bleak midwinter', expresses this perfectly: 'What can I give him, poor as I am? . . . Yet what I can I give him, give my heart'. This was certainly the way Jesus showed the depth of the relationship that existed between himself and his Father. His life consistently expressed the sacrificial worship of a loving and obedient son, whether he was on the mountain teaching others to pray (Mt. 6:9–13), pleading with his Father in the garden of Gethsamane (Mt. 26:39,42), or committing his dying moments into his Father's hands (cf. Heb. 5:7–8). The ultimate significance of sacrifice as a sign of the reality of a father-son relationship can hardly be summed up more eloquently than in Jesus' final giving of himself to God, 'Father, into your hands I commit my spirit' (Lk. 23:46).

The implications of this for Christian worship are far-reaching. Once one becomes aware of the possibility that sacrifice is about the expression of a loving relationship, neither worship nor sacrifice can be confined any longer to mere action, whether performed in church or elsewhere. On the contrary, to worship in a biblical way makes a claim on every part of a Christian's life. Worship that is acceptable to God will be influenced by sacrificial principles at the most fundamental level.

1. Worship as thanksgiving

Worship is to be seen as a grateful response for all that God has done and said on his people's behalf. It is true that this view has little in common with that approach to worship which attempts to persuade God to be gracious through some kind of offering. But biblically-based worship is based on the assumption that God has already taken a decisive initiative of love towards the worshipper and that it is left to the worshipper simply to say 'thank you'. This is the pattern of worship found in both Old and New Testaments. Just as Israel's sacrifices were a response to God's grace expressed in the Sinai covenant, so the NT church offered spiritual sacrifices to God because of the love Jesus had shown them at the cross. One should not make the mistake of imagining that the response made in worship is in any way equivalent to God's prior action, however. The thanksgiving of Christian worship can never be more than a pale reflection of what God has already given, however intensive or spiritually uplifting the experience or however magnificent the gift that is offered.

It must be admitted that this view of worship contrasts sharply with most contemporary understandings of the nature of sacrifice, which are usually to do with self-sacrifice and self-denial. People generally may speak, for example, of a son or daughter who cares sacrificially for an elderly housebound parent, or of a person sacrificing a financially rewarding career for a noble calling such as social work or Christian ministry. The real focus in such forms of sacrifice actually falls on the person involved and what they have given up, often to the almost total exclusion of God's role, whether he is viewed as giver or receiver. The extent to which sacrifice in the twentieth century is instinctively understood as self-giving has been eloquently demonstrated in several in-depth studies of recent examples of sacrifice. Such diverse examples as the 1916 Easter Rising in Dublin, Archbishop William Temple's social theology, and the life of the French mystic and philosopher Simone Weil were all motivated by the desire of those involved to give of themselves.[3] In such instances, sacrifice has become 'something we're willing to offer or the price we're willing to pay in order to gain well-being (salvation), be it personal, corporate, or national'.[4]

For the biblical writers, however, sacrifice could never be reduced to a human-centred enterprise nor was it possible to entertain the idea of purchasing credit with God. They saw sacrifice as a debt to be gladly repaid, not because anyone could begin to pay back what was owed to God, but as a way of making public the depth of one's gratitude. This is not in any sense to criticize the heroism of those who freely give of themselves for others, since self-giving is an essential element of Christian sacrifice. It is rather to insist that all forms of human sacrifice are as nothing compared with the self-giving of the Son of God, and that acceptable worship must centre on God and not on man.

This principle is well illustrated by the famous motto of C.T. Studd, an English Test cricketer of the Victorian era who became a leading missionary to China: 'If Jesus Christ be God and died for me, no sacrifice can be too great for me to make for him.' He recognized that his personal sacrifice for the people of China was no more than a grateful echo of Jesus' love for him, and so he was able to put his own giving into proper perspective. He also understood that the basic principle of Christian worship is first of all to receive what God has given in Jesus. Worshipping begins with receiving, in agreement with David's testimony that

'Everything comes from you, and we have given you only what comes from your hand' (1 Ch. 29:14). Without this recognition, true worship cannot take place, but once God's prior action is acknowledged, every act of worship becomes a thankoffering (cf. Ps. 50:14,23; Col. 3:17).

2. Covenant worship

Biblically-based worship must always be a covenant-related activity. The sacrifices of Bible times were never intended to be independent activities, for their meaning was based entirely on the covenant relationship that existed between God and his people. This view is applicable both to Israel, whose rituals all belong to the Sinai covenant, and to the worship of the early church, which was based on the new covenant between Christ and his church.

The implications of seeing worship against the background of the covenant are considerable. Perhaps the most significant feature is the confidence it offers worshippers about God's unchanging love towards them. The covenants of both Old and New Testaments provide absolute guarantees of God's permanent commitment to those whom he had saved, whether from slavery in Egypt or from the ultimate slavery of sin and death. Christians in particular can worship God because Jesus has established 'the new covenant in my blood, which is poured out for you' (Lk. 22:20). The letter to the Hebrews explains that Jesus' death established the new covenant. It shows that Jesus' death is the foundation sacrifice of the new covenant, since there is a direct analogy between the blood of Jesus and the blood sprinkled on the Israelites at Sinai during the foundation sacrifices of the Sinai covenant (Ex. 24:1–11; Heb. 9:15–28). Two consequences arise from seeing Jesus' death as the founding covenant sacrifice. The first is that it speaks of God's eternal commitment to his church, since at the cross God sealed the new covenant and accompanied it by an immutable oath (Heb. 6:13–20). The other is that Jesus' sacrifice becomes the basis on which Christian worship is made acceptable to God.

When worship is treated in this way, there is no excuse for Christians failing to bring offerings to God. On the contrary, such unparalleled security gives them every reason to draw near to God with fresh gifts of love. Because the blood of Jesus is eternally effective, the way to the Father is always open. Even when people are acutely conscious of having failed God in thought, word, and deed, they have no need to fear that God will reject their prayers and praise. God's own guarantee makes their covenant with him secure, and they may worship him freely.

The various sacrifices associated with the OT and NT covenants provide further models for Christian worship. For example, the service of Communion or the Lord's Supper offers the opportunity for everyone to share in the benefits of Christ's death, just as the Israelites rejoiced in the covenant blessings at the communion meals which followed the sacrifice of the peace/fellowship/shared offerings. Through bread and wine, all who participate in Communion share in the covenant blessings that Jesus won for them on the cross. It is also important to note that the Christ on whom believers feed by faith and from whom they receive fresh assurance and strength is the same Christ who died as a sacrificial offering. Just as the Israelites ate part of the very peace offerings that had been sacrificed on the altar, so Christ's own sacrifice is directly associated with what is eaten at the communion service. It is notable again in this context that worship is about receiving rather than giving.

The OT sacrifices of praise and thanksgiving provide further encouragement for believers to go on praising God for his covenant blessings in Christ. If the Communion service is a reminder of the negative achievements of the cross in removing everything to do with sin, praise is a positive means of entering into the inexhaustible benefits of the new covenant. For that reason, Hebrews exhorts Christians to offer a continual sacrifice of praise (Heb. 13:15–16) and Peter stresses the advantages of offering spiritual sacrifices to God (1 Pet. 2:5).

The covenant nature of worship also emphasizes that Christian worship must be at heart a corporate activity. Every worshipper belongs to a single family, in which all have the same status as children of God and the same privilege of addressing God as 'Abba, Father'. No-one has a special advantage and every human distinction is irrelevant. The covenant connection also means that worship can never be a purely private or individual concern, and even those who are forced to worship God on their own can draw strength from a sense of wider fellowship. It is therefore no accident that the invitation in the letter to the Hebrews to Christians to worship God advises them not to neglect the habit of meeting together (Heb. 10:19–25). Sacrificial worship encourages believers to acknowledge God's worth together rather than to do their own thing. It is meant to be like a symphony orchestra producing rich and melodious harmonies rather than soloists indulging in their own individual fantasies, or in biblical terminology, it emphasizes the ministry of a whole body in which every organ plays its proper role. Members need not only to acknowledge the value of their own contribution but that of others in worship. In this way, worship attributes worth to one another and to the church as a whole as well as to God. Where worship is given its proper role as the jewel in the church's crown, other activities and priorities will more easily fall into their intended places.

3. Worship as a way of life

Since the whole of life belongs to the sphere of worship, worship is much more a way of life than a series of ritual or liturgical acts. Neither worship nor sacrifice are regarded in the Bible as uniquely religious activities, except in the sense that they are offered to God. On the contrary, anything may be offered to God, including physical and spiritual things, the world of the secular as well as the spiritual, internal motives and external acts. Worship demands comprehensive commitment, which cannot be limited to any particular day of the week, or be concerned with some kinds of activities and not with others. The range of offerings in Israel, for example, stretched from ordinary kitchen ingredients such as flour, salt, and olive oil to all the produce of the field. The prophets were especially keen to emphasize that the people could not split their lives into religious and other compartments, insisting that people's behaviour in matters such as politics, ethics, business, and family life were an integral part of their worship before God (cf. Is. 1:13–18). The NT is equally practical, including such varied things as money, acts of kindness, and physical bodies as acceptable offerings (e.g. Rom. 12:1; 2 Cor. 8:5; Phil. 4:18; Heb. 13:16). Indeed, this almost routine approach to sacrifice may be one reason why many Christians seem to miss its significance in the NT. Whatever the reason for our contemporary neglect, the fact is that the NT increases rather than reduces the importance of sacrificial worship in Christianity. Nothing, not even life itself, is to be excluded, as is perfectly expressed in Frances Ridley Havergal's hymn of consecration: 'Take my life, and let it be consecrated, Lord, to Thee'.

This emphasis is of special significance today, for at least two reasons. In the first place, it directly challenges the commonly held view that Christian sacrifice is essentially a spiritual matter and that 'worship is the interior acknowledgement of God'.[5] This view is based on a selective interpretation of passages such as Ps. 51:16–17 or Col. 3:16, for although Christians are not required to offer sacrifices as the Israelites did, 'it is as part of the world and within the world that Christian worship is offered by the Christian'.[6] It is also a dangerously reductionist position, since it tends to deny that 'the earth is the LORD's, and everything in it' (Ps. 24:1). On the contrary, God wants gifts of every kind, whether we categorize them as spiritual or not, including our possessions and profits, abilities and ambitions, as well as praise and prayer. Secondly, worship that arises out of the context of a life offered to God affirms the value of the gifts of every Christian. God does not put a special premium on the offerings of those who are supposedly more spiritually advanced or of a more contemplative frame of mind. Ordinary things offered to God by so-called 'ordinary' Christians are equally as acceptable as gifts offered by those who are apparently more mature. What matters most is that a person's gifts are offered in the right spirit rather than that the offerer uses the right word or knows the correct actions. Jesus' assessment of the worth to God of the widow's mite is particularly relevant here. Though others despised her contribution, Jesus saw that 'she . . . put in all she had to live on' (Lk. 21:4), and commended her accordingly.

II. JESUS' SACRIFICE FOR TODAY

All this shows how important it is for Christian worship that the significance of what Jesus did on the cross is properly understood. There is a direct connection between the sacrifice of Jesus and the sacrifices offered by Christians. Jesus did not just make the outward form of the OT sacrificial system obsolete (cf. Heb. 8:13; 9:9–10), he also laid down a fresh pattern for sacrificial Christian living based on his own self-offering (cf. 1 Pet. 2:18–23). How then does Jesus' sacrifice affect Christian worship today?

Firstly and most importantly, Jesus represents the ultimate fulfilment of God's revelation about sacrifice. The entire Israelite sacrificial system comes together in him, in such a way that he does not merely fulfil individal sacrifices like the Passover or the sin offering, but reveals the true meaning of sacrifice as something greater than the sum of the parts. Jesus actually personifies not just the forms but the true spirit of biblical sacrifice. It is as though light shining from the cross produces an image in Jesus' likeness across the whole range of OT ceremonial.

As a living sacrifice in every sense of the phrase, the whole of Jesus' life as well as his death must be interpreted in sacrificial terms. Though his death clearly brings his sacrifice to a climax, he lived his entire life according to the principle, 'not my will, but yours be done' (Lk. 23:42). There can be no greater illustration of this than Jesus' fulfilment of the Suffering Servant prophecies of Isaiah (Is. 42:1–7; 49:1–6; 50:4–9; 52:13–53:12; cf. Zc. 12:10; 13:7–9). This mysterious, anonymous, figure represents the highest form of sacrifice in the OT through the offering of his life according to God's will as a unique human offering for sin (Is. 53:10; Zc. 12:10). This is the model which the gospel writers employ most frequently to characterize Jesus' life and to interpret the meaning of his impending death (cf. Mt. 12:18–21; Mk. 10:45).[7] The way in which Jesus lives and dies as God's Suffering Servant also serves as the pattern for Christians, as other parts of the NT make abundantly clear (cf. Rom. 12:1; 1 Pet. 2:18-23). As the Servant par excellence, Jesus' whole life is lived as an obedient sacrifice, and his disciples are expected to follow his example.[8]

Secondly, Jesus lived and died according to a scheme of sacrifice and worship that did much more than demonstrate the full meaning of the Levitical pattern. In the words of Driver, 'Hebrews does not present an atoning Christ who is merely an improvement on the sacrificial system of the old order. The work of Christ is a radical departure from sacrifice as it developed in Israel and was perpetuated in Judaism. It was a radical return to the original purpose of sacrifice.'[9] The most obvious feature of this alternative pattern is the link between the priesthood of Jesus and that of Melkisedek rather than that of Aaron (Heb. 5:6–10; 6:20–7:28). Though the details are not always easy to follow, the key distinction is that Jesus undertakes a priestly ministry 'on the basis of the power of an indestructible life' (Heb. 7:16). Aaron's priesthood, on the other hand, is fatally inflicted with the very human weaknesses for which it tries to atone. Where there are two kinds of priesthood, there are also two patterns of sacrifice. Jesus, for example, was not laid on an altar in the Jerusalem temple as might have been expected according to the levitical pattern, but nailed to a cross in a cemetery ('Golgotha' means 'the place of a skull'; Calvary is a Latin variant). Similarly, his suitability as a sacrificial lamb did not conform with the levitical laws requiring the lack of any physical mark or blemish. His perfection was of a different kind altogether, in that it was spiritual and moral rather than physical. As Isaiah's prophetic words explain, he had done 'no violence' nor was there 'any deceit' in his mouth, even though 'his appearance was so disfigured beyond that of any man' (Is. 52:14; 53:9).

These considerations make it plain that far from abolishing sacrificial worship, Jesus raised it to a much higher plane. Though the cross showed that the levitical system had outlived its usefulness, this was so only that it might be replaced by an infinitely superior pattern already present in OT times, but which Jesus had raised to new prominence and which he had infused with new meaning. What is more, Hebrews encourages Christians to adopt this new pattern for themselves enthusiastically. The invitation to every Christian to 'draw near' to God (Heb. 10:21), which is the proper technical term for priestly activity (cf. Ezk. 45:4), clearly implies that every believer has a priestly ministry to fulfil. Indeed, Christian priesthood and offering takes on a greater significance than in the old levitical scheme since they are to be exercised not before any earthly altar but in God's heavenly sanctuary.

Thirdly, the atoning qualities of Jesus' death are of unique significance as far as Christian worship is concerned. Though Christians may bring various kinds of offerings to God, they can add absolutely nothing to the atonement won by Jesus. He died as a sin offering to end all sin offerings (Rom. 8:3; 2 Cor. 5:21; Is. 53:10), the Lamb of God who finally removed the world's sin (Jn. 1:29, 36; 1 Cor. 5:7). The writer to the Hebrews could not have put it more succinctly: 'there is no longer any sacrifice for sin' (Heb. 10:18). Jesus died for every kind of sin, past, present, and future. He not only fulfilled the two main Israelite offerings for sin, the guilt or reparation offering and the sin or purification offering, but also died for sins which were not clearly covered by the earlier ceremonies, especially deliberate sins (cf. Lv. 4:1–5:13; Nu. 15:30–31). He far exceeded the limited scope of the OT offerings, defeating sin decisively and comprehensively.

In fact, the Bible makes it plain that Jesus did away with sin and evil in all its forms. He came not only to provide forgiveness for individual Christians, but 'to destroy the devil's work' (1 Jn. 3:8). That this included much more than personal atonement is already suggested by the OT purification offerings through which the impurities of various physical ailments and even places such as the Holy of Holies were purified (cf. Lv.

12–16). But with the death of Christ, the old order of things has completely passed away and the new has come (cf. 2 Cor. 5:17). Jesus' sacrifice inaugurates a new cosmos as well as a new covenant (cf. Rom. 8:18–25; Phil. 2:5–11; Col. 1:13–20). The Lamb is now upon the throne, and will finally sweep away death and all its accessories such as mourning, crying and pain (cf. Rev. 21:4).[10]

The consequences of this are breathtaking. Because Jesus' sacrifice has ensured the ultimate defeat and destruction of evil, Christians can be absolutely confident of one day bringing their gifts to God face to face. Christian sacrifice therefore has as much an eschatological dimension as an historical one, since it looks forward to Jesus' completion of what his death has set decisively in motion. To gather for worship Sunday by Sunday is not just about appreciating the benefits of the cross. It is also to anticipate being a part of heavenly worship: 'When I stand in glory, I will see his face, And there I'll serve my King for ever, in that Holy Place.'[11] It is also to join now with the worship described in the book of Revelation, for Christians today already have access to God's very presence. What, then, should be the chief characteristics of the gifts they bring to him?

III. SACRIFICIAL WORSHIP TODAY

1. Bringing gifts in worship

The basic feature of Christian worship should be that every believer brings sacrifices to God. The sacrificial vocabulary and ideas which are widely scattered through the NT make it quite clear that all Christians are to take over and transform Israel's priestly ministry (1 Pet. 2:5, 9; cf. Ex. 19:6; Rev. 1:6). The church will therefore have many more priests than did ancient Israel, and obliterate the distinction between priesthood and laity. Because all the laity or people (Gk. *laos*) have become priests, the two groups can no longer be differentiated in priestly terms. Christian worship should therefore be characterized by enjoying the priestly privilege of direct access to God and using the priestly opportunity of bringing an offering directly to the Lord. Believers need no leader or minister to represent them to God, and neither does the congregation need to watch from the pews while their leader worships on their behalf. All this is in line with the biblical principle that 'No-one should appear before the LORD empty-handed' (Dt. 16:16), and is confirmed by Paul's observation that everyone can bring something to Christian worhip, whether it is a hymn, a word of instruction, a revelation, a message in an unknown language or an interpretation (1 Cor. 14:26).

It must be admitted that by no means all Christians think of worship as an opportunity for each person to contribute. Part of the reason for this must be put down to a misunderstanding of the church's heritage from the Reformation. Many people, for example, instinctively interpret

Toplady's line, 'Nothing in my hand I bring, simply to thy cross I cling', to mean that Christians can offer nothing acceptable to God because the cross has brought an end to all sacrifice. Nonconformist and evangelical circles have also reacted against anything associated with sacrifice and sacerdotalism in favour of a priesthood of all believers which has been variously interpreted in terms of freedom of access to the Scriptures or democratic forms of church government. The priesthood of all believers, however, surely means much more than that. These kinds of reductionist views have deprived Christians of a vital form of ministry and seriously weakened the church's worship. Ashby has recently commented: 'it has been a serious fault in both patristic and contemporary, twentieth century, theology, that either sacrifice has been limited to one hour a week in a consecrated building and to a wafer and a drop of fortified wine, or else Calvary has been applied to the contemporary scene as a set of ethical precepts and advice for social action.'[12]

A more balanced and biblical view of worship has to recognize that Jesus came to fulfil the law of sacrifice rather than abolish it (Mat. 5:17). This means that although Jesus brought the sacrifices of atonement to an end, he transformed and renewed other types of sacrifice (cf. Rom. 12:1; 1 Pet. 2:5; Heb. 13:15–16). Jesus also renewed the profound relationship that exists between worship, sacrifice, and sonship. It is above all through gifts of sacrificial love that Christians may express to their heavenly Father what it means to be sons and daughters of God (cf. Jn. 15:13).

2. Spiritual sacrifices

What kind of 'spiritual sacrifices' (1 Pet. 2:5) or 'spiritual worship' (Rom. 12:2) should Christians offer? Such sacrifices are certainly not to be reduced to mere spiritual thoughts or pietistic words. Paul's appeal in the same context for Christians to offer their bodies is a clear indication that physical and material gifts are just as important to God as praise and prayer. A probable solution is suggested by the reference to a spiritual house and a holy priesthood in 1 Pet. 2:5. According to 1 Peter, spiritual sacrifices may be offered by anyone who belongs to this house and priesthood, that is, to the church. Since this includes all believers and does not refer to any privileged élite, any Christian on this basis may offer spiritual sacrifices. What makes the sacrifices spiritual is that they are offered by people who have become spiritual because of their faith in Christ and that they offer them by the Holy Spirit who makes their gifts 'acceptable to God through Jesus Christ' (1 Pet. 2:5). Though the form and content of one person's gifts will vary considerably from the gifts of others, the critical factor is the presence of an active spiritual relationship between God and those who worship him. This understanding of spiritual sacrifices is of course similar to that of the spiritual gifts whose use Paul encouraged in worship (cf. 1 Cor. 14). In their case too, the spirituality of the gifts comes from their being offered to God in the Spirit as well as having been given to the believer by the Spirit. Christian worship therefore ought to be characterized by ordinary Christians bringing their gifts and sacrifices to God, and doing so in total dependence on the Holy Spirit.

The most obvious of these gifts and sacrifices are those which are found in the context of public worship, such as praise and thanksgiving (Col. 3:16–17; Heb. 13:15–16), prayer and intercession (Heb. 4:16; Rev. 5:8; 8:3), and occasions for communion and celebration (1 Cor. 5:7–8; 1 Pet. 2:9). Each of these activities is described in sacrificial terms in the NT. In the light of this, ordinary church services should really be regarded as sacrificial occasions, not because great cost is necessarily involved, but because they are occasions when gifts are offered to God. When on the other hand, church services are treated as a mere routine, the vital God-given ministry of bringing sacrificial praise and worship will be neglected, with serious consequences for God, for Christians, and for the world. In such circumstances, God is deprived of his due, Christians become guilty of despising the love which took Jesus to the cross and of failing to enter the open door into God's presence, and the world loses an opportunity to hear about what God has done.

Evangelistic testimony is in fact often singled out as an important feature in the worship of Bible times, as when the psalmists called worshippers in the temple to 'declare his glory among the nations' (Ps. 96:3), or when Peter described the calling of Christian priests as being able to 'declare the praises of him who called them out of darkness into his wonderful light' (cf. 1 Pet. 2:9). The practice of the first Christians in proclaiming the good news to outsiders through their worship in the temple (cf. Acts 2:46–47; 5:42) ought to encourage unbelievers today to expect Christian worship to communicate to them in ways they can understand.

Sacrificial worship is not to be confined to meetings or services, however, since the Bible also understands various forms of social concern in a sacrificial way. By doing good to others and by sharing their possesions, Christians may offer themselves to God and to one another in Jesus' name (Heb. 13:16; cf. 10:24). Specific examples of this from the NT include giving financial support to Christian workers (Phil. 4:18) or offering oneself in Christian ministry so that others may come to faith (Rom. 15:16; 2 Tim. 4:6). It is significant that these activities enjoy the same value and status as praise and worship, since no distinction is made in biblical thought between worship offered directly to God and service offered to others. Both are equally important, and neither is superior to the other. Christian sacrifice is neither to be detached from its moorings in formal worship nor seen as primarily concerned with issues of practical Christian living.[13] The challenge to Christian worshippers today is the need to integrate what happens inside and outside church buildings, during church services and apart from them. Failure to make a proper connection will result in an unnatural and unbiblical imbalance.

3. In Spirit and in truth

Finally, it is important to clarify God's priority for Christian worship, which is about maintaining a proper perspective between the form and the spirit of worship. It is as easy today as in biblical times to fall under the joint condemnation of Isaiah and Jesus by becoming preoccupied with matters of form and order: 'These people honour me with their lips but their heart is far from me' (Is. 29:13; Mk. 7:6). To imagine that real worship can be attained through debates over such matters as orders of service, the singing of hymns and songs, preferences in musical style, or dress and vestments, is to be in danger of missing the point altogether, even if one wins an argument on such contentious issues. For the motive with which worship is offered is always of greater value to God than the manner in which the gift is given (cf. e.g. the attitude of both Hezekiah and God in 2 Ch. 30:18–20). Worship based on the principles of biblical sacrifice is about obedience and love for God above everything else, as Jesus' own life and teaching demonstrate: 'Greater love has no-one than this that he lay down his life for his friends' (Jn. 15:13; Phil. 2:8).

What Christian worship and sacrifice are really about therefore is nothing less than the offering of one's self to God. Paul's appeal to Christians 'to offer your bodies as living sacrifices' (Rom. 12:1) eloquently sums up the Bible's teaching on the subject. God looks in worship not just for gifts of praise, money, or selfless generosity, but for lives made wholly available to him. Worship calls not just for admiration nor even adoration, but for action based on the example of the cross. Just as Jesus was not only God's High Priest but made himself the ultimate Sacrifice, so God looks to every Christian both to exercise a priestly ministry and to offer their very selves on his altar. Only in this way can one begin to express the worthiness or 'worthship' of the God who gave everything in the person of his only Son. 'If Jesus Christ be God and died for me, no sacrifice can be too great for me to make for him.'

NOTES

1. K. Dearman, 'We bring the sacrifice of praise', *Songs of Fellowship* (Eastbourne: Kingsway, 1991, 574; T. Coelho, 'Father, we adore you', ibid., 99; C. Wesley, 'O Thou who camest from above'; G. Kendrick, 'From heaven you came', *Songs of Fellowship* 120.

2. S.W. Sykes, in S.W. Sykes (ed.), *Sacrifice and redemption: Durham essays in theology* (Cambridge: Cambridge University Press, 1991) 287–292.

3. These studies are to be found in the volume mentioned in the pevious note, 218–261.

4. J. Driver, *Understanding the atonement* (Scottdale: Herald, 1986) 145.

5. S.W. Sykes, 'Sacrifice and redemption', 286.

6. J. Dunn, *Romans 9–16* (WBC) (Dallas: Word, 1988) 709.

7. Cf. chap.8 and R.T. France, *Jesus and the Old Testament* (London: Tyndale, 1971) chap.4.

8. Abraham's offering of Isaac is another important OT model for the sacrifice of both Jesus and of Christians. See e.g. R.W.L. Moberly, 'Christ as the key to Scripture: Genesis

22 reconsidered', in R.S. Hess, etc. (eds.), *He swore an oath: biblical themes from Genesis 12–50* (Cambridge: Tyndale House, 1993) 143–173.
9. Driver, *Understanding* 142.
10. See further, Driver, *Understanding* 213–241.
11. M. Green, 'There is a Redeemer', *Songs of Fellowship* 544.
12. G. Ashby, *Sacrifice* (London: SCM, 1988) 128–129.
13. For a different view, cf. e.g. R.J. Daly, *The origins of the Christian doctrine of sacrifice* (Philadelphia: Fortress, 1978) chap.4; Driver, *Understanding* 129–130.

FOR FURTHER READING

R.J. Daly, *The origins of the Christian doctrine of sacrifice* (Philadelphia: Fortress, 1978).
J. Driver, *Understanding the atonement* (Scottdale: Herald, 1986).
R.W.L. Moberly, 'Christ as the key to Scripture: Genesis 22 reconsidered', in R.S. Hess, etc. (eds.), *He swore an oath: biblical themes from Genesis 12–50* (Cambridge: Tyndale House, 1993) 143–173.
D.G. Peterson, *Engaging with God: A biblical theology of worship* (Leicester: Apollos, 1992).
J.R.W. Stott, *The Cross of Christ* (Leicester: IVP, 1986).
S.W. Sykes (ed.), *Sacrifice and redemption: Durham essays in theology* (Cambridge: Cambridge University Press, 1991).
F. Young, *Sacrifice and the death of Christ* (London: SPCK, 1975), Part II.

General index

Index of biblical and other texts

(References are to the English Bible)